DEPARTMENT FOR EDUCATION AND EMPLOYMENT
WELSH OFFICE
SCOTTISH OFFICE EDUCATION AND INDUSTRY DEPARTMENT
DEPARTMENT OF EDUCATION FOR NORTHERN IRELAND
UNIVERSITIES FUNDING COUNCIL
HIGHER EDUCATION STATISTICS AGENCY

EDUCATION **S**TATISTICS FOR THE **U**NITED **K**INGDOM

1995 EDITION

London: HMSO

NOR: RD

Contents

Introduction

This new edition of 'Education Statistics for the United Kingdom' updates, to 1993/94 and, provisionally, to 1994/95 its description of education in the United Kingdom. Its value is as the primary source of education statistics for the UK as a whole, allowing comparisons to be made over time (sometimes as far back as 20 years) and in many of the tables between the 4 home countries. A summary of the main trends evident from the statistics is given in 'Summary of Main United Kingdom Statistics' immediately following this introduction.

CHANGES TO MAIN TABLES

We are receiving more and more requests from international organisations such as Eurostat and UNESCO for more up to date data and this year we have collected two years worth of data (1993/94 and 1994/95) for many of the tables. Apart from this increase in the number of tables other changes are that we have dropped tables 10 and 16 from last year's volume and introduced new tables 13, 22a and 22b. Existing expenditure table 7 has been restructured to fit one page of the volume and table 32 showing progress towards national targets for education and training has been extended to cater for lifetime targets.

CONTRIBUTIONS

The efforts of the statistics teams in DfEE, Welsh Office, Scottish Office Education and Industry Department and Department of Education Northern Ireland, who have contributed data for this volume, are greatly appreciated. In DfEE the team responsible for bringing all the data together and producing the volume were Alison Kennedy, Tony McLay, Dave Walton, Dave McVean, Lisa Smith and Irene Jordan.

Analytical Services Branch
Schools, Teachers and General Division (STG 1)
Room 113
Department for Education and Employment
Mowden Hall
Staindrop Road
Co. Durham
Darlington
DL3 9BG

Summary of Main United Kingdom Statistics

INTRODUCTION

1 This introduction summarises the main features in the detailed statistical tables. The figures cover the academic year 1994/95 and also show comparable data mainly for the previous academic years 1984/85 and 1990/91 to 1993/94 inclusive. Data on expenditure relate to financial years rather than academic years.

SUMMARY

2 The key findings mainly for 1993/94 and 1994/95 (unless otherwise stated) with figures generally relating to the UK as a whole are:

a For schools, the statistics show that some 9.5 million pupils were taught by over half a million teachers in 34 thousand schools. The pupil/teacher ratio for all schools combined (maintained and independent) was 17.5:1, the same as the previous year and also ten years ago.

b The participation rate of under 5s in all schools rose by 1 percentage point since 1993/94 to 57% in 1994/95, up from 46% in 1984/85.

c A higher proportion of 16 year olds (87%) than 17 year olds (70%) or 18 year olds (50%) were participating in post-compulsory education. The rates for individual ages are all higher than a decade before - up 13 percentage points for 16 years olds, 17 percentage points for 17 year olds and 11 percentage points for 18 year olds.

d Over the same period there has been a shift from part-time to full-time attendance with part-time rates for 16-18 year olds falling by 11 percentage points between 1984/85 and 1994/95 compared with a rise of 25 percentage points in the full-time rate over the same period.

e Total further education enrolments have increased by 3% between 1993/94 and 1994/95 to over 3.8 million of which 0.8 million were full-time and 3.1 million were part-time.

f Enrolments in higher education stood at 1.7 million in 1994/95 of which 49% were women. Because of changes in coverage and definitions of the 1994/95 data there is a discontinuity in the time series. Calculation of year on year changes are therefore not appropriate. Table D gives an indication of the effect of these changes in England only. See also Background.

g 560 thousand school pupils gained at least one General Certificate of Secondary Education (GCSE) at grades A-C (or equivalent qualifications) in 1993/94 and 190 thousand school pupils gained at least one GCE A level pass (or equivalent qualifications). The numbers of successful pupils increased by 1% compared with 1992/93.

h The proportions of school pupils achieving better grades continued to rise. In 1993/94 51% of pupils with GCSEs (or equivalent) at grades A-C gained at least 5 grades A-C compared with 47% in 1992/93. At GCE A level (or equivalent) standard just over 73% of successful pupils gained the equivalent of at least 2 GCE A level passes in 1993/94 compared with just under 73% in 1992/93.

i In terms of individuals' lifetime learning, 40% of the employed workforce in 1995 was qualified to NVQ Level 3, Advanced GNVQ or 2 GCE A level standard, 20 percentage points below the new National Target set for the year 2000. 23% of the employed workforce had vocational, professional, management or academic qualifications at NVQ Level 4 or above, 7 percentage points below the National Target set for 2000.

j At foundation level, 64% of 19-21 year olds in 1995 had 5 GCSEs at grades C or above, an Intermediate GNVQ, a NVQ Level 2 or equivalent qualifications, 21 percentage points below the new National Target set for the year 2000. The proportion of 21-23 year olds with 2 GCE A levels, an Advanced GNVQ, a NVQ Level 3 or equivalent qualification was 44%, 16 percentage points below the new National Target set for 2000.

k At the higher education level, in 1993/94 the latest year for which information is available, a total of 439 thousand people obtained qualifications, a rise of 8% compared with the previous year and 81% compared with 1983/84. Of these, 211 thousand were at first degree level.

l Net expenditure by public authorities on education was some £35 billion, real term increases of 3% compared with 1993-94 and 31% compared with 1984-85. Public expenditure on education in 1994-95 represented 5.2% of the Gross Domestic Product.

TABLES

Table A gives figures on schools, pupils, teachers, pupil/teacher ratios and under fives participation rates.

Table B shows participation rates for 16 to 18 year olds.

Table C shows enrolments on further and higher education courses.

Table D gives an indication (for England only) of the effect of the change in coverage and definition of the 1994/95 higher education data. It contains data on both new and old definitions to provide a consistent time series.

Table E gives information about non-vocational qualifications attained by school pupils.

Table F gives information about the progress towards the National Targets for Education and Training.

Table G gives figures on higher education qualifications.

Table H gives figures on expenditure on education.

BACKGROUND

1   Statistics for the education systems in England, Wales, Scotland and Northern Ireland are collected and processed separately in accordance with the particular needs of the responsible Departments ie the Department for Education and Employment, the Welsh Office Education Department, the Scottish Office Education and Industry Department and the Department of Education Northern Ireland. Each Department makes available a selection of statistics concerning the education services for which it is responsible.

2   The data collection arrangement for higher education changed in 1994/95 in that the main source of data became the Higher Education Statistical Agency (HESA) Student Record replacing the University Statistical Record (USR) and the Department's Further Education Statistical Record (FESR). The coverage and some of the definitions used in the HESA record differ from those in FESR and USR giving rise to a discontinuity in the time series. The main differences in definitions and coverage were explained in Press Notice 107/95, 'Student Enrolments in Higher Education Courses in England and in the United Kingdom: Academic Year 1994/95' published in May 1995. Table D contains data for England for 1994/95 on both old and new definitions to provide a consistent time series and an indication of the extent of the discontinuity. The old definitions applied reflect as closely as possible those used in earlier years. The figures update the provisional figures published in the above mentioned Press Notice.

3   Basic statistics for the whole of the United Kingdom are assembled to illustrate the size and nature of the educational task throughout the four countries and to facilitate international comparisons. They are published annually for the Department by Her Majesty's Stationery Office.

DEFINITIONS

4   The non-vocational qualifications usually taken by school pupils at the age of 16 are the General Certificate of Secondary Education (GCSE) in England, Wales and Northern Ireland and the Scottish Certificate of

Education - Standard Grades (SCE Standard Grades) in Scotland. The results and grades of the two qualifications are directly comparable.

5   It is possible to study at school for qualifications beyond GCSE and SCE Standard Grades. In England, Wales and Northern Ireland the qualifications which are gained normally after two further years of study are the General Certificate of Education (GCE) A levels and/or AS examinations. AS examinations are equal to half a GCE A level. They are at the same academic standard as GCE A levels, but have half the content.

6   In Scotland the additional period of study before qualifications are gained is normally one year rather than two. The qualifications are the Scottish Certificate of Education - Higher Grades (SCE H Grades). Three passes at SCE H Grade are regarded as equivalent to 2 passes at GCE A level.

7   In recent years school pupils have been able to take vocational courses in addition to or instead of the more traditional academic courses. The National Council for Vocational Qualifications (NCVQ) was set up in 1986 to reform and rationalise the vocational qualifications system in England, Wales and Northern Ireland. Its aim was to establish a new framework of National Vocational Qualifications (NVQs) based on five defined levels of achievement from foundation level (NVQ Level 1) to professional level (NVQ Level 5). NVQs attest to competence to do a particular job or a range of jobs based on clear standards set by employers. The competence-based system is being extended in Scotland through a new system of Scottish Vocational Qualifications (SVQs) along the lines of NVQs. SVQs are accredited by the Scottish Vocational Education Council. NCVQ also accredit GNVQs, which are broad based vocational qualifications designed to facilitate progression to employment and further training or Higher Education. GNVQs are currently available at three levels, Foundation, Intermediate and Advanced which are, respectively, equivalent to NVQ levels 1,2 and 3.

8   In 1991 the Confederation of British Industry drew up National Targets for Education and Training. These consisted of four foundation targets and four lifetime targets in total which aimed jointly to measure progress towards achieving a more flexible, highly skilled and qualified workforce. In 1995 an updated set of targets was launched for the year 2000. These consist of 3 foundation targets and 3 lifetime targets and are aimed at covering higher level skills which will be developed throughout life. Table F of this summary includes figures which measure progress towards 4 of the targets which are:

Foundation target 1:
By 2000, 85% of young people achieving five GCSEs at grade C or above, an Intermediate GNVQ or a NVQ Level 2.

Foundation target 3:
By 2000, 60% of young people achieving 2 GCE A levels, an Advanced GNVQ or a NVQ Level 3.

Lifetime target 1:
By 2000, 60% of the workforce qualified to NVQ Level 3, Advanced GNVQ or 2 GCE A Level standard.

Lifetime target 2:
By 2000, 30% of the workforce to have a vocational, professional, management or academic qualification at NVQ Level 4 or above.

Five GCSEs, SCE Standard Grades at grades A-C or an Intermediate GNVQ are equivalent to NVQ Level 2; two GCE A level passes, three SCE H Grades or an Advanced GNVQ are broadly equivalent to NVQ Level 3. NVQ Level 4 is first degree standard.

9   Education expenditure in the United Kingdom is based on the statements of income and expenditure of the Education Departments of the four countries as included in the Civil Appropriation Accounts presented annually to Parliament; on annual returns submitted by local education authorities and educational institutions; and on the statement of grants paid, up to 1992/93, through the Universities Funding Council and the Polytechnics and Colleges Funding Council and from 1993/94 through the respective Further Education and Higher Education Funding Councils. Private expenditure on education is excluded.

TABLE A: SCHOOLS, PUPILS AND TEACHERS IN THE UNITED KINGDOM [1] , [2] , [3]: 1984/85 TO1994/95

	1984/85	1990/91	1991/92	1992/93	1993/94	1994/95 [4]	% change 84/85-94/95	% change 93/94-94/95
Number of schools (000s)								
nursery	1	1	1	1	1	1	18	2
primary [5]	25	24	24	24	24	24	-6	-1
secondary [5][6]	5	5	5	5	4	4	-15	-
all maintained mainstream [5][6]	32	30	30	30	30	29	-6	-1
all independent [7][8][9][10]	3	3	2	2	2	2	-5	-
special [5]	2	2	2	2	2	2	-12	-2
all schools	36	35	34	34	34	34	-7	-1
Number of pupils (000s)								
nursery	57	60	61	62	62	62	9	1
primary [5]	4,514	4,812	4,850	4,923	4,998	5,062	12	1
secondary [5][6]	4,244	3,473	3,535	3,606	3,588	3,651	-14	2
all maintained mainstream [5][6]	8,815	8,346	8,445	8,590	8,647	8,775	-	1
all independent [7][8][9][10]	582	604	605	596	591	591	1	-
special [5][11]	132	113	113	113	114	114	-14	-
all schools	9,529	9,062	9,162	9,300	9,352	9,479	-1	1
Number of teachers (000s) [12]								
nursery	3	3	3	3	3	3	12	4
primary [5]	205	221	223	224	226	231	13	3
secondary [5][6]	268	232	233	234	228	230	-14	1
all maintained mainstream [5][6]	475	456	458	461	457	464	-2	2
all independent [7][8][9][10]	50	56	57	57	57	59	20	4
special [5][11]	19	20	20	20	19	19	-3	-2
all schools	544	532	535	538	533	542	-	2
							(difference)	(difference)
Pupil/teacher ratios (rates) [12]								
nursery	21.8	21.5	21.6	21.5	21.6	21.7	-0.1	0.1
primary [5]	22.0	21.8	21.8	21.9	22.2	21.9	-0.1	-0.3
secondary [5][6]	15.9	15.0	15.2	15.4	15.7	15.9	-	0.2
all maintained mainstream [5][6]	18.5	18.3	18.4	18.6	18.9	18.9	0.4	-
all independent [7][8][9][10]	11.7	10.7	10.6	10.4	10.3	9.9	-1.8	-0.4
special [5][11]	6.8	5.7	5.7	5.8	5.9	6.0	-0.8	0.1
all schools	17.5	17.0	17.1	17.3	17.5	17.5	-	-
							(% point difference)	(% point difference)
Pupils under 5 attending school (percentages)								
participation rate [13]	46	52	53	55	55	57	10	1

Source: Education Statistics for the United Kingdom

[1]   Pupils and teachers include full-time equivalents of part-time.

[2]   Teachers (including Heads) at school.

[3]   From 1 April 1993 excludes sixth form colleges in England and Wales which were reclassified as further education colleges.

[4]   Provisional. Includes some 1993/94 data for Wales and Northern Ireland.

[5]   From 1990/91 includes grant maintained schools, of which there were 415 primary, 632 secondary and 2 special in England and Wales in 1994/95.

[6]   From 1989/90 includes voluntary grammar schools in Northern Ireland, previously shown under non-maintained.

[7]   Excludes non-maintained special schools but includes independent special schools.

[8]   From 1989/90 includes City Technology Colleges (CTCs), of which there were 15 in England in 1994/95.

[9]   Excludes independent nursery schools having less than 5 pupils of compulsory school age.

[10]   Comprising independent (including special), direct grant and, up to 1988/89, voluntary grammar (Northern Ireland).

[11]   Both maintained and non-maintained (run by charitable bodies). Excludes independent special.

[12]   Includes qualified and unqualified teachers in schools.

[13]   As a percentage of all children aged 3 and 4 at 31 December of academic year.

-   = between -0.5% and +0.5%

TABLE B: POST-COMPULSORY PARTICIPATION RATES OF 16-18 YEAR OLDS IN EDUCATION IN THE UNITED KINGDOM: 1984/85 TO 1994/95

	1984/85	1990/91	1991/92	1992/93	1993/94	1994/95 [1]	% point difference 84/85-94/95	% point difference 93/94-94/95
Participation rates in education [2][3]								
16 year olds (percentages) [4]								
full-time [5]	48	62	68	71	74	73	24	-1
part-time [6][7]	26	20	18	16	15	15	-11	-
full and part-time	74	82	85	88	89	87	13	-2
17 year olds (percentages) [4]								
full-time [5]	32	43	50	54	58	59	27	1
part-time [6][7]	22	18	17	14	12	11	-11	-1
full and part-time	54	62	66	68	69	70	17	1
18 year olds (percentages) [4]								
full-time [5]	17	25	29	33	37	38	21	2
part-time [6][7]	22	16	16	14	12	11	-11	-1
full and part-time	40	40	45	48	49	50	11	1
16 - 18 year olds (percentages) [4]								
full-time [5]	32	43	48	53	56	57	25	1
part-time [6][7]	23	18	17	15	13	12	-11	-1
full and part-time	56	61	65	67	69	69	14	-

Source: Education Statistics for the United Kingdom

[1]   Provisional. 1994/95 data postdates the publication of GSS Press Notice 284/95. This explains the difference in figures when compared with table 2 of the Press Notice.
[2]   Includes Youth Training (YT) in public sector colleges and adult education centres.
[3]   Excludes nursing and paramedic enrolments.
[4]   Ages at 31 August at the beginning of the academic year.
[5]   Includes sandwich students.
[6]   Includes estimated age detail for students in adult education centres (in England and Wales) and non-vocational further education in Scotland and Northern Ireland.
[7]   Excludes youth clubs and centres and students on some courses of further education run by other bodies for whom age detail was not available.

TABLE C: FURTHER AND HIGHER EDUCATION ENROLMENTS IN THE UNITED KINGDOM: 1984/85 TO 1994/95

(i) Further education enrolments (home and overseas) (000s) [1]

	1984/85	1990/91	1991/92	1992/93	1993/94[5][6]	1994/95[2][3][5][6]	% change 84/85-94/95	% change 93/94-94/95
full-time [4]	400	480	550	586	738	758	..	3
part-time [7]	3,126	3,340	3,298	3,201	3,012	3,042	..	1
all further education	3,526	3,820	3,848	3,787	3,750	3,800	..	1
							(% point difference)	(% point difference)
% of all FE who are female	59	63	63	62	62	62	..	1

(ii) Higher education enrolments (home and overseas) (000s) [8]

	1984/85	1990/91	1991/92	1992/93	1993/94	1994/95[2][6][9]	% change 84/85-94/95	% change 93/94-94/95
full-time [4]	590	747	844	958	1,064	1,144	..	..
part-time [10]	319	428	456	486	515	557	..	..
all higher education	909	1,175	1,300	1,444	1,579	1,701	..	..
							(% point difference)	(% point difference)
% of all HE who are female	40	46	46	47	48	49	..	..

Source: Education Statistics for the United Kingdom

[1]   Includes Youth Training (YT) in public sector colleges and adult education centres.

[2]   Provisional.

[3]   Includes 1993/94 data for non-vocational further education in Scotland and Northern Ireland.

[4]   Includes sandwich students.

[5]   Includes sixth form colleges in England and Wales which were reclassified as FE colleges from 1 April 1993.

[6]   1993/94 and 1994/95 data postdate the publication of GSS Press Notice 284/95. This explains the difference in figures when compared with table 3 of the Press Notice.

[7]   Includes students in adult education centres (in England and Wales) and non-vocational further education in Scotland and Northern Ireland (estimated at 1,226,900 in 1994/95).

[8]   Excludes nursing and paramedic enrolments.

[9]   Higher Education Institution figures are based on new definitions in the Higher Education Statistical Agency (HESA) record.

[10]   Includes the Open University.

-   = between -0.5% and +0.5%

.. = not available

TABLE D: HIGHER EDUCATION ENROLMENTS [1] IN ENGLAND: 1993/94 TO 1994/95

	1993/94 [2]	1994/95 [3]	1994/95 [4]	% change 1993/94 to 1994/95 [3]	1993/94 [2]	1994/95 [3]*	1994/95 [4]	% change 1993/94 to 1994/95 [3]
	First years				All years			
Higher education enrolments (000s)								
home students								
postgraduate								
full-time	47	51	51	7	63	71	71	12
part-time	45	48	49	7	91	101	103	11
all postgraduates	92	99	100	7	155	172	174	11
undergraduate								
full-time	289	289	294	-	697	737	742	6
part-time	149	145	155	-3	239	231	243	-3
all undergraduates	438	435	450	-1	936	968	985	3
overseas students	59	65	71	9	103	114	120	11
all higher education	590	599	620	1	1,194	1,255	1,278	5

Source: Education Statistics for the United Kingdom

[1] Excludes the Open University.
[2] Figures are revisions of those published in Press Notice 107/95.
[3] Figures are based on definitions applied in 1993/94.
[4] Figures are based on new definitions in the Higher Education Statistical Agency (HESA) record.

- = between -0.5% and +0.5%

TABLE E: NON-VOCATIONAL QUALIFICATIONS ATTAINED BY SCHOOL PUPILS IN THE UNITED KINGDOM [1] : 1983/84 TO 1993/94

	1983/84	1989/90	1990/91	1991/92	1992/93	1993/94	% change 83/84-93/94	% change 92/93-93/94
GCE/GCSE/CSE/SCE attainment of school pupils (000s)		school leavers only			all pupils			
GCE A levels or equivalent [2]								
2 + passes [3]	121	124	124	132	136	139	..	2
1 pass [4]	33	29	27	54	52	51	..	-2
1 or more passes	154	153	151	186	187	190	..	1
Population aged 17 (000s) [5]	947	819	770	730	702	679	-28	-3
GCSEs or equivalent								
5 or more higher grades [6]	70	63	59	256	262	288	..	10
1-4 higher grades [6][7]	234	180	162	299	293	272	..	-7
1 or more higher grades	304	243	221	555	555	560	..	1
Population aged 15 (000s) [5]	901	724	698	676	650	667	-26	3

Source: Education Statistics for the United Kingdom.

[1] Excludes sixth form colleges in England which were reclassified as further education colleges from 1 April 1993.
[2] SCE Higher grades and GCE AS passes. 2 GCE AS passes are counted as 1 GCE A level. 3 SCE Higher grade passes are counted as 2 GCE A levels.
[3] 3 or more SCE Higher grade passes in Scotland.
[4] 1 or 2 SCE Higher grade passes in Scotland.
[5] Ages at 31 August at the beginning of the academic year.
[6] Grades A-C at GCSE/GCE O-level and grade 1 at CSE. Includes Scottish O/S-grades 1-3/A-C.
[7] Includes students with 1 GCE AS pass only.

.. = not available.
- = between -0.5% and +0.5%.

TABLE F: NATIONAL TARGETS [1] FOR EDUCATION AND TRAINING IN THE UNITED KINGDOM: 1985 TO 1995

Spring of each year

	1985	1991 [2]	1992 [2]	1993	1994	1995	% point difference 1994 to 1995
Foundation learning targets for the year 2000 (percentages) [3]							
proportion of 19-21 year olds in the UK achieving 5 GCSEs at grade C or above, an Intermediate GNVQ or a NVQ level 2 (or equivalent) (target 85% by 2000) [4]	45	54	59	62	65	64	-
proportion of 21-23 year olds in the UK achieving 2 GCE A levels, an Advanced GNVQ or a NVQ level 3 (or equivalent) (target 60% by 2000) [4]	26	30	35	37	41	44	4
Lifetime learning targets for the year 2000 (percentages) [3]							
proportion of the employed workforce qualified to NVQ level 3, Advanced GNVQ or 2 GCE A level standard (or equivalent) (target 60% by 2000) [4]	27	31	33	38	40	40	-
proportion of the employed workforce having vocational, professional, management or academic qualifications at NVQ level 4 or above (target 30% by 2000)	15	17	20	22	23	23	-

Source: Labour Force Survey (LFS)

[1]   An updated set of targets for the year 2000 was launched in 1995. These cover higher level skills (identified by employers as the foundation for effective transition to work) which will be developed throughout life.
[2]   Revised data.
[3]   See paragraph 8 of this summary for targets
[4]   Data prior to 1993 use assumptions for the number of GCSEs and GCE A levels achieved and are thus not directly comparable with subsequent data.

-   = between -0.5% and +0.5%.

TABLE G: HIGHER EDUCATION QUALIFICATIONS OBTAINED IN THE UNITED KINGDOM: 1983/84 TO 1993/94

	1993/84	1989/90	1990/91	1991/92 [1]	1992/93	1993/94[2] [3]	% change 83/84 - 93/94	% change 92/93 - 93/94
Higher education qualifications [4] obtained (000s)								
below degree level [5][6]	72	107	111	125	143	153	*112*	*7*
first degree level [6][7]	133	152	162	179	189	211	*59*	*11*
post-graduate level [6][8]	37	57	65	73	74	76	*104*	*2*
all HE qualifications	243	316	338	376	406	439	*81*	*8*

Source: Education Statistics for the United Kingdom

[1] Includes estimated data on qualifications awarded by the CNAA.

[2] Provisional. Includes 1992/93 data for the Open University and for USR below degree level and higher diplomas and certificates of post-graduate level.

[3] 1993/94 data postdates the publication of GSS Press Notice 284/95. This explains the difference in figures when compared with table 7 of the Press Notice.

[4] Excludes successful completions of nursing and paramedical courses at Department of Health establishments (32,100 in 1993/94) and all private sector graduates.

[5] Includes Higher TEC/SCOTEC, BEC/SCOTBEC, BTEC/SCOTVEC Certificates and Diplomas, HND/HNC, first university diplomas and certificates, CNAA diplomas and certificates below degree level and estimates of successful completions of sub-degree level public sector professional courses.

[6] Trends in qualification numbers and enrolments may not be directly comparable because qualifications may have been awarded after the end of the last year of study.

[7] Includes university degrees and estimates of university validated degrees (GB), CNAA degrees (and equivalent) and successful completions of degree level public sector professional courses.

[8] Includes university and CNAA post-graduate certificates and diplomas, Masters degrees and PhDs (or equivalents) and estimates of successful completions of post-graduate level public sector professional courses. Post-Graduate Certificates in Education are also included.

TABLE H: EDUCATION EXPENDITURE IN THE UNITED KINGDOM: 1984-85 TO 1994-95

£ billion (cash)

	1984-85	1990-91	1991-92	1992-93	1993-94	1994-95 estimated	% change in real terms [1] 84-85 - 94-95	% change in real terms [1] 93-94 - 94-95
Net expenditure on education	16	27	29	32	34	35	*31*	*3*
							(% point difference)	(% point difference)
as a percentage of GDP [2]	*5.0*	*4.8*	*5.1*	*5.3*	*5.3*	*5.2*	*0.2*	*-0.1*

Source: DfEE Statistical Bulletin 5/95, April 1995; HM Treasury

[1] Percentage changes calculated in 1994-95 prices based on June 1995 GDP deflator.

[2] Gross Domestic Product at market prices. Includes adjustments to remove the distortion caused by the abolition of domestic rates.

International Comparisons

1   The Department for Education and Employment supply summary statistics for the United Kingdom to the Organisation for Economic Co-operation and Development (OECD), Statistical Office of the European Communities (EUROSTAT) and the United Nations Educational, Scientific and Cultural Organisation (UNESCO). Most educational activity is assigned to 7 categories or ISCED[1] levels. The correspondence between figures supplied and tables in the UK Volume or other publications is described in a note obtainable from the address at the end of this section.

2   Comparative tables have been compiled using data supplied by various countries to the international bodies and for the first time, in particular, data derived from OECD's own publication, 'Education at a Glance'. There are inevitably a number of problems of comparability and interpretation in using these tables and readers are advised to read the footnotes carefully. The main needing attention are:

a   The underlying educational systems need to be understood and the statistics adjusted to a standardised form, if at all possible. As an aid to understanding the differences between some of the various countries, up to date information about the different education systems in the European Community is available from Epic Europe, The Mere, Upton Park, Slough Berkshire SL1 2DQ.

b   The ages at which different stages of education are undertaken varies. In particular the range of compulsory education differs.

c   Part-time study should be taken into account, and numbers of enrolments adjusted to full-time equivalents in certain contexts.

d   The range of public and private provision, and the definition of the public/private sectors, will vary from country to country.

e   Institutions may cover more than one of the education levels, so that estimates are required to assign the figures between levels.

f   To obtain comparisons for a common year, it is often necessary to adjust figures for academic or financial years. Financial data require updating using consumer price indices and converting to a common basis using purchasing power parities. The dates at which enrolment counts are taken can also affect the figures.

g   In higher education, participation rates are difficult to compare because of varying course-lengths and drop-out rates. Comparisons of new entrants and qualifiers are generally more meaningful.

h   Comparisons between countries of the different levels within higher education are not always very helpful because different countries can interpret the definitions of sub-degree, first degree and post-graduate courses differently. In most cases, it is best to combine the figures for all three levels. Further problems arise in using figures for the United States, where, for instance, the figures for sub-degree higher education may cover some courses akin to further education in the UK; and Japan, where some further education colleges (senshu) run courses more akin to higher education.

Six sets of international comparisons are presented in tables AA to FF as follows:

AA   -   Covers pre-primary education and day care;

BB   -   Covers education and training at ages 16-18. Most countries have included apprenticeships and training schemes; for comparability, the UK figures contain an estimate of Youth Training with employers although this is not covered routinely in education statistical returns.

CC   -   Compares participation and qualifications in higher education. The UK figures exclude private sector and correspondence courses in higher education. These would add a few percentage points to the UK rates. The new entrant rates for some countries may be inflated by the inclusion of first year students rather than true new (i.e. first time) entrants to HE courses. The table may also over-estimate the percentage of the population entering tertiary education at the normal age, to the extent that students who are older or younger than the theoretical entry age began tertiary education during the reference year.

DD   -   Compares public expenditure on education.

EE and FF - Show destinations of UK students participating in both the ERASMUS and LINGUA programmes and the home states of non-UK students participating in these schemes in UK institutions.

---

1 International Standard Classification of Education

4 ERASMUS (European Action Scheme for the Mobility of University Students) is an EC (European Community) initiative to promote co-operation among higher education institutions in the European Union and, since the start of the 1992/93 academic year, EFTA (European Free Trade Association) member countries also. The programme started in 1987. One of its principal aims is to prepare young people for working within the Community by offering students an opportunity to live and study in another member country.

5 ERASMUS is based on agreements between higher education institutions in the various participating member states which guarantee that the host institutions do not charge any tuition fee to their home institutions. Participating institutions guarantee academic recognition for the study period abroad, which is fully integrated and normally lasts between 3 and 12 months. Normal student facilities are available to incoming students.

6 The programme covers all academic subjects. To gain from the experience of studying abroad, ERASMUS students should have a reasonable command of the language spoken at the host institution. Many students first study the language of their chosen host country immediately prior to moving to the host country, and follow this up with an intensive immersion language course on arrival.

7 Higher education institutions apply to the European Commission for funds to support their programmes and to provide ERASMUS top-up grants for their students. A sum of money is allocated by the EC for ERASMUS student mobility programmes. In this country the UK ERASMUS Student Grants Council allocates block grants to institutions to reflect the applications approved by the EC. The institutions allocate a grant to individual students. This is paid to the student in addition to any grant received from his/her home country.

8 The European Community also runs a similar programme called LINGUA (Action Programme to Promote Foreign Language Competence). LINGUA is currently restricted to EC member states and is targeted at language students, particularly those intending to become language teachers.

9 These programmes are reciprocal so students from other member states can, and do, participate in higher education, in the United Kingdom.

10 A note on the ISCED levels and on the derivation of data for international returns can be obtained from Schools Teachers and General Division (STG 1), Analytical Services Branch, at the address given in the Introduction to this volume (telephone 01325 392753). More detailed information on outward student mobility from the UK, under the ERASMUS and LINGUA programmes, is available in a booklet published by the UK ERASMUS Student Grants Council.

Participation in Pre-Primary Education and Day Care

- The distinction made between education for under fives and Day Care is not always clearly made in all countries. Thus the figures quoted below for education for some countries may also include what other countries regard as Day Care.

- Participation in pre-compulsory education is usually highest among children just before they reach compulsory school age. Age 6 is the usual compulsory school starting age. The exceptions are UK and Netherlands at 5, Denmark, Finland and Norway at 7 and in some states of the USA, 8.

- In Belgium and France virtually all 3 to 5year olds participated in education. The United Kingdom with a participation rate of 68 percent in education in 1992 was among the highest of the countries compared.

- Almost all countries including the UK have increased the participation in education of 3 to 5year olds since 1982.

TABLE AA: PARTICIPATION IN EDUCATION OF 3 TO 5 YEAR OLDS, 1992: AGE PARTICIPATION RATES

Percentages

| | Age at which compulsory schooling starts | Education | | | | | | | Day care |
| | | Age | 3 | 4 | 5 | 3 to 5 | | 3 to 4 | | 3 to 5 |
		Year		1992		1982	1992	1982	1992	1987[1]
Austria	6		29	66	86	..	60	..	47	..
Belgium	6		98	99	100	97	99	96	98	-
Canada	6		-	46	99	34	48	13	23	9[2]
Denmark	7		38	54	61	..	51	..	46	..
Finland	7		24	28	32	..	28	..	26	33[2]
France	6		99	100	100	97	100	95	100	-
Germany, Fed.	6		31	69	79	60	59	51	49	-
Ireland	6		1	56	100	50	54	27	29	14[2]
Japan	6		23	58	66	45	49	33	41	29[2]
Netherlands	5		-	98	99	66	66	50	49	17[2]
Norway	7		44	57	65	..	55	..	50	43
Portugal[3]	6		28	44	63	..	45	..	36	..
Spain	6		37	96	100	..	78	..	67	-
Sweden	6		45	51	61	..	52	..	48	20
UK	5		32	74	100	64	68	45	53	27[4]
USA	6-8[5]		29	53	89	52	56	36	41	..

1   Full-time and part-time combined.
2   Day care data: 1985 for Canada, 1983 for Finland, Ireland and Netherlands, 1986 for Japan.
3   1991 data.
4   DfEE estimates (via General Household Survey) including day nurseries, playgroups, mother and toddler clubs, but avoiding double-counting with education.
5   Varies between states.

Education and Training of 16 to 18 year olds

- In all countries, participation rates are higher among 16 year olds and lower for 18 year olds. The UK's 16 year old rate (91%) is in the mid-range for OECD countries although our 18 year old rate is amongst the lowest.

- Consistent distinction between full-time and part-time study is a problem in international comparisons, e.g. Germany, France and some other countries record all participants on apprenticeship programmes as being in full-time education and training. There are thus larger differences between countries in full-time participation rates than in overall rates. The UK has the lowest full-time participation rates but the highest part-time participation rates.

TABLE BB: PARTICIPATION IN EDUCATION AND TRAINING[1] OF 16 TO 18 YEAR OLDS BY AGE AND MODE OF STUDY 1992: AGE PARTICIPATION RATES

Percentages

	Minimum leaving age	Age 16			Age 17			Age 18		
		Full-Time	Part-Time	All	Full-Time	Part-Time	All	Full-Time	Part-Time	All
Belgium	15	97	2	99	94	2	97	78	-	78
Canada	16	96	-	96	81	-	81	61	-	61
Denmark	16	92	-	92	80	-	80	69	-	69
Finland	16	95	-	95	86	-	86	82	-	82
Germany, Fed.	15	95	-	96	93	-	94	84	-	84
France	15/16	92	-	92	89	-	89	79	-	79
Greece	14/15	88	-	88	62	-	62	45	-	45
Ireland	16	88	1	89	77	-	77	58	-	58
Japan	15	95	1	97	90	1	92	..	..	..
Netherlands	16	97	-	98	92	1	94	79	3	81
New Zealand	16	88	1	89	67	3	70	41	6	47
Norway	16	93	-	93	87	-	87	78	-	78
Spain	16	76	-	76	67	-	67	54	-	54
Sweden	16	89	-	90	87	1	88	61	4	64
Switzerland	14/15	85	-	85	82	-	82	75	-	75
Turkey	14	39	-	39	37	-	37	26	-	26
United Kingdom[2]	16	75	15	91	57	20	77	34	18	52
USA	16-18[3]	91	-	91	75	-	76	54	4	58

1 Includes apprenticeships and similar schemes such as YT. Also includes an estimate of participation in part-time higher education.
2 The UK figures do not match those in table B of the Summary because the latter excludes YT with employers.
3 Varies between states.

Source: OECD, Education at a Glance, 1995

Higher Education

- The UK participation rate for 18-21 year olds, at 18% for full-time and part-time combined, is towards the lower end of the range. Participation rates can be influenced by a number of factors including varying course lengths and drop out rates.

- The full-time new entrant rates to higher education in 1992 varied from 34 per 100 of the relevant year group in Austria to 55 per 100 in Japan. The UK, at 37 per 100, had the second lowest rate after Austria. However, in the UK, entry to part-time courses is relatively more important than in most other countries. Taking account of part-time entrants, the UK rate in 1992 rises to 52 per 100 and has since risen to 62 per 100 in 1994.

- Qualification rates provide an approximate measure of the proportion of young people obtaining Bachelor's and Master's degrees. In some countries the Master's degree is the first degree in higher education. The graduation rates for Master's degrees in these countries are therefore generally higher than those in the UK but lower than our graduation rates for Bachelor's degrees.

TABLE CC: HIGHER EDUCATION: PARTICIPATION AND QUALIFICATION RATES, 1992

	Typical Length of Course (Years)		Participation[1] of 18-21 year olds in HE	New Entrant Rate[2]	Qualification Rates[3]	
	First Degree	Sub Degree	Full-time and Part-time	All HE	Bachelors	Masters[4]
Australia[5]	3-4	3	42	526	26	..
Austria	4-6	2-3	..	34	.	8
Belgium	4	3	31	53	-	14
Canada	4	3	..	..	32	5
Denmark	3-5	1-3	9	53	22	8
Finland[7]	5-6	3-4	15	..	7	12
France	4-5	2-3	29	48	..	15
Germany, Fed.	6	2	10	48	.	13
Italy	4-6	2-4	..	42	1	10
Japan[8]	4	2-3	..	55	23	2
Netherlands	4	4	20	40	18	9
Spain	3-5	3	23	43	8	12
Sweden	4	0-3	11	52	11	.
UK[9]	3-4	1-3	18	37(52)[10](62)[11]	20[12]	7
USA	4	2	39	65[6]	27	9

1   Number of students aged 18-21 as a percentage of the population aged 18-21.

2   Full-time courses. Excludes postgraduates and those already qualified in higher education irrespective of age. The denominator is the population in the theoretical entry age group within a country.

3   Annual flow of students qualifying, divided by the average population of the theoretical graduation age group.

4   In some countries, masters degree is considered as a first degree.

5   Includes Technical and Further Education (TAFE) enrolments, some of which are classified as below HE level.

6   1991 data.

7   Masters is normally the first degree, but Bachelor's degree is being planned in many fields.

8   Includes advanced students in special training schools (SENSHUs) some of whose courses may be below sub-degree level.

9   Excludes private HE.

10   Full-time and part-time entrants in 1992.

11   Full-time and part-time entrants in 1994.

12   Includes estimated public sector professional.

Expenditure on Education

- Public expenditure on primary and secondary education in the UK accounts for a higher percentage of GDP (4.1%) than in most EU and OECD countries.

- Although total public expenditure on education in the UK relative to GDP (5.2%) is comparatively low, education accounts for a larger share of total public expenditure in the UK (11.9%) than in many EU countries.

- On comparisons of expenditure per student, the UK spends more per head at the tertiary level than in any other EU country - although, usually, for a shorter period. As a consequence total public expenditure on tertiary education relative to GDP (at 1.1%) is lower in the UK than in most OECD countries.

TABLE DD: EXPENDITURE ON EDUCATION, 1992

	Start of Fiscal year	Public education expenditure as a % of GDP (%)			Public education expenditure as a % of total public expenditure (%)			Expenditure[1] per student in public institutions (£ per FTE student)		
		Prim & Second[2]	HE	All Levels[3]	Prim & Second[2]	HE	All Levels[3]	Primary	Secondary[2]	Tertiary
Austria	Jan	3.7	1.2	5.8	7.2	2.3	11.3	2,490	3,990	3,620
Australia	Jul	3.0	1.9	5.5	7.7	4.9	14.0	..	..	4,100
Belgium	Jan	3.4	0.9	6.0	6.0	1.5	10.5	1,490[4]	3,200[4]	4,100[4]
Canada	Apr	..	2.4	7.2	..	4.7	14.0	..	..	7,680
Denmark	Jan	4.5	2.0	7.6	7.5	3.3	12.5	2,620	3,070	4170
Finland	Jan	5.0	2.2	8.3	8.4	3.7	13.9	2,390	3,000	5,380
France	Jan	3.8	0.9	5.5	7.3	1.7	10.6	1,800[4]	3,380[4]	3,580[5]
Germany, Fed,	Jan	2.6	1.0	4.1	5.4	2.2	8.5	1,850	2,650	4,070
Ireland	Jan	3.7	1.3	5.6	9.1	3.2	13.7	1,100	1,720	4,520
Italy	Jan	3.4	0.8	5.1	6.4	1.6	9.5	2,520	2,920	3,640
Japan	Apr	2.8	0.3	3.6	8.7	1.0	11.3	2,190	2,420	4,440[5]
Netherlands	Jan	3.3	1.8	5.6	5.6	3.0	9.5	1,590[4]	2,060[4]	5,420[4]
New Zealand	Jul	3.2	2.0	6.5	..	..	..	1,260	1,630	3,780
Spain	Jan	3.3	0.8	4.6	7.5	1.9	10.4	1,260[4]	1,740[4]	2,340
Sweden	Jul	5.1	1.6	7.7	7.7	2.4	11.7	3,010	3,760	4,430
Switzerland	Jan	4.1	1.2	5.7	11.9	3.4	16.5	1,590	..	8,020
United Kingdom	Apr	4.1	1.1	5.2	9.3	2.4	11.9	1,940	2,730	6,450[4]
United States	Oct	3.9	1.3	5.4	10.1	3.5	14.2	3,480	4,020	8,640[5]

1 At purchasing power parity for the calendar year shown.
2 Includes Further Education.
3 Includes expenditure for pre-primary education and other miscellaneous expenditure.
4 All publicly funded institutions (public and government-dependent private).
5 All institutions (both public and private).

EC ERASMUS Students Programme

- The ERASMUS programme continues to grow. In 1992/93 (the most recent year for which complete figures are available) 11,990 EC and EFTA students came to the UK to study, whilst 8,110 UK students studied in Europe. By 1994/95 the number of UK students studying in Europe had risen to 11,540, including 1,090 studying in EFTA countries.

- France and Germany remain the favourite destinations for UK ERASMUS students although other countries (such as Spain and the Netherlands) are becoming increasingly popular. A similar pattern applies to students coming to the UK to study via ERASMUS.

TABLE EE: ERASMUS STUDENT MOBILITY TO AND FROM THE UNITED KINGDOM, 1989/90 TO 1994/95

Percentages

| | 1989/90 | | 1990/91 | | 1991/92 | | 1992/93 | | 1993/94 | | 1994/95[2] | |
	To UK	From UK	To UK	From UK	To UK	From UK[1]	To UK	From UK[1]	To UK	From UK	To UK	From UK[1]
France	33	38	32	41	30	39	27	41	..	40	..	38
Germany	27	23	25	22	26	20	25	19	..	20	..	19
Spain	12	11	13	11	12	12	13	11	..	12	..	14
Italy	12	11	11	8	12	9	13	8	..	8	..	7
Netherlands	6	8	8	7	8	9	8	9	..	9	..	10
Denmark	2	3	3	3	3	3	4	3	..	3	..	3
Belgium	3	3	3	4	4	3	4	4	..	4	..	4
Greece	3	2	2	1	3	1	3	2	..	2	..	2
Ireland	1	2	1	1	1	2	1	2	..	2	..	2
Portugal	1	1	2	1	2	1	2	1	..	2	..	2
Luxembourg	-	-	-	-	-	-	-	-	..	-	..	-
Total Student Numbers (100%)	5,320	4,140	7,430	5,020	9,060	6,130	11,220	7,820	..	9,100	..	10,450
EFTA	..	..	..	..	..	..	770	290	..	600	..	1,090

1 A small number of students attended more than one country.

2 Data are estimated.

EC LINGUA Students Programme

- The LINGUA programme, for which separate data have been available since 1990/91, continues to grow rapidly. In 1990/91, there were less than 200 students both coming to the UK to study and going to other member EC states. In 1992/93 (the most recent year for which complete figures are available) 970 EC students came to the UK and 830 UK students went to other member states. In 1994/95, 1,450 students from the UK participated in the scheme.

- As with ERASMUS, France and Germany are among the favourite destinations for the UK LINGUA students, although Spain is popular too.

TABLE FF: LINGUA STUDENT MOBILITY TO AND FROM THE UNITED KINGDOM, 1990/91 TO 1994/95

| | 1990/91 | | 1991/92 | | 1992/93 | | 1993/94 | | 1994/95[2] | |
	To UK	From UK	To UK	From UK[1]	To UK	From UK[1]	To UK	From UK	To UK	From UK[1]
France	9	27	16	24	25	34	..	37	..	35
Germany	7	6	29	23	28	21	..	18	..	22
Spain	23	44	29	33	24	26	..	27	..	24
Italy	21	4	6	5	6	7	..	7	..	8
Netherlands	7	7	2	4	3	2	..	3	..	3
Denmark	10	3	3	1	2	1	..	-	..	1
Belgium	6	3	5	2	6	4	..	3	..	4
Greece	7	2	5	2	4	1	..	1	..	1
Ireland	-	2	-	1	-	1	..	1	..	1
Portugal	10	3	5	6	3	3	..	2	..	2
Luxembourg	-	-	-	-	-	-	..	-	..	-
Total Student Numbers (100%)	180	190	580	480	970	830	..	1,260	..	1,450

1 A small number of students attended more than one country.

2 Data are estimated.

Main United Kingdom Tables

TABLES

POPULATION
Population (1) at 1 January by age and gender at beginning of the academic year (2)

Thousands

	1981	1986	1991	1996	1994 UK	England	Wales	Scotland	N I	1995 UK	England	Wales	Scotland	N I
PERSONS (3)		United Kingdom												
2	656	718	783	766	792	660	39	66	26	784	654	38	66	26
3	639	713	765	784	781	653	38	65	25	792	660	39	66	26
4	665	727	751	792	771	644	38	64	26	781	653	39	65	25
5	689	736	752	782	785	652	40	66	27	771	644	38	64	26
6	718	716	724	772	766	634	39	66	27	785	652	40	67	27
7	763	657	725	786	753	623	38	65	26	766	634	39	66	27
8	814	640	720	766	753	623	39	65	26	753	623	38	65	26
9	875	666	734	753	725	599	37	63	26	753	624	39	65	26
10	864	690	743	754	727	600	37	64	26	726	599	37	63	26
11	890	720	722	727	722	595	37	65	26	728	601	37	64	26
12	904	764	663	729	737	606	38	67	26	723	595	37	65	26
13	922	815	647	724	746	615	39	65	27	738	607	38	67	26
14	937	874	673	739	725	597	37	65	26	747	616	39	65	27
15	962	866	698	748	667	549	33	60	25	727	599	37	65	26
16	967	892	727	728	651	536	33	58	24	669	551	33	60	25
17	943	905	770	671	679	557	34	63	25	654	538	33	58	24
18	929	924	820	656	704	580	35	64	25	682	559	34	63	25
19	910	942	880	684	734	607	36	66	25	707	582	35	65	25
20	882	970	870	709	779	643	38	72	26	737	610	36	66	25
21-24	3,302	3,789	3,664	3,243	3,494	2,907	163	318	106	3,377	2,805	159	307	106
25-29	3,822	4,127	4,722	4,586	4,756	4,003	209	418	126	4,682	3,938	206	412	126
30 and over	31,811	32,355	33,347	35,496	34,692	29,012	1,767	3,056	857	35,087	29,350	1,784	3,086	867
Total Aged 2 & over	54,864	55,206	55,898	57,396	56,939	47,495	2,845	5,020	1,579	57,168	47,695	2,855	5,030	1,588
MALES														
2	336	368	402	392	405	338	20	34	13	402	335	19	34	13
3	328	366	392	402	401	335	20	33	13	406	338	20	34	13
4	341	373	386	406	396	330	19	33	13	401	335	20	33	13
5	353	377	386	401	403	335	20	34	14	396	330	20	33	13
6	369	368	371	396	393	326	20	34	14	404	335	20	34	14
7	393	337	372	404	387	320	20	33	14	393	326	20	34	14
8	418	329	369	394	387	320	20	33	13	387	320	20	33	14
9	449	342	376	387	372	308	19	32	14	387	321	20	33	13
10	444	354	381	388	374	309	19	33	13	373	308	19	32	14
11	457	370	371	373	371	306	19	33	13	374	309	19	33	13
12	464	393	341	375	378	311	19	34	13	372	307	19	33	13
13	474	419	333	372	383	316	20	33	14	379	312	19	35	13
14	481	449	346	380	373	307	19	33	13	384	316	20	33	14
15	495	445	358	384	343	283	17	31	13	374	308	19	33	13
16	497	457	374	375	336	276	17	30	12	344	284	17	31	13
17	483	463	396	345	350	287	18	32	13	337	278	17	30	12
18	473	474	421	338	362	298	18	33	13	351	288	18	33	13
19	462	481	450	353	378	312	19	34	13	364	300	18	33	13
20	449	496	444	365	401	331	20	37	14	379	313	19	34	13
21-24	1,675	1,921	1,863	1,665	1,791	1,489	84	162	55	1,733	1,439	82	157	55
25-29	1,929	2,084	2,388	2,341	2,423	2,043	106	211	63	2,387	2,011	104	209	63
30 and over	14,885	15,179	15,717	16,907	16,455	13,794	833	1,427	401	16,679	13,987	842	1,444	406
Total Aged 2 & over	26,655	26,845	27,235	28,144	27,861	23,275	1,386	2,430	771	28,005	23,400	1,391	2,437	776
FEMALES														
2	320	350	382	374	386	322	19	32	13	382	319	19	32	12
3	311	347	373	382	380	318	19	32	12	386	322	19	32	13
4	324	355	366	386	375	314	18	31	12	381	318	19	32	12
5	335	359	366	381	382	317	19	32	13	376	314	18	31	12
6	349	348	353	376	373	309	19	32	13	382	317	19	32	13
7	371	319	353	382	366	303	18	32	13	373	308	19	32	13
8	396	311	350	373	366	303	19	32	13	366	303	19	32	13
9	426	324	358	366	353	291	18	31	13	366	303	19	32	13
10	420	335	362	367	353	292	18	31	13	353	292	18	31	13
11	434	350	351	353	351	288	18	32	13	354	292	18	31	13
12	440	371	322	354	359	295	18	33	13	351	289	18	32	13
13	448	396	314	351	363	299	19	32	13	359	295	18	33	13
14	456	426	327	360	352	290	18	31	13	363	299	19	32	13
15	468	421	339	364	324	266	16	29	12	353	290	18	31	13
16	470	434	353	353	316	260	16	28	12	325	267	16	29	12
17	460	441	374	326	329	270	17	31	12	317	261	16	28	12
18	456	450	399	318	342	281	17	31	12	330	271	16	31	12
19	448	461	430	332	357	295	18	32	12	343	283	17	32	12
20	434	474	426	344	378	312	19	35	12	358	296	18	32	12
21-24	1,627	1,868	1,800	1,578	1,704	1,418	79	156	51	1,644	1,366	77	150	51
25-29	1,892	2,043	2,334	2,245	2,333	1,960	103	207	63	2,295	1,927	101	204	63
30 and over	16,927	17,174	17,630	18,588	18,238	15,218	935	1,629	456	18,408	15,363	942	1,642	461
Total Aged 2 & over	28,212	28,357	28,663	29,252	29,078	24,221	1,460	2,590	808	29,163	24,295	1,464	2,593	812

(1) Estimated and projected population numbers based on demographic data provided by the Office of Population Censuses and Surveys and the Government Actuary's Department.
(2) 31 August of the previous year.
(3) Males and Females may not sum to Persons totals due to rounding.

2

ALL INSTITUTIONS
Number of schools or departments by type and establishments of further and higher education

	Academic years					
	1980/81	1985/86	1990/91	1992/93	1993/94	1994/95 (1)
UNITED KINGDOM						
Public sector mainstream						
Nursery	1,251	1,262	1,364	1,406	1,451	1,477
Primary	26,504	24,756	24,135	23,829	23,673	23,523
of which grant maintained			.	75	265	415
Secondary (2)	5,542	5,161	4,790	4,648	4,496	4,478
of which grant maintained			50	266	564	633
of which 6th form colleges	101	109	116	119		
Non-maintained mainstream	2,640	2,538	2,508	2,476	2,478	2,470
of which City Technology Colleges (CTCs)	.	.	7	14	15	15
Special - maintained	}				1,670	1,641
of which grant maintained	}					2
	} 2,011	1,923	1,830	1,768		
- non maintained	}				72	73
ALL SCHOOLS	37,948	35,640	34,627	34,127	33,840	33,662
Universities (including Open University) (3)	48	48	48	48	88	110
Other higher education institutions				111	69	110
	} 806	753	698			
Further education colleges (4)	}			577	682	701
of which 6th form colleges					117	114
Adult education centres (England and Wales)	4,628 (5)	2,874	2,656	1,538 (6)	1,647	4,390 (7)
ENGLAND						
Public sector mainstream						
Nursery	588	560	566	561	552	551
Primary	21,018	19,549	19,047	18,828	18,683	18,551
of which grant maintained			.	75	260	410
Secondary (2)	4,654	4,286	3,897	3,773	3,629	3,614
of which grant maintained			50	262	554	622
of which 6th form colleges	100	108	114	117		
Non-maintained mainstream	2,342	2,274	2,289	2,263	2,268	2,261
of which City Technology Colleges (CTCs)	.	.	7	14	15	15
Special - maintained	}				1,238	1,218
of which grant maintained	}				.	2
	} 1,593	1,493	1,380	1,327		
- non maintained	}				72	73
ALL SCHOOLS	30,195	28,162	27,179	26,752	26,442	26,268
Universities (including Open University) (3)	37	37	37	37	72	94
Other higher education institutions				85	49	90
	} 532	496	460			
Further education colleges	}				462	448
of which 6th form colleges					115	114
Adult education centres	4,067 (4)	2,616	2,315	1,538	1,450	4,192 (7)
WALES						
Public sector mainstream						
Nursery	69	59	54	52	52	..
Primary	1,908	1,774	1,717	1,697	1,698	..
of which grant maintained			.	.	5	..
Secondary (2)	239	237	230	229	227	..
of which grant maintained				4	10	..
of which 6th form colleges	1	1	2	2		..
Non-maintained mainstream	72	69	71	65	64	..
Special	73	67	61	61	59	..
ALL SCHOOLS	2,361	2,206	2,133	2,104	2,100	..
Universities	1	1	1	1	1	1
Other higher education institutions				9	9	9
	} 46	41	38			
Further education colleges	}			25	28	27
of which 6th form colleges					2	
Adult education centres	561 (4)	258	341	..	197	198
SCOTLAND						
Public sector mainstream						
Nursery	515	559	659	705	758	783
Primary	2,522	2,425	2,372	2,347	2,341	2,336
Secondary	444	440	424	412	408	405
of which grant maintained						1
Non-maintained mainstream	138	106	131	130	125	125
Special	319	339	343	334	327	317
ALL SCHOOLS	3,938	3,869	3,929	3,928	3,959	3,966
Universities (3)	8	8	8	8	13	13
Other higher education institutions				15	9	9
	} 89	73	64			
Further education colleges	}			46	46	47
Evening centres	109	115	110	129	122	162
NORTHERN IRELAND						
Grant aided mainstream						
Nursery	79	84	85	88	89	91
Primary	1,056	1,008	999	957	951	938
Secondary	205	198	239	234	232	232
Non-maintained mainstream	88	89	17	18	21	20
Special	26	24	46	46	46	47
ALL SCHOOLS	1,454	1,403	1,386	1,343	1,339	1,328
Universities	2	2	2	2	2	2
Other higher education institutions	4	2	2	2	2	2
Further education colleges	26	26	24	24	24	17

(1) Provisional. Includes 1993/94 schools data for Wales.
(2) From 1 April 1993 excludes sixth form colleges in England and Wales which were reclassified as further education colleges.
(3) From 1993/94 includes former polytechnics and colleges which became universities as a result of the Further and Higher Education Act 1992.
(4) Includes Evening Centres for Scotland.
(5) Includes youth clubs and centres; these were excluded from 1985/86.
(6) England only.
(7) From 1994/95 includes all institutions where formal provision exists. Previous years counted administrative centres only in England.

FINANCE
New student awards, by type (1)

		1970/71	1975/76	1980/81	1985/86	1990/91 (2)	1992/93 (2)		1993/94	
				Academic years					**Thousands**	
Postgraduate awards										
Made by										
Education Departments and the Research Councils		8.2	8.6	10.4	9.5	11.5	11.3		11.8	(3)
Local education authorities (4)		1.2	1.9	2.2	3.9	3.9	3.2		1.9	(3)
Teacher training awards		50.7	46.7	21.2	18.9	26.2	35.2	(5)	37.1	(5)
Full value higher education awards (6)	}						289.4	(5)	312.1	(5)
	}	108.9	131.0	154.1	174.0	232.4				
Full value further education awards (6)	}						32.8	(5)	23.9	(5)
Lesser value further and higher education awards (7)		26.0	33.8	55.5	90.2	81.2	97.6		127.2	
Total		195.0	222.0	243.4	296.6	355.2	469.4		514.1	

(1) See section 8 of the explanatory notes.
(2) Includes revised data.
(3) Includes 1992/93 data for Northern Ireland.
(4) Discretionary awards for postgraduate study made under Section 2 of the Education Act 1962 (excluding initial teacher training) in England and Wales.
(5) England figures include placement year sandwich students.
(6) Full value awards are those paid at between 50% and 100% of the mandatory rate.
(7) Lesser value awards are those paid at less than 50% of the mandatory rate.

FINANCE
Current student awards, by type (1)

		1970/71	1975/76	1980/81	1985/86	1990/91 (2)	1992/93 (2)		1993/94	
				Academic years					**Thousands**	
Postgraduate awards										
Made by										
Education Departments and the Research Councils		15.9	17.7	19.0	18.9	19.5	21.2		21.4	(3)
Local education authorities (4)		1.4	2.1	2.3	4.4	4.2	3.3		2.0	(3)
Teacher training awards		132.5	121.4	44.1	39.4	51.5	66.2	(5)	69.9	(5)
Full value higher education awards (6)	}						730.0	(5)	813.3	(5)
	}	285.2	322.6	402.9	469.9	588.8				
Full value further education awards (6)	}						50.3	(5)	42.3	(5)
Lesser value further and higher education awards (7)		32.8	44.8	77.3	131.6	114.9	156.9		177.6	
Total		467.8	508.6	545.7	644.3	778.9	1,027.9		1,126.5	

See footnotes at Table 3 above.

FINANCE
5
Summary of net education and related expenditure

Financial year 1 April to 31 March (1)						£ million
	1975-76	1980-81	1985-86	1990-91	1992-93 (2)	1993-94 (3)
Local education authorities						
Education						
Recurrent	4,579.5	8,975.9	12,264.6	18,573.3	22,799.7	21,256.2
Capital	535.6	568.9	495.5	821.0	883.7	731.9
Total (4)	5,571.0	10,314.1	13,553.7	20,256.0	23,683.4	21,988.1
Related						
Recurrent	832.0	1,410.6	1,846.1	2,234.6	2,500.8	2,733.3
Capital	28.8	17.2	20.3	23.7	13.1	20.5
Total (4)	884.2	1,462.2	1,902.1	2,299.7	2,513.9	2,753.7
Central Government						
Education						
Recurrent	768.8	1,503.4	2,054.5	3,870.6	3,669.6	6,780.9
Capital	154.8	170.1	218.5	512.1	595.1	814.3
Total (4)	930.3	1,679.6	2,278.1	4,387.8	4,264.6	7,595.3
Related						
Recurrent	47.5	99.2	101.5	197.4	453.7	580.0
Capital	8.5	6.5	3.1	2.0	3.7	2.8
Total	56.0	105.7	104.6	199.4	457.4	582.7
All public authorities						
Education						
Recurrent	5,348.3	10,479.3	14,319.2	22,443.9	26,469.3	28,037.2
Capital	690.4	739.0	714.0	1,333.2	1,478.8	1,546.2
Total (4)	6,038.7	11,218.3	15,033.2	23,777.1	27,948.1	29,583.4
Related						
Recurrent	879.6	1,509.8	1,947.6	2,432.0	2,954.5	3,313.2
Capital	37.3	23.7	23.4	25.7	16.8	23.2
Total	916.9	1,533.5	1,971.0	2,457.7	2,971.3	3,336.5
All expenditure						
Recurrent	6,227.9	11,989.2	16,266.8	24,875.9	29,423.8	31,350.4
Capital	727.7	762.6	737.4	1,358.9	1,495.5	1,569.4
Total (4)	7,441.5	13,561.6	17,838.6	27,143.0	30,919.3	32,919.8
SET/VAT (5),(6) incurred on above expenditure	53	189	284	493	656	579
All public expenditure on education (7)(8) (including school meals and milk)	7,009	12,941	17,288	26,728	31,575	33,499
Gross national product (GNP, at market prices) (5)	112,195	237,839	367,195	557,122	608,073	644,911
Gross domestic product (GDP, at market prices) (5), (9)	109,215	233,460	358,362	556,781	605,156	640,314
Education expenditure as a percentage of GDP	6.4	5.5	4.8	4.8	5.2	5.2
GDP deflator (5), (8)	24.345	48.196	65.637	87.807	97.084	100.000
GDP in real terms (10)	448,614	484,397	545,976	634,096	623,332	640,314
Total education expenditure in real terms (10)	28,790	26,851	26,339	30,439	32,523	33,499

(1) In Scotland prior to 1975-76 the financial year for most education authorities was 16 May to 15 May. In 1975-76 the local authority financial year ended 31 March and the expenditure was therefore grossed up from 10.5 to 12 months for that year only.

(2) Revised central government figures for recurrent (+7.2m) and capital (+0.5m)

(3) Provisional.

(4) Includes loan charge expenditure up to 1991-92, excluded from 1991-92 as not available on a UK basis.

(5) Source: Central Statistical Office.

(6) Current and Capital VAT.

(7) Excludes additional adjustment to allow for Capital consumption made for National Accounts purposes amounting to £941m in 1993-94.

(8) Excludes loan charges.

(9) Includes adjustments to remove the distortion caused by the abolition of domestic rates which have led to revisions to the historical series.

(10) At 1993-94 prices.

6

FINANCE
Summary of net education and related expenditure by type of service

	Financial year 1 April to 31 March					£ million
	1975-76	**1980-81**	**1985-86**	**1990-91**	**1992-93 (1)**	**1993-94 (2)**
Nursery and Primary schools						
Recurrent	1,560.8	2,891.7	3,775.7	6,457.6	8,262.4	8,706.4
Capital	187.6	179.8	171.8	353.1	384.1	408.6
Total (3)	1,888.1	3,301.6	4,180.2	7,087.1	8,635.5	9,115.0
Secondary schools						
Recurrent	1,873.4	3,694.8	5,060.7	7,147.4	8,346.8	8,619.9
Capital	268.2	274.6	222.7	464.7	517.6	490.3
Total (3)	2,354.9	4,338.7	5,644.2	7,975.4	8,875.5	9,110.2
Special schools						
Recurrent	186.7	443.5	666.7	1,120.7	1,353.7	1,419.9
Capital	35.0	26.0	17.2	36.1	32.2	31.1
Total (3)	238.7	503.2	717.0	1,189.8	1,385.9	1,451.0
Universities (4)						
Student grants (tuition fees)	30.1	217.1	159.8	385.8	1,546.9	.
Grants to universities - recurrent	547.9	1,047.4	1,445.4	1,879.6	1,814.0	.
Capital	105.6	117.0	140.4	210.7	235.6	.
Total	683.6	1,381.5	1,745.6	2,476.0	3,596.6	.
Other higher,further and adult education						
Student grants (tuition fees)	19.7	138.7	167.6	477.9	241.8	.
Other recurrent (inc Training of Teachers - tuition)	859.6	1,530.9	2,307.7	3,649.9	3,894.3	.
Capital	90.7	131.2	151.1	229.6	284.5	.
Total (3)	1,048.0	1,935.7	2,790.6	4,493.6	4,420.6	.
Higher Education Funding Council (5)						
Student grants (tuition fees) (6)	.	.	.	.	.	1,795.0
Other recurrent	.	.	.	.	.	3,112.9
Total recurrent						4,908.0
Capital	.	.	.	.	.	405.6
Total	.	.	.	.	.	5,313.6
Further Education Funding Council (7)						
Student grants (tuition fees) (8)	.	.	.	.	.	123.7
Other recurrent	.	.	.	.	.	2,948.1
Total recurrent						3,071.8
Capital	.	.	.	.	.	193.8
Total	.	.	.	.	.	3,265.6
Continuing Education (9)						
Recurrent	.	.	.	.	.	380.4
Capital	.	.	.	.	.	5.6
Total (3)	.	.	.	.	.	386.1
School Welfare (10)						
Recurrent	8.8	20.5	36.6	155.3	270.4	345.9
Capital	0.5	-	-	1.7	-	-
Total (3)	9.5	20.5	36.9	163.4	270.4	345.9
Meals and milk						
Recurrent	383.1	479.2	532.1	506.1	161.4	148.5
Capital	16.4	3.0	1.4	1.7	1.5	1.8
Total (3)	412.7	501.4	548.9	524.1	162.9	150.3
Youth service						
Recurrent	72.3	147.9	238.8	347.7	393.2	393.9
Capital	18.7	19.2	20.3	18.7	12.8	18.6
Total (3)	98.9	182.0	279.1	385.2	406.0	412.5
Transport of pupils						
Recurrent	..	..	..	393.3	416.7	443.7
Capital	..	..	..	3.2	1.8	2.3
Total (3)	99.6	215.0	279.4	396.5	418.4	446.1
Maintenance grants/allowances to students/pupils (11)(12)	318.4	645.4	857.3	1,027.5	1,705.0	1,971.5
Other and miscellaneous expenditure						
Recurrent	267.5	517.1	739.0	1,327.2	1,017.0	940.4
Capital	4.2	10.7	11.2	39.4	25.4	11.6
Total (3)	279.2	535.0	758.1	1,424.4	1,034.7	952.0
TOTAL EXPENDITURE						
Recurrent	6,227.9	11,989.2	16,266.8	24,875.9	29,423.8	31,350.4
Capital	727.7	762.6	737.4	1,358.9	1,495.5	1,569.4
Total (3)	7,441.5	13,561.6	17,838.6	27,143.0	30,919.3	32,919.8

(1) Includes 1991-92 data for Wales.
(2) Provisional.
(3) Includes loan charge expenditure up to 1991-92. Not available on a UK basis from 1991-92 onwards.
(4) Includes expenditure on University departments of education for England and Wales.
(5) Includes expenditure on Higher Education Institutions in Northern Ireland.
(6) Expenditure on mandatory awards - tuition fees - can include fees in respect of non-HEFC institutions.
(7) Includes expenditure on Further Education Institutions in Northern Ireland.
(8) Expenditure on mandatory awards - tuition fees - can include fees in respect of non-FEFC institutions.
(9) Includes expenditure on Further Education for Adults and Other Continuing Education.
(10) Expenditure mainly on other education support services.
(11) From 1986-87, excludes the secondment of teachers on further training.
(12) From 1990-91 includes student loans expenditure.

7 FINANCE
Net education and related expenditure (1) by type of service

Financial year 1 April 1993 - 31 March 1994 (2)(3) £ million

	Local education authorities	Central govern-ment	Total
(i). EDUCATION EXPENDITURE			
Nursery and primary schools			
Salaries and wages			
Teaching staff	5,529.4	-	5,529.4
Other staff	1,189.1	-	1,189.1
Other recurrent expenditure	1,970.5	17.5	1,988.0
Total recurrent expenditure	8,688.9	17.5	8,706.4
Capital expenditure	322.5	86.1	408.6
Total expenditure	9,011.5	103.5	9,115.0
Secondary schools			
Salaries and wages			
Teaching staff	5,205.4	-	5,205.4
Other staff	708.3	-	708.3
Other recurrent expenditure	2,491.1	215.1	2,706.2
Total recurrent expenditure	8,404.8	215.1	8,619.9
Capital expenditure	360.3	130.0	490.3
Total expenditure	8,765.1	345.1	9,110.2
Special schools			
Salaries and wages			
Teaching staff	669.3	-	669.3
Other staff	325.4	-	325.4
Other recurrent expenditure	419.4	5.8	425.2
Total recurrent expenditure	1,414.1	5.8	1,419.9
Capital expenditure	30.0	1.1	31.1
Total expenditure	1,444.1	6.9	1,451.0
HEFC (4)			
Grants to students - tuition fees (5)	1,573.4	221.6	1,795.0
Other recurrent expenditure	0.2	3,112.7	3,112.9
Total recurrent expenditure	1,573.6	3,334.3	4,908.0
Capital expenditure	0.0	405.6	405.6
Total expenditure	1,573.6	3,739.9	5,313.6
FEFC (6)			
Grants to students - tuition fees (7)	66.9	56.8	123.7
Other recurrent expenditure	72.9	2,875.2	2,948.1
Total recurrent expenditure	139.8	2,932.1	3,071.8
Capital expenditure	7.8	185.9	193.8
Total expenditure	147.6	3,118.0	3,265.6
Continuing Education (8)			
Recurrent expenditure	337.4	43.1	380.4
Capital expenditure	5.3	0.3	5.6
Total expenditure	342.7	43.4	386.1
Other education expenditure			
Administration			
Salaries and wages			
Teaching staff	52.6	-	52.6
Other staff	479.3	12.9	492.2
Other Administration	69.7	143.4	213.1
Total	601.6	156.4	757.9
Other recurrent expenditure (9)	96.1	76.8	172.8
Total recurrent expenditure	697.6	233.1	930.8
Capital expenditure	5.9	5.3	11.2
Total expenditure	703.5	238.4	941.9
TOTAL EDUCATION EXPENDITURE			
Salaries and wages			
Teaching staff	11,456.7	-	11,456.7
Other staff	2,702.0	12.9	2,715.0
Other recurrent expenditure	7,097.5	6,768.0	13,865.5
Total recurrent	21,256.2	6,780.9	28,037.2
Total capital	731.9	814.3	1,546.2
Total education expenditure	21,988.1	7,595.3	29,583.4

	Local education authorities	Central govern-ment	Total
(ii). RELATED EXPENDITURE			
School welfare(10)			
Salaries and wages			
Teaching staff	127.9	-	127.9
Other staff	184.3	-	184.3
Other recurrent expenditure (9)	33.8	-	33.8
Total recurrent expenditure	345.9	-	345.9
Capital expenditure	-	-	-
Total expenditure	345.9	-	345.9
Meals and milk			
Salaries and wages			
Teaching staff	-	-	-
Other staff	37.4	-	37.4
Other recurrent expenditure(9)	111.1	-	111.1
Total recurrent expenditure	148.5	-	148.5
Capital expenditure	1.8	-	1.8
Total expenditure	150.3	-	150.3
Youth service			
Salaries and wages			
Teaching staff	50.8	-	50.8
Other staff	188.5	1.2	189.7
Other recurrent expenditure	145.1	8.4	153.5
Total recurrent expenditure	384.3	9.6	393.9
Capital expenditure	16.3	2.3	18.6
Total expenditure	400.6	11.9	412.5
Transport of pupils			
Recurrent expenditure	443.7	-	443.7
Capital expenditure	2.3	-	2.3
Total expenditure	446.1	-	446.1
Maintenance grants and allowances to pupils and students			
Student loans	-	345.9	345.9
Higher education	1,116.9	143.3	1,260.3
Training of teachers: grants and allowances to students	110.6	13.3	123.9
Further education	142.0	58.2	200.2
Schools (inc. special education)	41.2	-	41.2
Total maintenance grants and loans	1,410.8	560.7	1,971.5
Miscellaneous expenditure			
Salaries and wages			
Teaching staff	-	-	-
Other staff	-	1.0	1.0
Other recurrent expenditure	-	8.6	8.6
Total recurrent expenditure	-	9.6	9.6
Capital expenditure	-	0.4	0.4
Total expenditure	-	10.1	10.1
TOTAL RELATED EXPENDITURE			
Salaries and wages			
Teaching staff	178.6	-	178.6
Other staff	410.2	2.2	412.4
Other recurrent expenditure	1,700.8	577.8	2,278.5
Total recurrent	2,733.3	580.0	3,313.2
Total capital	20.5	2.8	23.2
Total related expenditure	2,753.7	582.7	3,336.5
(iii). ALL EDUCATION EXPENDITURE			
Salaries and wages			
Teaching staff	11,635.3	-	11,635.3
Other staff	3,112.2	15.1	3,127.3
Other recurrent expenditure	8,798.3	7,345.7	16,144.1
Total recurrent expenditure	23,989.5	7,360.9	31,350.4
Total capital expenditure	752.3	817.1	1,569.4
Total expenditure	24,741.9	8,178.0	32,919.8

(1) Recurrent expenditure except where stated. The totals shown under recurrent expenditure are net expenditure figures. Salaries and wages of 'Teaching' and 'Other' staff are however gross amounts expended by local authorities. Any income has been deducted from 'Other'.
(2) Provisional.
(3) Excludes loan charges expenditure.
(4) Includes expenditure by Higher Education institutions in Northern Ireland.
(5) Expenditure on mandatory awards - tuition fees - can include fees in respect of students at non-HEFC institutions.
(6) Includes expenditure by Further Education institutions in Northern Ireland.
(7) Expenditure on mandatory awards - tuition fees - can include fees in respect of students at non-FEFC institutions.
(8) Includes expenditure on Further Education for Adults and Continuing Education not covered by FEFC.
(9) Scotland, Wales and Northern Ireland only. Other recurrent expenditure on Other Education, School Welfare and Meals and milk in England has been recharged across the other expenditure headings.
(10) Expenditure mainly on other education support services in England and Wales.

8 TEACHING STAFF

New entrants, total enrolments and successful students for initial (1) teacher training by gender and type of course (2)

Thousands

	1980/81	1985/86	1990/91	1991/92	1992/93	1993/94	1994/95 (3)
UNITED KINGDOM							
New entrants (4)							
Universities (5)	6.2	5.0	8.2	9.9	9.4	21.4	22.1
Courses for graduates (6)	5.7	4.3	7.1	8.6	7.8	14.5	15.3
Courses for undergraduates (7)	0.6	0.6	1.1	1.2	1.6	6.8	6.8
Other Teacher Training	15.7	14.3	20.8	23.1	25.0	15.3	13.5
Courses for graduates (6)	7.0	4.8	7.0	8.8	8.7	5.8	6.0
Courses for undergraduates (7)	8.7	9.5	13.9	14.3	16.3	9.4	7.5
Enrolments (4)							
Universities (5)	7.7	6.6	11.1	13.2	13.9	38.1	39.2
Courses for graduates (6)	5.7	4.4	7.1	9.0	8.7	15.1	15.4
Courses for undergraduates (7)	2.0	2.2	4.0	4.1	5.2	23.0	23.8
Other Teacher Training	35.1	33.0	44.4	48.9	54.6	34.4	34.2
Courses for graduates (6)	7.0	4.8	7.1	9.2	9.1	6.0	6.2
Courses for undergraduates (7)	28.0	28.1	37.3	39.7	45.5	28.4	28.0
Successfully completing (8)(9)							
Universities	6.0	4.8	6.4	7.8	15.0	15.0	..
Courses for graduates	5.4	4.3	5.7	7.1	10.9	11.3	..
Courses for undergraduates	0.6	0.5	0.7	0.7	4.1	3.6	..
Other Teacher Training	16.2	11.4	13.6	15.9	11.4	12.6	..
Courses for graduates	6.6	4.2	6.4	8.3	5.9	6.2	..
Courses for undergraduates	9.6	7.1	7.2	7.6	5.6	6.4	..
All successfully completing (8)(9)(10)	22.2	16.2	20.0	23.7	27.0	28.1	..
of which articled/SCITT/distance learning	.	.	..	..	0.2	0.1	..
of which licensed/overseas teachers	.	.	..	..	0.6	0.5	..
ENGLAND AND WALES (10)							
All new entrants	18.9	17.3	25.7	29.5	31.0	33.4	32.4
Males	7.1	5.1	7.1	8.7	8.8	10.0	9.8
Females	11.8	12.2	18.6	20.8	22.2	23.4	22.5
All enrolments	35.8	34.9	48.8	54.7	60.8	65.0	66.0
Males	10.9	8.5	11.3	13.2	14.5	16.1	16.5
Females	24.9	26.4	37.5	41.4	46.4	48.9	49.5
All successfully completing (11)	19.0	13.5	17.6	21.0	24.0	24.9	..
Males	5.3	4.1	4.8	6.0	6.5	7.2	..
Females	13.7	9.4	12.8	15.0	17.4	17.7	..
SCOTLAND (11)							
All new entrants	2.4	1.4	2.6	2.7	2.6	2.5	..
Males	0.8	0.3	0.6	0.7	0.7	0.7	..
Females	1.7	1.1	2.0	2.1	1.8	1.7	..
All enrolments	4.9	3.0	4.8	5.4	5.7	5.5	..
Males	1.3	0.6	0.8	1.0	1.1	1.2	..
Females	3.6	2.4	4.0	4.4	4.5	4.3	..
All successfully completing	2.3	1.2	1.8	2.0	2.3	2.4	..
Males	0.7	0.3	0.4	0.5	0.6	0.6	..
Females	1.6	0.9	1.3	1.5	1.7	1.8	..
NORTHERN IRELAND							
All new entrants	0.6	0.6	0.7	0.8	0.8	0.8	0.7
Males	0.2	0.1	0.2	0.2	0.2	0.2	0.2
Females	0.4	0.5	0.6	0.6	0.6	0.6	0.5
All enrolments	2.1	1.6	1.9	1.9	2.0	1.9	1.9
Males	0.6	0.3	0.3	0.3	0.4	0.4	0.4
Females	1.5	1.3	1.5	1.6	1.6	1.6	1.5
All successfully completing	0.9	0.6	0.7	0.7	0.8	0.8	..
Males	0.3	0.2	0.1	0.2	0.2	0.2	..
Females	0.6	0.4	0.5	0.6	0.6	0.6	..

(1) All courses leading to Qualified Teacher Status.
(2) See paragraphs 9.1 - 9.9 of the explanatory notes.
(3) Provisional. Includes 1993/94 data for Wales and Scotland.
(4) At the start of the academic year. University entrants are calendar year of first year shown.
(5) From1993/94 includes former polytechnics and colleges which became universities as a result of the Further and Higher Education Act 1992.
(6) From 1993/94 England figures include School Centred ITT (SCITT), Articled teachers and the Open University.

(7) From 1990/91 includes licensed/overseas trained teachers for England.
(8) Completers at the end of the academic year.
(9) Including students in England and Wales who failed their BEd degree course but have received qualified teacher status on the basis of a non-degree qualification obtained in an earlier year.
(10) England and Wales.
(11) Numbers for males and females are estimated from 1980.

9 TEACHING STAFF

Teachers and lecturers by type of establishment, gender and graduate status: percentage trained

(i) Full-time

	1980/81 All (000s)	1980/81 Grads (%)	1985/86 (1) All (000s)	1985/86 (1) Grads (%)	1990/91 (2) All (000s)	1990/91 (2) Grads (%)	1991/92 (2)(3) All (000s)	1991/92 (2)(3) Grads (%)	1992/93 (2) All (000s)	1992/93 (2) Grads (%)	1993/94 (2)(4) All (000s)	1993/94 (2)(4) Grads (%)	1993/94 (2)(4) Grads (%) trained (5)
UNITED KINGDOM													
PERSONS													
Public sector mainstream													
Primary (6)	222	17	201	25	209	36	209	39	210	41	212	44	98
Secondary (7)(8)	281	54	266	62	233	66	230	67	229	68	223	69	93
Non-maintained mainstream (7)(9)	43	63	43	69	44	70	46	71	45	72	46	73	..
Special - maintained	19	22	19	31	19	37	19	38	19	39	17	40	96
- non-maintained											1	44	94
All schools	565	39	529	47	505	53	504	55	503	56	498	58	..
FHE establishments (10)	89	43	93	46	90	48	89	49	84	49	..	..	..
Universities (11)	34	99	31	99	32	99	30	99	31	99	32	99	..
All establishments (12)	693	42	657	50	631	55	624	56	618	57	..	..	..
MALES													
Public sector mainstream													
Primary (6)	48	24	41	34	38	45	37	47	37	49	36	52	99
Secondary (7)(8)	154	58	143	65	121	70	118	71	116	72	111	73	93
Non-maintained mainstream (7)(9)	20	78	21	82	21	84	21	86	20	86	20	87	..
Special - maintained	6	25	6	35	6	43	6	44	6	46	5	47	96
- non-maintained											-	48	93
All schools	229	51	211	60	185	65	181	67	179	68	173	69	..
FHE establishments (10)	70	43	69	46	62	48	60	48	56	49	..	..	..
Universities (11)	30	99	28	99	27	99	25	99	26	99	26	99	..
All establishments (12)	332	54	310	60	276	64	266	66	260	67	..	..	..
FEMALES													
Public sector mainstream													
Primary (6)	174	15	160	23	171	34	172	37	173	39	175	42	98
Secondary (7)(8)	127	49	123	58	112	62	113	63	113	65	111	66	94
Non-maintained mainstream (7)(9)	23	50	22	56	24	58	25	59	25	60	26	62	..
Special - maintained	13	20	13	29	13	34	13	35	13	37	12	37	96
- non-maintained											1	40	95
All schools	336	30	318	39	320	46	323	48	324	50	325	51	..
FHE establishments (10)	19	42	24	46	28	49	29	49	28	49	..	..	..
Universities (11)	4	99	4	99	5	99	5	99	5	98	6	99	..
All establishments (12)	361	32	347	40	355	47	358	48	357	50	..	..	..
ALL SCHOOLS													
ENGLAND AND WALES (2)													
Persons	490	39	460	47	440	53	439	55	437	57	432	58	..
Males	202	50	186	59	163	65	161	66	158	67	153	69	..
Females	288	30	274	40	276	47	278	48	279	50	280	52	..
SCOTLAND (2)(9)													
Persons	57	49	..	..	47	48	47	48	47	51	47	51	..
Males	20	67	..	..	15	71	15	71	14	73	14	73	..
Females	37	31	..	..	32	38	32	38	32	41	32	41	..
NORTHERN IRELAND (2)(9)													
Persons	19	42	18	49	19	58	18	60	19	62	19	65	..
Males	7	54	7	60	7	69	6	70	6	72	6	74	..
Females	12	33	11	43	12	52	12	55	12	58	13	60	..

(ii) Part-time (13)

	1980/81	1985/86	1990/91	1991/92	1992/93	Persons	Males	Females
GREAT BRITAIN (PERSONS)								
Public sector mainstream								
Primary (6)	..	..	..	..	..	16	3	13
Secondary (7)(8)	..	..	..	..	..	15	8	8
Non-maintained mainstream (7)(9)	..	..	..	..	..	8	1	7
Special - maintained	..	..	..	..	..	1	..	1
- non-maintained	..	..	..	..	..			
All schools	17	18	30	32	33	41	12	29
FHE establishments (10)(14)	22 (15)	23	28	30	30	..	..	..
Universities (11)	..	..	..	..	..			
All establishments	41	43	58	62	63	..	..	..

(1) UK includes 1984/85 schools data for Scotland.
(2) Includes some estimated data for each of the countries.
(3) Includes 1992/93 data for Scotland.
(4) Provisional.
(5) GB only.
(6) Includes nursery schools.
(7) From 1989/90 voluntary grammar schools are recorded in the maintained sector.
(8) From 1 April 1993 excludes sixth form colleges which were reclassified as further education colleges.
(9) Excludes independent schools in Scotland and Northern Ireland

(10) Excludes Ulster Polytechnic. See Paragraph 9.13 of the explanatory notes for graduate shortfall.
(11) Excludes Open University.
(12) Includes teachers classified as miscellaneous.
(13) See paragraphs 9.10 - 9.15 of the explanatory notes.
(14) From 1990/91 includes staff in some formerly independent (now public sector) colleges.
(15) England and Wales only.

TEACHING STAFF
Full-time teachers and lecturers by type of establishment (1), gender and age: average salary summary, 1992/93

Thousands

Age Band	Under 25	25-29	30-34	35-39	40-44	45-49	50-54	55-59	60 and over	Total	Average salary (2) (£)
UNITED KINGDOM											
PERSONS											
Public sector schools											
Nursery and Primary	9	25	16	30	48	41	24	14	3	210	19,900
Secondary	5	20	26	39	53	44	26	12	3	229	21,400
Special	-	1	1	3	4	4	2	1	-	17	22,500
Total schools	14	46	44	73	106	89	52	27	6	458	20,800
Universities (3)	-	2	3	4	5	6	5	4	2	32	26,500
MALES											
Public sector schools											
Nursery and Primary	1	3	3	6	9	8	4	2	1	37	22,300
Secondary	2	7	12	19	29	24	14	7	2	116	22,400
Special	-	-	-	1	1	1	1	-	-	5	24,000
Total schools	2	11	15	26	40	34	18	9	3	158	22,500
Universities (3)	-	1	2	3	4	5	5	3	2	26	27,400
FEMALES											
Public sector schools											
Nursery and Primary	8	22	13	25	39	33	20	12	2	173	19,400
Secondary	4	13	14	20	24	20	12	5	1	113	20,400
Special	-	1	1	2	3	3	2	1	-	12	21,800
Total schools	12	35	28	47	66	55	34	18	4	299	19,900
Universities (3)	-	1	1	1	1	1	1	-	-	6	22,700
ENGLAND AND WALES											
Public sector mainstream (4)											
Males	2	9	13	21	33	29	15	7	2	132	22,400
Females	10	30	23	36	53	46	28	15	3	244	19,800
SCOTLAND											
Public sector mainstream (4)											
Males	-	1	1	3	4	3	2	1	-	14	..
Females	1	3	3	6	7	5	4	2	-	31	..
NORTHERN IRELAND											
Grant-aided mainstream (4)											
Males			1	1	2	1	1	-	-	6	21,500
Females	1	2	1	2	2	2	1	1	-	12	18,500

(1) Information on teachers in non-university FHE establishments is not available.
(2) Rounded to the nearest £100. The average salary is calculated on the basis of England, Wales and Northern Ireland only. No salary details were available for teachers in Scotland.
(3) Full-time teaching and research staff paid wholly from general university funds. The average salary is that of non-clinical staff.
(4) Excludes special schools.

SCHOOLS
Full-time and part-time pupils in school, by age (1) and gender

(i) Public sector schools (2)   Thousands

	1970/71	1975/76	1980/81	1985/86 (3)	1990/91 (4)	1991/92 (5)	1992/93	1993/94	1994/95 (6)
PERSONS									
2-4 (7)	351	545	753	872	954	985	1,021	1,042	1,069
5-10	5,336	5,257	4,555	3,911	4,136	4,148	4,189	4,262	4,315
11	789	907	844	682	660	681	676	664	670
12-14	2,259	2,573	2,591	2,304	1,817	1,860	1,951	2,019	2,022
15	476	813	877	785	637	612	586	599	645
16	226	384	234	242	252	265	272	218	215
17	123	140	135	135	160	169	178	144	147
18 and over	42	44	15	21	25	27	27	15	16
MALES									
14	373	428	447	417	316	304	310	338	347
15	244	415	446	400	326	313	299	305	329
16	116	194	109	116	120	128	132	106	105
17	64	71	66	66	76	79	84	68	69
18 and over	25	25	9	11	13	14	14	8	8
FEMALES									
14	357	410	429	399	301	290	297	322	333
15	232	398	431	385	311	299	287	294	316
16	110	189	125	126	132	137	140	112	110
17	59	69	69	69	84	90	94	76	77
18 and over	17	19	6	9	12	13	13	7	7
UNITED KINGDOM (4)	9,602	10,662	10,005	8,952	8,640	8,748	8,900	8,963	9,099
ENGLAND	7,823	8,714	8,185	7,306	7,045	7,140	7,276	7,321	7,450
WALES	500	563	532	483	469	475	482	487	..
SCOTLAND	966	1,054	970	861	787	791	797	806	811
NORTHERN IRELAND (4)	313	332	318	302	340	342	342	348	350

(ii) All schools

	1970/71	1975/76	1980/81	1985/86 (3)	1990/91 (4)	1991/92 (5)	1992/93	1993/94	1994/95 (6)
PERSONS									
2-4 (7)	384	576	792	917	1,012	1,045	1,082	1,103	1,133
5-10	5,545	5,453	4,752	4,096	4,346	4,356	4,392	4,462	4,514
11	844	965	903	737	714	735	727	713	717
12-14	2,443	2,768	2,777	2,487	1,975	2,021	2,112	2,179	2,178
15	534	876	940	845	691	664	638	651	699
16	273	432	280	286	295	308	313	259	257
17	157	175	168	169	197	206	215	180	184
18 and over	53	56	21	28	32	34	35	23	24
MALES									
14	373	428	447	417	316	332	338	367	376
15	244	415	446	400	326	341	327	333	358
16	116	194	109	116	120	151	154	128	128
17	64	71	66	66	76	100	104	88	90
18 and over	25	25	9	11	13	18	18	12	13
FEMALES									
14	386	439	457	428	326	314	322	347	358
15	259	427	459	412	336	323	311	318	341
16	131	211	144	145	151	156	159	131	130
17	73	84	82	84	100	106	111	92	94
18 and over	21	24	8	12	15	16	16	11	11
UNITED KINGDOM (4)	10,232	11,301	10,633	9,565	9,260	9,368	9,513	9,571	9,707
ENGLAND (8)	8,361	9,258	8,720	7,830	7,617	7,712	7,842	7,883	8,012
WALES	512	576	545	495	482	487	493	498	..
SCOTLAND	1,006	1,094	1,005	894	821	826	832	841	846
NORTHERN IRELAND (4)	353	374	363	346	341	343	346	349	351

(1)   Age at beginning of January of second year shown up to and including 1975/76 and at 31 August of first year shown for 1980/81 and later years. Age data for Scotland has been adjusted to 31 August 1980 for 1980/81. Age data for Northern Ireland are at 1 July from 1992/93 for grant-aided schools. It remains the same - January - for the independent schools.

(2)   Includes grant-maintained schools. From 1 April 1993 excludes 6th form colleges in England and Wales, reclassified as further education colleges.

(3)   Includes 1984/85 data for Scotland.

(4)   From 1989/90 Northern Ireland voluntary grammar schools formerly allocated to the independent sector are recorded as public sector schools.

(5)   From 1991/92 the figures for Independent schools in England include pupils aged less than 2 years.

(6)   Provisional. Includes 1993/94 data for Wales.

(7)   From 1980/81 includes the so-called rising fives (i.e. those pupils who became 5 during the autumn term).

(8)   The ages of pupils in non-maintained schools in England have been estimated for 1980/81.

SCHOOLS
Full-time and part-time pupils by age, gender and school type, 1993/94

Thousands

| | Maintained schools | | | | | | Non-maintained | | | |
| | Primary Schools | | | | | | | | | |
Age at 31 August 1993 (5)	Nursery Schools	Nursery Classes	Other Classes	Secondary Schools (1)	Special Schools	Total Schools	Special schools (2)	Other schools (3),(4)	Total Schools	ALL SCHOOLS
PERSONS										
2 - 4 (6)	84.7	345.5	603.9	-	7.9	1,042.0	0.2	60.9	61.0	1,103.0
5	0.3	0.4	745.6	-	4.6	750.9	0.1	30.0	30.1	781.0
6	-	-	725.2	-	5.3	730.5	0.2	30.0	30.2	760.7
7	-	-	706.8	-	6.0	712.8	0.2	31.5	31.7	744.5
8	-	-	700.8	-	7.0	707.8	0.2	34.0	34.2	742.1
9	-	-	636.1	37.3	7.6	681.0	0.3	35.4	35.7	716.7
10	-	-	628.0	42.5	8.7	679.3	0.4	37.8	38.2	717.5
11	-	-	87.2	566.9	10.0	664.2	0.5	48.8	49.3	713.4
12	-	-	1.2	664.8	10.8	676.7	0.5	50.8	51.3	728.1
13	-	-	-	671.4	11.7	683.1	0.6	52.7	53.3	736.4
14	-	-	-	648.1	11.4	659.5	0.7	53.8	54.5	714.1
15	-	-	-	587.8	10.8	598.5	0.6	51.7	52.3	650.8
16	-	-	-	214.3	3.6	217.9	0.5	40.8	41.3	259.2
17	-	-	-	141.0	2.6	143.6	0.4	36.3	36.7	180.3
18	-	-	-	12.4	1.8	14.2	0.3	5.7	6.0	20.2
19 and over	-	-	-	1.1	0.1	1.2	0.2	1.6	1.8	3.0
TOTAL	85.0	345.9	4,834.9	3,587.5	110.0	8,963.3	6.0	601.7	607.7	9,571.0
of which										
ENGLAND	52.5	295.1	3,946.6	2,933.6	93.4	7,321.3	5.5	556.0	561.6	7,882.8
WALES	3.6	23.8	261.9	194.4	3.6	487.3	-	10.8	10.8	498.1
SCOTLAND	23.7	24.4	438.4	311.3	8.6	806.3	0.4	34.0	34.4	840.7
NORTHERN IRELAND	5.3	2.6	187.9	148.3	4.4	348.4	-	0.9	0.9	349.4
MALES										
2 - 4 (6)	43.8	176.5	308.1	-	4.9	533.3	0.1	30.5	30.6	563.9
5	0.2	0.3	380.2	-	3.0	383.6	0.1	15.4	15.4	399.1
6	-	-	371.1	-	3.5	374.6	0.1	15.3	15.4	390.0
7	-	-	361.6	-	3.9	365.5	0.1	16.3	16.4	381.9
8	-	-	357.4	-	4.6	362.1	0.2	18.0	18.1	380.2
9	-	-	323.1	19.1	5.1	347.3	0.2	18.6	18.8	366.1
10	-	-	320.3	21.8	6.0	348.1	0.3	20.2	20.5	368.5
11	-	-	44.6	288.1	6.8	339.6	0.4	25.5	25.9	365.4
12	-	-	0.7	337.4	7.3	345.4	0.4	26.6	27.0	372.4
13	-	-	-	341.2	8.0	349.2	0.4	27.7	28.2	377.4
14	-	-	-	329.8	7.8	337.5	0.5	28.6	29.1	366.6
15	-	-	-	297.6	7.3	304.8	0.4	27.5	27.9	332.7
16	-	-	-	103.7	2.2	105.8	0.3	22.2	22.6	128.4
17	-	-	-	66.4	1.5	67.9	0.2	19.7	19.9	87.8
18	-	-	-	6.5	1.0	7.6	0.2	3.2	3.4	10.9
19 and over	-	-	-	0.5	0.1	0.6	0.1	0.9	1.0	1.6
TOTAL	43.9	176.8	2,467.1	1,812.1	72.9	4,572.8	3.9	316.2	320.1	4,892.9
FEMALES										
2 - 4 (6)	41.0	168.9	295.8	-	3.0	508.7	0.1	30.4	30.4	539.1
5	0.1	0.1	365.4	-	1.6	367.2	0.1	14.6	14.7	381.9
6	-	-	354.1	-	1.8	355.9	0.1	14.7	14.8	370.7
7	-	-	345.2	-	2.1	347.3	0.1	15.2	15.3	362.6
8	-	-	343.4	-	2.4	345.8	0.1	16.0	16.1	361.8
9	-	-	313.1	18.1	2.6	333.7	0.1	16.8	16.9	350.7
10	-	-	307.8	20.7	2.7	331.2	0.1	17.6	17.7	349.0
11	-	-	42.6	278.8	3.2	324.6	0.2	23.2	23.4	348.0
12	-	-	0.5	327.3	3.5	331.3	0.2	24.2	24.4	355.7
13	-	-	-	330.2	3.7	333.9	0.2	24.9	25.1	359.0
14	-	-	-	318.4	3.7	322.0	0.2	25.2	25.4	347.4
15	-	-	-	290.2	3.5	293.7	0.2	24.2	24.4	318.1
16	-	-	-	110.6	1.4	112.0	0.2	18.6	18.8	130.8
17	-	-	-	74.6	1.1	75.7	0.1	16.6	16.8	92.5
18	-	-	-	5.9	0.8	6.7	0.1	2.5	2.6	9.3
19 and over	-	-	-	0.6	-	0.7	0.1	0.7	0.8	1.5
TOTAL	41.1	169.1	2,367.8	1,775.4	37.1	4,390.5	2.1	285.5	287.6	4,678.1

(1) Excludes sixth form colleges in England and Wales which were reclassified as further education colleges.
(2) For Scotland grant-aided special schools only.
(3) Includes pupils in grant-aided and independent schools in Scotland.
(4) Age 2-4 includes pupils less than 2 years of age in England.
(5) 1 July for Northern Ireland and 31 December for Scotland.
(6) Includes the so-called rising fives (ie those pupils who became 5 during the autumn term).

SCHOOLS
Full-time and part-time pupils by age, gender and school type, 1994/95 (1)

12b (13)

Thousands

| | Maintained schools | | | | | | Non-maintained | | | |
| | Primary Schools | | | | | | | | | |
Age at 31 August 1993 (6)	Nursery Schools	Nursery Classes	Other Classes	Secondary Schools (2)	Special Schools	Total Schools	Special schools (3)	Other schools (4),(5)	Total Schools	ALL SCHOOLS
PERSONS										
2 - 4 (7)	85.1	355.8	620.3	-	8.2	1,069.4	0.2	63.9	64.0	1,133.5
5	0.4	0.5	735.1	-	4.5	740.4	0.1	29.4	29.5	769.9
6	-	-	744.4	-	5.1	749.6	0.2	30.6	30.8	780.4
7	-	-	722.3	-	6.1	728.4	0.2	32.0	32.2	760.6
8	-	-	704.5	0.2	6.9	711.6	0.2	33.5	33.7	745.3
9	-	-	658.8	38.3	7.8	704.9	0.3	35.8	36.1	741.0
10	-	-	629.9	41.4	8.4	679.6	0.3	37.3	37.6	717.2
11	-	-	77.7	582.2	10.0	670.0	0.5	46.8	47.3	717.3
12	-	-	1.1	652.8	10.7	664.6	0.6	49.1	49.7	714.3
13	-	-	-	666.5	11.3	677.8	0.6	51.1	51.7	729.5
14	-	-	-	668.2	11.8	680.1	0.6	53.2	53.8	733.9
15	-	-	-	633.7	11.1	644.9	0.7	53.7	54.4	699.3
16	-	-	-	211.6	3.5	215.0	0.5	41.9	42.3	257.4
17	-	-	-	144.1	2.5	146.6	0.4	36.6	36.9	183.6
18	-	-	-	12.6	1.7	14.4	0.3	5.6	5.9	20.3
19 and over	-	-	-	1.1	0.1	1.2	0.2	1.8	2.0	3.2
TOTAL	85.5	356.3	4,894.3	3,652.6	109.8	9,098.6	5.9	602.1	608.1	9,706.6
of which										
ENGLAND	52.6	304.1	4,006.8	2,993.3	92.9	7,449.7	5.5	556.6	562.1	8,011.8
WALES	..	..	..	..	..	..	..	..	..	..
SCOTLAND	24.0	25.8	438.0	314.9	8.7	811.4	0.4	33.8	34.2	845.6
NORTHERN IRELAND	5.3	2.6	187.6	150.0	4.6	350.2	-	0.9	0.9	351.1
MALES										
2 - 4 (7)	44.2	182.0	317.1	-	5.2	548.4	0.1	32.0	32.1	580.6
5	0.2	0.3	375.6	-	2.9	379.1	0.1	14.9	15.0	394.0
6	-	-	379.6	-	3.3	383.0	0.1	15.8	15.9	398.8
7	-	-	369.6	-	4.0	373.7	0.1	16.4	16.5	390.2
8	-	-	359.9	0.1	4.5	364.5	0.2	17.6	17.8	382.3
9	-	-	336.4	19.6	5.3	361.3	0.2	19.0	19.2	380.5
10	-	-	319.7	21.2	5.7	346.6	0.2	19.7	19.9	366.6
11	-	-	39.9	296.4	6.9	343.2	0.3	24.6	24.9	368.2
12	-	-	0.6	331.7	7.3	339.5	0.4	25.7	26.1	365.6
13	-	-	-	338.2	7.7	345.9	0.4	26.7	27.1	373.0
14	-	-	-	339.2	8.1	347.3	0.4	28.0	28.4	375.8
15	-	-	-	321.3	7.5	328.9	0.5	28.5	29.0	357.8
16	-	-	-	102.9	2.1	105.0	0.3	22.5	22.8	127.8
17	-	-	-	67.8	1.4	69.2	0.2	20.0	20.3	89.5
18	-	-	-	6.8	1.0	7.8	0.2	3.3	3.4	11.2
19 and over	-	-	-	0.5	-	0.6	0.1	1.0	1.1	1.7
TOTAL	44.5	182.3	2,498.4	1,845.9	72.9	4,644.0	3.9	315.7	319.5	4,963.5
FEMALES										
2 - 4 (7)	40.9	173.8	303.3	-	3.1	521.0	0.1	31.8	31.9	552.9
5	0.1	0.2	359.5	-	1.6	361.4	-	14.5	14.5	375.9
6	-	-	364.8	-	1.8	366.6	0.1	14.9	15.0	381.6
7	-	-	352.7	-	2.0	354.7	0.1	15.6	15.7	370.4
8	-	-	344.6	0.1	2.3	347.1	0.1	15.9	16.0	363.0
9	-	-	322.4	18.7	2.6	343.6	0.1	16.8	16.9	360.5
10	-	-	310.1	20.2	2.7	333.0	0.1	17.5	17.7	350.7
11	-	-	37.9	285.8	3.1	326.7	0.2	22.2	22.4	349.1
12	-	-	0.5	321.1	3.4	325.1	0.2	23.5	23.7	348.7
13	-	-	-	328.2	3.6	331.9	0.2	24.4	24.6	356.5
14	-	-	-	329.0	3.8	332.8	0.2	25.2	25.4	358.2
15	-	-	-	312.4	3.7	316.1	0.2	25.1	25.4	341.4
16	-	-	-	108.6	1.4	110.0	0.2	19.3	19.5	129.5
17	-	-	-	76.3	1.1	77.4	0.1	16.5	16.7	94.0
18	-	-	-	5.8	0.8	6.6	0.1	2.4	2.5	9.1
19 and over	-	-	-	0.6	-	0.6	0.1	0.8	0.9	1.5
TOTAL	41.0	174.0	2,395.9	1,806.8	36.9	4,454.6	2.0	286.5	288.5	4,743.1

(1) Provisional. Includes 1993/94 data for Wales.
(2) Excludes sixth form colleges in England and Wales which were reclassified as further education colleges.
(3) For Scotland grant-aided special schools only.
(4) Includes pupils in grant-aided and independent schools in Scotland.
(5) Age 2-4 includes pupils less than 2 years of age in England.
(6) 1 July for Northern Ireland and 31 December for Scotland.
(7) Includes the so-called rising fives (ie those pupils who became 5 during the autumn term).

SCHOOLS
Full-time and part-time pupils by age, gender and school type, 1970/71 to 1994/95

Thousands

| | Maintained Schools | | | | | | Non-maintained | | | Total |
| | Nursery Schools (1) | Primary Schools | | Secondary Schools | Special schools | maintained schools | Total Special Schools | Other schools | non-maintained schools | All schools |
		Nursery Classes	Other Classes							
1970/71										
Persons	50.7		5,930.9	3,705.3	103.3	9,790.3		439.8	439.8	10,230.1
Males	26.2		3,033.7	1,894.4	62.9	5,017.3		237.8	237.8	5,255.1
Females	24.5		2,897.2	1,810.9	40.4	4,773.0		202.1	202.1	4,975.1
1975/76										
Persons	74.8		6,026.7	4,604.9	149.8	10,856.3		444.3	444.3	11,300.6
Males	38.5		3,081.6	2,346.2	91.1	5,557.4		241.8	241.8	5,799.2
Females	36.3		2,945.1	2,258.7	58.7	5,298.9		202.6	202.6	5,501.4
1979/80 (2)										
Persons	88.1		5398.1	4636.2	140.4	10263.0	8.8	620.2	629.0	10,892.0
Males	45.6		2763.8	2347.1	86.5	5242.9	5.4	336.3	341.7	5584.6
Females	42.5		2634.4	2289.2	53.9	5020.0	3.3	283.9	287.2	5306.9
1985/86										
Persons	96.0		4,637.1	4,095.5	123.0	8,951.5	7.3	606.4	613.7	9,565.2
Males	49.2		2,371.5	2,074.9	77.8	4,573.3	4.6	325.6	330.3	4,903.5
Females	46.8		2,265.6	2,020.6	45.2	4,378.2	2.7	280.8	283.4	4,661.7
1990/91										
Persons	104.9		4,954.5	3,473.3	107.7	8,640.4	6.4	613.4	619.7	9,260.2
Males	54.0		2,529.4	1,753.6	70.6	4,407.7	4.2	323.8	328.0	4,735.6
Females	50.9		2,425.1	1,719.7	37.1	4,232.8	2.2	289.6	291.8	4,524.5
1991/92										
Persons	106.4		4,998.5	3,534.5	108.1	8,747.5	6.2	614.3	620.5	9,368.0
Males	54.9		2,551.6	1,783.8	71.1	4,461.4	4.1	324.2	328.3	4,789.7
Females	51.5		2,446.9	1,750.8	37.0	4,286.1	2.1	290.1	292.2	4,578.3
1992/93										
Persons	85.5	338.4	4,761.5	3,605.8	109.0	8,900.3	6.1	606.8	612.9	9,513.2
Males	44.2	173.1	2,430.1	1,819.4	36.9	4,538.8	4.0	319.5	323.5	4,862.3
Females	41.4	165.3	2,331.4	1,786.4	72.1	4,361.5	2.1	287.3	289.4	4,650.9
1993/94 (3)										
Persons	85.0	345.9	4,834.9	3,587.5	110.0	8,963.3	6.0	601.7	607.7	9,571.0
Males	43.9	176.8	2,467.1	1,812.1	72.9	4,572.8	3.9	316.2	320.1	4,892.9
Females	41.1	169.1	2,367.8	1,775.4	37.1	4,390.5	2.1	285.5	287.6	4,678.1
1994/95 (4)										
Persons	85.5	356.3	4,894.3	3,652.6	109.8	9,098.6	5.9	602.1	608.1	9,706.6
Males	44.5	182.3	2,498.4	1,845.9	72.9	4,644.0	3.9	315.7	319.5	4,963.5
Females	41.0	174.0	2,395.9	1,806.8	36.9	4,454.6	2.0	286.5	288.5	4,743.1

(1) Prior to 1992/93 nursery schools included some nursery classes in primary schools for Scotland.
(2) 1979/80 data shown in time series as 1980/81 data are not available.
(3) From 1 April 1993 excludes sixth form colleges in England and Wales which were reclassified as Further Education colleges.
(4) Provisional. Includes 1993/94 data for Wales.

	1970/71 (1)	1975/76 (1)	1980/81	1985/86	1990/91	1992/93	1993/94 (2)	1994/95 (2)(3)
UNITED KINGDOM								
Pupils (thousands) (4)								
Public sector mainstream (5)	9,472.8	10,435.8	9,749.1	8,657.7	8,346.0	8,590.4	8,646.8	8,774.7
Nursery	35.2	47.1	55.5	56.9 (6)	60.4	61.6	61.6	62.2
Primary (7)	5,882.9	5,940.3	5,087.3	4,520.8	4,812.3	4,923.0	4,997.7	5,061.6
Secondary (8)	3,554.7	4,448.4	4,606.3	4,080.0	3,473.3	3,605.8	3,587.5	3,650.9
Non-maintained mainstream	605.6	614.6	629.0 (9)	597.1	603.8	596.4	591.0	590.6
Special - maintained }							108.6	108.2
}	103.3	149.5	147.2	130.0	112.5	113.2		
- non maintained }							5.5	5.5
All schools	10,181.7	11,199.9	10,525.3 (9)	9,384.8 (6)	9,062.3	9,300.0	9,351.9	9,479.1
Teachers (thousands) (4)(10)								
Public sector mainstream (5)	418.6	515.7	512.0	468.9	455.7	460.9	456.7	463.9
Nursery	1.3	2.1	2.6	2.6 (6)	2.8	2.9	2.8	2.9
Primary (7)	217.4	249.5	227.8	205.8	220.6	224.4	225.5	231.2
Secondary (8)	199.9	264.1	281.6	260.5	232.3	233.6	228.4	229.8
Non-maintained mainstream	43.3	43.7	47.9 (9)	51.8	56.3	57.3	57.2	59.4
Special - maintained }							18.0	17.6
}	9.9	17.1	19.8	19.6	19.6	19.6		
- non maintained }							1.2	1.2
All schools	471.8	576.5	579.1 (9)	540.3 (6)	531.7	537.8	533.2	542.1
Pupils per teacher (10)								
Public sector mainstream (5)	22.6	20.2	19.0	18.5	18.3	18.6	18.9	18.9
Nursery	26.6	22.1	21.5	21.7 (6)	21.5	21.5	21.6	21.7
Primary (7)	27.1	23.8	22.3	22.0	21.8	21.9	22.2	21.9
Secondary (8)	17.8	16.8	16.4	15.7	15.0	15.4	15.7	15.9
Non-maintained mainstream	14.0	14.1	13.1 (9)	11.5	10.7	10.4	10.3	9.9
Special - maintained }							6.0	6.2
}	10.5	8.7	7.4	6.6	5.7	5.8		
- non maintained }							4.5	4.7
All schools	22.0	19.4	18.2 (9)	17.4 (6)	17.0	17.3	17.5	17.5
ENGLAND								
Pupils per teacher								
Public sector mainstream								
Nursery	19.1	21.1	19.7	19.6	18.9	19.0	18.9	19.0
Primary	27.0	24.0	22.6	22.1	22.0	22.2	22.5	22.2
Secondary	17.9	17.0	16.6	15.9	15.3	15.8	16.1	16.3
Non-maintained mainstream	13.7	13.4	12.5	11.3	10.8	10.4	10.3	9.9
Special - maintained }							6.2	6.3
}	10.2	8.6	7.6	6.8	5.8	5.9		
- non maintained }							4.5	4.7
All schools	21.4	19.4	18.2	17.4	17.2	17.4	17.7	17.7
WALES								
Pupils per teacher (10)								
Public sector mainstream								
Nursery	19.9	19.4	19.0	20.2	20.6	20.3	20.6	..
Primary	25.0	22.8	21.7	22.1	22.3	22.1	22.3	..
Secondary	18.3	17.1	16.6	16.1	15.4	15.7	15.9	..
Non-maintained mainstream	13.8	12.3	12.1	10.7	9.8	9.7	9.6	..
Special	10.4	10.9	7.7	7.0	6.3	6.2	6.4	..
All schools	21.4	19.6	18.5	18.2	18.2	18.2	18.4	..
SCOTLAND								
Pupils per teacher								
Public sector mainstream								
Nursery	36.6	24.5	25.3	..	25.7	25.5	25.9	25.8
Primary	27.9	22.4	20.3	20.4	19.5	19.3	19.5	19.3
Secondary	16.1	15.1	14.4	13.5	12.2	12.6	12.8	12.9
Non-maintained mainstream	17.3	16.3	13.0	12.2	10.5	11.3	10.5	10.1
Special	11.6	9.7	6.2	5.4	4.5	4.3	4.5	4.5
All schools	22.1	18.6	16.7	..	15.2	15.4	15.5	15.4
NORTHERN IRELAND								
Pupils per teacher (10)								
Grant-aided mainstream								
Nursery	27.6	30.0	23.5	23.5	24.7	24.4	24.7	..
Primary (7)	28.9	26.4	23.6	23.4	22.9	22.3	21.7	..
Secondary (8)	18.6	17.2	15.2	14.9	14.7	15.2	15.1	..
Non-maintained mainstream	17.9	17.4	16.5 (9)	15.8	11.0	10.0	10.0	..
Special	10.7	9.8	8.4	8.1	6.9	6.9	6.8	..
All schools	23.5	21.3	18.9 (9)	18.5	18.1	18.1	17.8	..

(1) Excludes independent schools in Scotland. See paragraph 10.1 of the explanatory notes.
(2) From 1 April 1993 excludes sixth form colleges in England and Wales which were reclassified as further education colleges.
(3) Provisional. Includes 1993/94 data for Wales and Northern Ireland.
(4) Both pupils and teachers include full-time equivalents of part-time. See paragraph 10.2 of the explanatory notes.
(5) From 1989/90 includes grant-maintained schools.
(6) Data on nursery schools for Scotland are for 1984/85.
(7) Includes preparatory departments attached to Grammar schools in Northern Ireland.
(8) Includes Voluntary grammar schools in Northern Ireland from 1989/90, formerly allocated to the non-maintained sector.
(9) Excludes Northern Ireland independent schools data in 1980/81.
(10) Includes qualified teachers only in Wales and Northern Ireland.

THIS PAGE HAS BEEN LEFT BLANK

SCHOOLS

15a (15)

Schools and pupils by size of school or department (1) and school type, 1993/94

(i) Number of schools

	25 and under	26 to 50	51 to 100	101 to 200	201 to 300	301 to 400	401 to 600	601 to 800	801 to 1000	1001 to 1500	1501 and over	Total
UNITED KINGDOM												
Public Sector mainstream (2)												
Nursery	102	566	605	176	2	-	-	-	-	-	-	1,451
Primary (3)	419	1,522	3,036	7,172	7,055	3,076	1,329	83	3	3	-	23,698
Secondary (4)(5)	10	7	22	58	151	276	828	994	953	1,075	122	4,496
Non-maintained mainstream (6)(7)(8)	233	256	385	698	325	164	176	109	73	55	4	2,478
Special (9)	346	418	644	313	20	1	-	-	-	-	-	1,742
All schools	1,110	2,769	4,692	8,417	7,553	3,517	2,333	1,186	1,029	1,133	126	33,865
ENGLAND(10)												
Public Sector mainstream (2)												
Nursery	10	258	257	27	-	-	-	-	-	-	-	552
Primary	115	916	2,199	5,879	6,001	2,511	1,009	52	1	-	-	18,683
Secondary (5)	-	1	6	37	120	224	666	809	780	881	105	3,629
Non-maintained mainstream (6)(7)	192	223	348	664	305	149	165	103	70	48	1	2,268
Special	110	339	566	280	14	1	-	-	-	-	-	1,310
All schools	427	1,737	3,376	6,887	6,440	2,885	1,840	964	851	929	106	26,442
WALES												
Public Sector mainstream (2)												
Nursery	1	15	29	7	-	-	-	-	-	-	-	52
Primary	57	208	272	558	407	149	44	3	-	-	-	1,698
Secondary (5)	-	-	-	-	-	10	41	58	42	73	3	227
Non-maintained mainstream	11	6	10	17	8	8	1	3	-	-	-	64
Special	8	20	23	8	-	-	-	-	-	-	-	59
All schools	77	249	334	590	415	167	86	64	42	73	3	2,100
SCOTLAND												
Public Sector mainstream (2)												
Nursery	85	256	273	142	2	-	-	-	-	-	-	758
Primary	228	269	321	505	509	324	179	6	-	-	-	2,341
Secondary	10	6	13	15	8	19	54	84	91	97	11	408
Non-maintained mainstream (8)	20	23	22	16	11	7	10	3	3	7	3	125
Special (9)	225	50	38	13	1	-	-	-	-	-	-	327
All schools	568	604	667	691	531	350	243	93	94	104	14	3,959
NORTHERN IRELAND												
Grant-aided mainstream(4)												
Nursery	6	37	46	-	-	-	-	-	-	-	-	89
Primary (3)	19	129	244	230	138	92	97	22	2	3	-	976
Secondary (4)	-	-	3	6	23	23	67	43	40	24	3	232
Non-maintained mainstream (11)	10	4	5	1	1	-	-	-	-	-	-	21
Special	3	9	17	12	5	-	-	-	-	-	-	46
All schools	38	179	315	249	167	115	164	65	42	27	3	1,364

(1) In this table (apart from the independent sector) schools in Scotland with more than one department have been counted once for each department, eg a school with nursery, primary and secondary departments has been counted 3 times.

(2) Includes self-governing (grant maintained) schools.

(3) Includes 25 preparatory departments attached to Grammar Schools in Northern Ireland.

(4) Includes Voluntary Grammar Schools previously recorded as non-maintained in Northern Ireland.

(5) Excludes sixth form colleges in England and Wales which were reclassified as further education colleges.

(6) Includes direct grant nursery and independent schools for England.

(7) Includes City Technology Colleges.

(8) Includes all grant-aided schools/departments and independent schools for Scotland.

(9) Education authority schools/departments only for Scotland (see paragraph 10.8 of explanatory notes).

(10) Excludes part-time pupils except in nursery schools, where each part-time pupil is counted as 0.5 in both pupil count and school size.

(11) Northern Ireland independent schools only.

(12) Includes pupils in Nursery classes in primary schools in Scotland.

(13) Full-time pupils only in England: all pupils in the rest of the United Kingdom.

CONTINUED

SCHOOLS
Schools and pupils by size of school or department (1) and school type, 1993/94

	(ii) Number of pupils (13)											Thousands
	25 and under	26 to 50	51 to 100	101 to 200	201 to 300	301 to 400	401 to 600	601 to 800	801 to 1000	1001 to 1500	1501 and over	Total
UNITED KINGDOM												
Public Sector mainstream (2)												
Nursery (12)	1.8	22.6	41.4	21.6	0.4	-	-	-	-	-	-	87.7
Primary (3)	7.1	59.3	227.4	1,122.5	1,716.8	1,058.0	607.5	55.2	2.7	3.4	-	4,859.9
Secondary (4) (5)	0.1	0.3	1.6	9.6	39.2	98.2	422.9	691.7	853.8	1,266.5	203.6	3,587.5
Non-maintained mainstream (6)(7)(8)	3.5	9.9	29.1	101.8	79.4	56.9	87.6	75.0	64.8	63.1	9.0	580.0
Special (9)	4.2	16.3	46.2	41.0	4.7	0.4	-	-	-	-	-	112.8
All schools	16.6	108.4	345.7	1,296.6	1,840.5	1,213.4	1,117.9	822.0	921.3	1,333.1	212.6	9,228.0
ENGLAND (10)												
Public Sector mainstream (2)												
Nursery	0.2	10.3	17.1	3.1	-	-	-	-	-	-	-	30.8
Primary	2.3	36.5	165.9	926.1	1,458.5	863.4	457.9	34.0	0.8	-	-	3,945.3
Secondary (5)	-	-	0.5	6.3	31.1	79.7	341.8	563.1	698.9	1,037.9	174.3	2,933.6
Non-maintained mainstream (6)(7)	2.8	8.7	26.5	97.0	74.6	51.7	82.2	70.9	62.0	55.0	2.6	533.9
Special	1.7	13.4	40.8	36.5	3.4	0.4	-	-	-	-	-	96.3
All schools	7.1	69.0	250.8	1,069.0	1,567.6	995.1	881.8	668.0	761.8	1,092.9	176.8	7,539.9
WALES												
Public Sector mainstream (2)												
Nursery	-	0.6	2.1	0.8	-	-	-	-	-	-	-	3.6
Primary	1.1	7.9	20.2	85.3	97.7	51.2	20.5	1.9	-	-	-	285.7
Secondary (5)	-	-	-	-	-	3.6	20.4	40.4	37.6	86.8	5.6	194.4
Non-maintained mainstream	0.2	0.2	0.7	2.6	1.9	2.7	0.5	1.9	-	-	-	10.8
Special	0.1	0.8	1.6	1.1	-	-	-	-	-	-	-	3.6
All schools	1.4	9.5	24.6	89.9	99.6	57.4	41.4	44.3	37.6	86.8	5.6	498.1
SCOTLAND												
Public Sector mainstream (2)												
Nursery (12)	1.4	9.8	18.8	17.7	0.4	-	-	-	-	-	-	48.1
Primary	3.4	10.0	23.5	77.8	126.0	111.4	82.3	4.0	-	-	-	438.4
Secondary	0.1	0.2	0.8	2.3	2.1	6.8	27.2	58.1	81.8	113.8	17.9	311.3
Non-maintained mainstream (8)	0.3	0.8	1.6	2.1	2.7	2.5	4.9	2.2	2.7	8.1	6.4	34.4
Special (9)	2.3	1.8	2.5	1.8	0.2	-	-	-	-	-	-	8.6
All schools	7.5	22.7	47.3	101.7	131.5	120.6	114.4	64.2	84.5	121.9	24.4	840.7
NORTHERN IRELAND												
Grant-aided mainstream (4)												
Nursery	0.2	1.8	3.3	-	-	-	-	-	-	-	-	5.3
Primary (3)	0.4	5.0	17.8	33.2	34.6	32.1	46.8	15.3	1.9	3.4	-	190.5
Secondary (4)	-	-	0.3	1.0	5.9	8.1	33.5	30.2	35.5	28.0	5.8	148.3
Non-maintained mainstream (11)	0.1	0.2	0.3	0.2	0.2	-	-	-	-	-	-	0.9
Special	0.1	0.4	1.2	1.7	1.1	-	-	-	-	-	-	4.4
All schools	0.7	7.3	23.0	36.0	41.8	40.3	80.3	45.5	37.3	31.5	5.8	349.4

See Table 15a (i) for footnotes.

SCHOOLS
15b(15)
Schools and pupils by size of school or department (1) and school type, 1994/95 (2)

(i) Number of schools

	25 and under	26 to 50	51 to 100	101 to 200	201 to 300	301 to 400	401 to 600	601 to 800	801 to 1000	1001 to 1500	1501 and over	Total
UNITED KINGDOM (2)												
Public Sector mainstream (3)												
Nursery	105	585	609	176	2	-	-	-	-	-	-	1,477
Primary (4)	380	1,433	3,027	6,894	7,052	3,184	1,482	88	6	2	-	23,548
Secondary (5)	7	8	21	59	151	243	781	969	965	1,136	138	4,478
Non-maintained mainstream (6)(7)(8)	219	268	400	685	311	176	164	114	71	57	5	2,470
Special (9)	326	422	624	320	21	1	-	-	-	-	-	1,714
All schools	1,037	2,716	4,681	8,134	7,537	3,604	2,427	1,171	1,042	1,195	143	33,687
ENGLAND (10)												
Public Sector mainstream (3)												
Nursery	9	261	255	26	-	-	-	-	-	-	-	551
Primary	89	822	2,194	5,582	6,021	2,621	1,157	57	2	-	-	18,551
Secondary	-	-	6	40	123	193	616	790	785	941	120	3,614
Non-maintained mainstream (6)(7)	180	231	364	653	290	161	153	109	68	51	1	2,261
Special	109	335	545	286	15	1	-	-	-	-	-	1,291
All schools	393	1,649	3,364	6,587	6,449	2,976	1,926	956	855	992	121	26,268
WALES												
Public Sector mainstream												
Nursery	..	..	..	..	..	..	..	..	..	..	..	..
Primary	..	..	..	..	..	..	..	..	..	..	..	..
Secondary	..	..	..	..	..	..	..	..	..	..	..	..
Non-maintained mainstream	..	..	..	..	..	..	..	..	..	..	..	..
Special	..	..	..	..	..	..	..	..	..	..	..	..
All schools	..	..	..	..	..	..	..	..	..	..	..	..
SCOTLAND												
Public Sector mainstream (3)												
Nursery	89	270	279	143	2	-	-	-	-	-	-	783
Primary	215	278	322	515	502	313	184	7	-	-	-	2,336
Secondary	7	8	12	13	7	17	60	77	93	99	12	405
Non-maintained mainstream (8)	20	26	21	14	12	7	10	2	3	6	4	125
Special (9)	206	57	39	14	1	-	-	-	-	-	-	317
All schools	537	639	673	699	524	337	254	86	96	105	16	3,966
NORTHERN IRELAND												
All grant-aided mainstream (5)												
Nursery	6	39	46	-	-	-	-	-	-	-	-	91
Primary (4)	13	125	239	239	122	101	97	21	4	2	-	963
Secondary (5)	-	-	3	6	21	23	64	44	45	23	3	232
Non-maintained mainstream (11)	8	5	5	1	1	-	-	-	-	-	-	20
Special	3	10	17	12	5	-	-	-	-	-	-	47
All schools	30	179	310	258	149	124	161	65	49	25	3	1,353

(1) In this table (apart from the independent sector) schools in Scotland with more than one department have been counted once for each department, eg a school with nursery, primary and secondary departments has been counted 3 times.

(2) Provisional. Includes 1993/94 data for Wales.

(3) Includes self-governing (grant maintained) schools.

(4) Includes 25 preparatory departments attached to Grammar Schools in Northern Ireland.

(5) Includes Voluntary Grammar Schools previously recorded as non-maintained in Northern Ireland.

(6) Includes direct grant nursery and independent schools for England.

(7) Includes City Technology Colleges.

(8) Includes all grant-aided schools/departments and independent schools for Scotland.

(9) Education authority schools/departments only for Scotland (see paragraph 10.8 of explanatory notes).

(10) Excludes part-time pupils except in nursery schools, where each part-time pupil is counted as 0.5 in both pupil count and school size.

(11) Northern Ireland independent schools only.

(12) Includes pupils in Nursery classes in primary schools in Scotland.

(13) Full-time pupils only in England: all pupils in the rest of the United Kingdom.

CONTINUED

15b(15) SCHOOLS
Schools and pupils by size of school or department (1) and school type, 1994/95(2)

| | (ii) Number of pupils (13) | | | | | | | | | | | Thousands |
	25 and under	26 to 50	51 to 100	101 to 200	201 to 300	301 to 400	401 to 600	601 to 800	801 to 1000	1001 to 1500	1501 and over	Total
UNITED KINGDOM (2)												
Public Sector mainstream (3)												
Nursery (2)	1.8	23.5	41.9	21.8	0.5	-	-	-	-	-	-	89.4
Primary (4)	6.4	55.9	227.3	1,077.3	1,711.9	1,096.6	678.0	58.6	5.4	2.4	-	4,919.8
Secondary (5)	0.1	0.3	1.5	9.7	39.3	86.1	397.8	673.7	866.4	1,345.7	231.5	3,652.2
Non-maintained mainstream (6)(7)(8)	3.3	10.2	30.1	100.4	76.1	60.5	81.0	78.7	63.3	65.2	10.5	579.3
Special (9)	3.7	16.3	45.2	42.0	4.9	0.4	-	-	-	-	-	112.4
All schools	15.2	106.1	346.0	1,251.1	1,832.7	1,243.6	1,156.8	811.0	935.0	1,413.2	242.1	9,353.0
ENGLAND (10)												
Public Sector mainstream (3)												
Nursery	0.2	10.5	17.0	3.0	-	-	-	-	-	-	-	30.7
Primary	1.8	32.9	166.0	877.3	1,459.7	902.7	562.2	37.5	1.7	-	-	4,005.8
Secondary	-	-	0.5	6.8	32.0	68.6	315.7	549.0	704.7	1,115.1	200.5	2,992.9
Non-maintained mainstream (6)(7)	2.7	8.9	27.5	95.8	71.1	55.3	75.5	75.4	60.5	58.4	2.5	533.5
Special	1.5	13.2	39.7	37.1	3.6	0.4	-	-	-	-	-	98.5
All schools	6.3	65.4	250.8	1,020.0	1,566.3	1,026.9	917.4	661.8	766.9	1,173.5	202.9	7,658.4
WALES												
Public Sector mainstream												
Nursery	..	..	..	..	..	..	..	..	..	..	..	..
Primary	..	..	..	..	..	..	..	..	..	..	..	..
Secondary	..	..	..	..	..	..	..	..	..	..	..	..
Non-maintained maintained	..	..	..	..	..	..	..	..	..	..	..	..
Special	..	..	..	..	..	..	..	..	..	..	..	..
All schools	..	..	..	..	..	..	..	..	..	..	..	..
SCOTLAND												
Public Sector mainstream (3)												
Nursery (12)	1.4	10.4	19.5	18.0	0.5	-	-	-	-	-	-	49.8
Primary	3.2	10.3	23.6	79.8	124.3	107.8	84.4	4.7	-	-	-	438.0
Secondary	0.1	0.3	0.8	2.0	1.8	6.0	30.3	53.9	83.6	116.5	19.7	314.9
Non-maintained mainstream (8)	0.3	0.9	1.6	1.8	2.9	2.5	4.9	1.4	2.8	6.8	8.1	34.1
Special (9)	1.9	1.9	2.6	2.0	0.2	-	-	-	-	-	-	8.7
All schools	7.0	23.9	48.1	103.5	129.7	116.4	119.6	60.0	86.3	123.3	27.7	845.4
NORTHERN IRELAND												
All grant-aided mainstream (5)												
Nursery	0.1	1.9	3.3	-	-	-	-	-	-	-	-	5.3
Primary (4)	0.3	4.9	17.5	34.9	30.2	34.9	46.9	14.6	3.7	2.4	-	190.2
Secondary (5)	-	-	0.2	1.0	5.5	7.9	31.4	30.4	40.4	27.3	5.8	150.0
Non-maintained mainstream (11)	0.1	0.2	0.3	0.1	0.2	-	-	-	-	-	-	0.9
Special	0.1	0.4	1.3	1.7	1.1	-	-	-	-	-	-	4.6
All schools	0.6	7.3	22.6	37.7	37.0	42.9	78.3	45.0	44.1	29.7	5.8	351.1

See table 15b(i) for footnotes.

SCHOOLS
Pupils with special needs

(i) Numbers of public sector and assisted special schools (1), full-time pupils and teachers

		1975/76	1980/81	1985/86	1990/91	1992/93		1993/94	1994/95 (2)	
Hospital schools										
Schools										
Public sector		152	132	89	48	41		39	32	
Assisted		7	4	2	-	-		-	-	
Total		159	136	91	48	41		39	32	
of which:	England	151	131	87	47	40		38	31	
	Wales	8	5	4	1	1		1	..	
Full-time pupils (thousands)		9.5	7.1	4.4	0.9	0.5		0.6	0.2	(3)
Full-time teachers (thousands)		1.2	1.2	0.7	0.4	0.3		0.3	0.2	
Other special schools or departments (4)										
Schools										
Public sector		1,627	1,763	1,726	1,695	1,653		1,631	1,611	
Assisted		120	112	95	87	81		79	79	
Total		1,747	1,875	1,821	1,782	1,734		1,710	1,690	
of which:	Day	1,276	1,412	1,464	1,522	1,500	(5)	1,508	1,499	
	Boarding	471	463	357	260	234	(5)	202	191	
of which:	England	1,394	1,462	1,406	1,333	1,287		1,272	1,261	
	Wales	66	68	63	60	60		58	..	
	Scotland (4)	264	319	328	343	341		334	324	
	Northern Ireland (6)	23	26	24	46	46		46	47	
Full-time pupils (thousands) (4)(7)		139.5	139.2	126.0	110.8	111.7		112.6	112.6	
of which:	England	119.8	120.3	107.7	94.5	95.1		95.7	95.3	
	Wales	4.3	4.6	4.1	3.6	3.6		3.5	..	
	Scotland (4)	13.1	11.8	11.7	8.7	8.8		9.0	9.1	
	Northern Ireland (6)	2.3	2.5	2.6	4.0	4.2		4.4	4.6	
FTE number of Teachers (thousands) (4)		15.8	18.4	18.5	19.1	19.2		18.8	18.5	(8)

(1)   See paragraphs 10.6 to 10.9 of the explanatory notes.

(2)   Provisional. Includes 1993/94 data for Wales.

(3)   From 1994/95 England figures exclude pupils who are also registered elsewhere and are not comparable with earlier years.

(4)   Includes all Scottish special schools. In the 1985/86 column, data for Scotland relate to 1984/85.

(5)   Includes estimated split for Scotland.

(6)   From 1987 onwards figures include schools and pupils which were previously the responsibility of the Northern Ireland Department of Health and Social Security.

(7)   See paragraph 10.9 of the explanatory notes.

(8)   Includes 1993/94 data for Northern Ireland.

(ii) Pupils with statements of special needs in other public sector schools — Thousands

		1988/89	1989/90	1990/91	1991/92	1992/93	1993/94	1994/95 (2)
Public sector primary schools (9)(11)		31.8	35.0	40.3	45.3	53.3	61.2	67.4
Public sector secondary schools (9)(10)(11)		25.7	29.4	34.8	41.6	49.2	59.0	66.9
Total United Kingdom		57.4	64.4	75.2	86.9	102.5	120.2	134.3
of which:	England	47.3	54.3	62.0	71.2	85.0	100.3	112.8
	Wales	7.5	7.1	8.9	10.5	11.5	12.7	12.7
	Scotland	1.1	1.3	2.3	3.0	3.6	4.6	5.7
	Northern Ireland	1.6	1.7	2.0	2.2	2.5	2.7	3.2

(9)   Includes pupils in middle schools deemed primary or secondary as appropriate.

(10)   From 1 April 1993 excludes sixth form colleges in England and Wales which were reclassified as further education colleges.

(11)   From 1991/92 includes estimated primary/secondary split for Wales.

SCHOOLS
Pupils and schools in public sector secondary education by school type and country

	1980/81 Pupils		1985/86 Pupils		1990/91 Pupils		1992/93 Pupils		1993/94(1) Pupils		Schools	1994/95(1)(2) Pupils		Schools
	000s	%	000s	%	000s	%	000s	%	000s	%		000s	%	
ENGLAND														
Maintained secondary schools														
Middle deemed secondary	268	7.0	224	6.6	182	6.4	167	5.6	161	5.5	416	159	5.3	410
Modern	229	6.0	143	4.2	94	3.3	103	3.5	91	3.1	142	90	3.0	141
Grammar	131	3.4	103	3.0	102	3.6	112	3.8	116	4.0	153	123	4.1	157
Technical	10	0.3	2	0.1	2	0.1	2	0.1	2	0.1	3	3	0.1	4
Comprehensive	3,168	82.5	2,894	85.4	2,446	85.7	2,553	86.1	2,528	86.2	2,868	2,580	86.2	2,856
Other	34	0.9	22	0.7	28	1.0	28	0.9	36	1.2	47	37	1.2	46
Total	3,840	100.0	3,389	100.0	2,853	100.0	2,965	100.0	2,934	100.0	3,629	2,993	100.0	3,614
of which grant maintained	.	.	.	.	36	1.3	221	8	485	17	554	553	18.5	622
WALES														
Maintained secondary schools														
Middle deemed secondary	-	0.1	-	0.1	-	-	-	-	-	-	-	..	..	..
Modern	4	1.8	1	0.6	-	-	-	-	-	-	-	..	..	..
Grammar	3	1.3	1	0.5	-	-	-	-	-	-	-	..	..	..
Comprehensive	231	96.6	215	98.5	184	99.2	191	99.1	194	100.0	227	..	..	..
Other	1	0.3	1	0.3	1	0.8	2	0.9	-	-	-	..	..	..
Total	240	100.0	218	100.0	185	100.0	193	100.0	194	100.0	227	..	..	..
of which grant maintained	.	.	.	.	.	.	-	2	-	4	10	..	..	..
SCOTLAND														
Public sector secondary schools														
Selective	1	0.1	..	..	-	-	-	-	-	-	-	-	-	-
Comprehensive	392	96.0	..	..	294	100.0	303	100.0	311	100.0	408	315	100.0	405
Part comprehensive/ part selective	16	3.8	..	..	-	-	-	-	-	-	-	-	-	-
Total	408	100.0	361	100.0	294	100.0	303	100.0	311	100.0	408	315	100.0	405
of which grant maintained	.	.	.	.	.	.	.	.	.	.	.	-	-	1
NORTHERN IRELAND														
All grant-aided secondary schools														
Secondary intermediate	105	88.6	99	88.2	87	61.4	88	60.5	89	60.1	161	90	59.7	161
Grammar (3)	14	11.4	13	11.8	54	38.6	58	39.5	59	39.9	71	61	40.3	71
Total	119	100.0	113	100.0	141	100.0	146	100.0	148	100.0	232	150	100.0	232

(1) From 1 April 1993 excludes sixth form colleges in England and Wales which were reclassified as further education colleges.
(2) Provisional.
(3) Includes voluntary grammar schools from 1989/90, formerly allocated to the independent sector.

18(19)

POST-COMPULSORY EDUCATION
Educational and economic activities of 16-18 year olds (1) in Great Britain

(i) January 1995 (2)

AGE	16			17			18			16 to 18		
	Persons	Males	Females	Persons	Males	Females	Persons	Males	Females	Persons	Males	Females
Population (thousands)	644	332	312	629	325	305	656	338	318	1,930	995	935
Percentage of age group												
In full-time education	71	68	75	58	54	63	39	37	40	56	53	59
School	38	37	39	28	26	29	3	3	3	23	22	24
Further education (3)	33	31	35	29	26	31	15	14	15	25	24	27
Higher education (3)	-	-	-	2	2	2	21	20	22	8	7	8
On YT (4)	11	11	10	12	13	11	6	7	6	10	10	9
Other (5)	18	20	15	29	33	26	55	56	54	34	37	32
Of which Part-time day education (6)	5	6	4	4	6	3	5	6	3	5	6	3

(ii) January 1994

AGE	16			17			18			16 to 18		
	Persons	Males	Females	Persons	Males	Females	Persons	Males	Females	Persons	Males	Females
Population (thousands)	627	324	304	654	337	317	679	349	330	1,960	1,010	950
Percentage of age group												
In full-time education	72	69	76	56	52	61	37	36	38	55	52	58
School	40	38	41	26	25	28	3	3	3	22	22	23
Further education (3)	33	30	35	28	25	31	15	14	15	25	23	27
Higher education (3)	-	-	-	2	1	2	20	19	20	7	7	8
On YT (4)	12	13	10	13	15	11	6	7	5	10	12	9
Other(5)	16	18	14	31	33	28	57	57	56	35	36	33
Of which Part-time day education (6)	4	5	3	5	7	3	5	7	3	5	6	3

(iii) January 1993

AGE	16			17			18			16 to 18		
	Persons	Males	Females	Persons	Males	Females	Persons	Males	Females	Persons	Males	Females
Population (thousands)	652	336	316	677	348	328	706	363	343	2,034	1,047	988
Percentage of age group												
In full-time education	70	65	74	53	48	58	34	32	35	51	48	55
School	46	44	48	31	29	32	4	4	4	26	25	28
Further education (3)	23	21	26	21	18	24	12	11	12	18	16	20
Higher education (3)	-	-	-	2	1	2	18	17	18	7	6	7
On YT (4)	7	13	10	13	16	12	6	7	5	9	12	9
Other (5)	24	22	16	34	36	30	60	60	60	40	40	36
Of which Part-time day education (6)	5	6	4	6	9	4	7	10	4	6	8	4

(1)   Age as at 31 August of the preceding year.
(2)   Provisional.
(3)   Full-time and sandwich students in public sector institutions except on full-time YT within colleges.
(4)   Includes those in further education establishments attending YT courses.
(5)   Includes those aged 16-18 who attended evening only or open and distance learning courses, the unemployed and those mainly in employment (outside YT).
(6)   Public sector part-time day study only, excludes those attending YT courses.
(7)   Includes those on YOP in 1976 and 1981 and those in further education establishments attending YTS/YOP courses.

18(19) POST-COMPULSORY EDUCATION

Educational and economic activities of 16-18 year olds (1) in Great Britain

(iv) January 1992

AGE	16			17			18			16 to 18		
	Persons	Males	Females	Persons	Males	Females	Persons	Males	Females	Persons	Males	Females
Population (thousands)	677	348	330	704	361	343	745	382	363	2,126	1,091	1,035
Percentage of age group												
In full-time education	66	61	71	48	43	53	29	28	30	47	43	50
School	44	42	46	28	27	30	4	4	3	24	23	26
Further education (3)	22	19	25	18	15	21	10	9	11	17	14	19
Higher education (3)	-	-	-	1	1	1	15	15	15	6	6	6
On YT (4)	9	11	7	16	20	12	8	12	4	11	14	8
Other (5)	25	28	22	36	37	35	63	60	66	42	42	42
Of which Part-time day education (6)	6	8	4	8	11	4	8	12	4	7	10	4

(v) January 1991

AGE	16			17			18			16 to 18		
	Persons	Males	Females	Persons	Males	Females	Persons	Males	Females	Persons	Males	Females
Population (thousands)	701	361	341	743	382	361	793	407	387	2,238	1,149	1,089
Percentage of age group												
In full-time education	59	53	65	41	37	46	24	24	25	41	37	45
School	40	38	42	25	24	27	3	3	3	22	21	23
Further education (3)	18	15	23	15	12	18	8	8	9	14	11	16
Higher education (3)	-	-	-	1	1	1	13	13	13	5	5	5
On YT (4)	14	16	11	19	23	14	7	10	3	13	16	9
Other (5)	28	31	24	40	40	40	69	66	72	46	46	46
Of which Part-time day education (6)	8	10	5	9	13	5	8	12	4	8	12	4

(vi) January 1976 - 1990

	16 to 18											
AGE	January 1976			January 1981			January 1986			January 1990		
	Persons	Males	Females	Persons	Males	Females	Persons	Males	Females	Persons	Males	Females
Population (thousands)	2,409	1,231	1,178	2,748	1,405	1,343	2,633	1.349	1,284	2,386	1,223	1,163
Percentage of age group												
In full-time education	27	26	28	28	26	31	31	29	33	36	34	39
School	16	16	16	16	16	17	17	17	17	19	19	20
Further education (3)	8	7	9	9	7	11	11	8	13	13	11	15
Higher education (3)	3	3	3	3	3	3	3	4	3	4	4	4
On YT (7)	-	-	-	5	5	5	10	12	9	15	18	11
Other (5)	73	74	73	66	68	64	58	59	57	49	48	49
Of which Part-time day education (6)	14	22	5	13	19	5	8	12	5	7	10	4

See table 18(i) - (iii) for footnotes.

THIS PAGE HAS BEEN LEFT BLANK

POST-COMPULSORY EDUCATION
Numbers and percentages continuing their education aged 16 and over, by age, gender and type of course, 1993/94

19a(20)

	(i) PERSONS (1)							Home students
	Age at 31 August 1994 (2)							
	16	17	18	Total 16-18	19-20	21-24	25 and over (3)	All Ages (4)
NUMBERS (Thousands)								
Total population	651	679	704	2,034	1,514	3,494	.	.
FULL-TIME AND SANDWICH STUDENTS								
Schools	259	180	20	460	3	-	-	463
Further education	220	200	106	526	57	43	102	729
Higher education	1	10	133	144	352	274	185	955
Universities (5)	-	8	107	115	284	223	135	757
Undergraduates	-	8	107	115	283	184	105	688
Postgraduates	-	-	-	-	-	39	30	69
Other HE	-	3	26	29	69	52	49	198
Undergraduates	-	3	26	29	68	47	44	188
Postgraduates	-	-	-	-	-	5	5	10
Total full-time and sandwich students	480	391	259	1,130	412	318	287	2,147
PART-TIME STUDENTS								
Further education	99	80	82	261	166	405	1,874	2,710
Day students	62	56	54	172	86	163	790	1,213
Adult education centres (6)(7)	19	2	4	24	27	97	348	496
Other	43	54	51	148	58	67	442	717
Evening only students	37	24	28	89	81	241	1,084	1,497
Adult education centres (6)(7)	26	9	10	45	43	150	521	759
Other	11	15	17	44	38	91	563	737
Higher education (8)	-	1	5	6	25	68	381	480
Universities	-	-	1	1	8	33	172	214
Undergraduates	-	-	1	1	7	26	87	121
Postgraduates	-	-	-	-	-	8	85	93
Other HE	-	1	4	5	17	31	101	154
Undergraduates	-	1	4	5	17	30	88	141
Postgraduates	-	-	-	-	-	1	12	13
Open University	-	-	-	-	-	3	108	111
Total part-time students	99	81	87	267	191	472	2,254	3,190
All full-time and part-time students	579	472	346	1,397	603	790	2,541	5,337
AS PERCENTAGE OF THE POPULATION								
FULL-TIME AND SANDWICH STUDENTS								
Schools	39.8	26.6	2.9	22.6	0.2	-	..	..
Further education	33.8	29.5	15.1	25.9	3.8	1.2	..	..
Higher education	0.1	1.5	18.9	7.1	23.3	7.8	..	..
Universities (5)	-	1.1	15.3	5.7	18.7	6.4	..	..
Undergraduates	-	1.1	15.3	5.7	18.7	5.3	..	..
Postgraduates	-	-	-	-	-	1.1	..	..
Other HE	-	0.4	3.6	1.4	4.5	1.5	..	..
Undergraduates	-	0.4	3.6	1.4	4.5	1.3	..	..
Postgraduates	-	-	-	-	-	0.1	..	..
Total full-time and sandwich students	73.7	57.5	36.8	55.6	27.2	9.1	..	..
PART-TIME STUDENTS								
Further education	15.2	11.8	11.6	12.8	11.0	11.6	..	..
Day students	9.5	8.2	7.7	8.5	5.7	4.7	..	..
Adult education centres (6)(7)	2.9	0.3	0.5	1.2	1.8	2.8	..	..
Other	6.6	7.9	7.2	7.3	3.9	1.9	..	..
Evening only students	5.7	3.6	3.9	4.4	5.3	6.9	..	..
Adult education centres (6)(7)	3.9	1.4	1.5	2.2	2.8	4.3	..	..
Other	1.7	2.2	2.5	2.1	2.5	2.6	..	..
Higher education (8)	-	0.1	0.7	0.3	1.7	1.9	..	..
Universities	-	-	0.2	0.1	0.5	1.0	..	..
Undergraduates	-	-	0.2	0.1	0.5	0.7	..	..
Postgraduates	-	-	-	-	-	0.2	..	..
Other HE	-	0.1	0.7	0.3	1.1	0.9	..	..
Undergraduates	-	0.1	0.6	0.2	1.1	0.9	..	..
Postgraduates	-	-	-	-	-	-	..	..
Open University	-	-	-	-	-	0.1	..	..
Total part-time students	15.2	11.9	12.4	13.1	12.6	13.5	..	..
All full-time and part-time students	89.0	69.5	49.2	68.7	39.9	22.6	..	..

(1)   Includes gender unrecorded for England, Wales and Scotland.
(2)   At 1 July for Northern Ireland schools and further education and 31 December for Northern Ireland higher education and Scotland schools.
(3)   Includes ages unknown for Northern Ireland.
(4)   Includes ages unknown for Wales, Scotland and Northern Ireland.

19a(20) POST-COMPULSORY EDUCATION
Numbers and percentages continuing their education aged 16 and over, by age, gender and type of course, 1993/94

	(ii) MALES							Home students
	Age at 31 August 1994 (2)							
	16	17	18	Total 16-18	19-20	21-24	25 and over (3)	All Ages (4)
NUMBERS (Thousands)								
Total population	336	350	362	1,048	779	1,791	.	.
FULL-TIME AND SANDWICH STUDENTS								
Schools	128	88	11	227	2	-	-	229
Further education	109	95	53	257	31	23	44	355
Higher education	-	5	66	71	176	148	91	486
Universities (5)	-	4	56	60	148	125	69	401
Undergraduates	-	4	56	60	147	102	52	362
Postgraduates	-	-	-	-	-	22	17	39
Other HE	-	1	10	12	29	23	22	86
Undergraduates	-	1	10	12	29	22	19	81
Postgraduates	-	-	-	-	-	2	2	4
Total full-time and sandwich students	237	188	130	556	209	171	134	1,070
PART-TIME STUDENTS								
Further education	50	46	46	143	76	143	571	934
Day students	36	38	37	110	46	57	211	423
Adult education centres (6)(7)	8	1	1	10	8	24	66	108
Other	28	37	36	100	38	32	144	315
Evening only students	15	8	9	32	31	87	360	511
Adult education centres (6)(7)	10	3	3	17	16	53	147	234
Other	4	5	6	16	14	33	214	277
Higher education (8)	-	-	3	4	17	38	188	247
Universities	-	-	1	1	5	19	84	109
Undergraduates	-	-	1	1	5	15	39	59
Postgraduates	-	-	-	-	-	4	46	50
Other HE	-	-	3	3	13	18	48	82
Undergraduates	-	-	3	3	13	18	43	76
Postgraduates	-	-	-	-	-	-	6	6
Open University	-	-	-	-	-	1	55	56
Total part-time students	50	47	50	147	93	182	758	1,181
All full-time and part-time students	288	235	180	702	302	352	893	2,251
AS PERCENTAGE OF THE POPULATION								
FULL-TIME AND SANDWICH STUDENTS								
Schools	38.2	25.1	3.0	21.7	0.2	-	..	..
Further education	32.3	27.3	14.6	24.5	4.0	1.3	..	..
Higher education	-	1.4	18.2	6.8	22.6	8.3	..	..
Universities (5)	-	1.1	15.4	5.7	19.0	7.0	..	..
Undergraduates	-	1.1	15.4	5.7	18.9	5.7	..	..
Postgraduates	-	-	-	-	-	1.2	..	..
Other HE	-	0.3	2.9	1.1	3.7	1.3	..	..
Undergraduates	-	0.3	2.9	1.1	3.7	1.2	..	..
Postgraduates	-	-	-	-	-	0.1	..	..
Total full-time and sandwich students	70.7	53.8	35.9	53.0	26.8	9.5	..	..
PART-TIME STUDENTS								
Further education	14.9	13.2	12.8	13.6	9.8	8.0	..	..
Day students	10.6	10.8	10.2	10.5	5.8	3.2	..	..
Adult education centres (6)(7)	2.4	0.2	0.4	1.0	1.0	1.3	..	..
Other	8.2	10.6	9.8	9.5	4.9	1.8	..	..
Evening only students	4.3	2.4	2.6	3.1	3.9	4.8	..	..
Adult education centres (6)(7)	3.1	0.9	0.9	1.6	2.1	3.0	..	..
Other	1.3	1.5	1.7	1.5	1.8	1.9	..	..
Higher education (8)	-	-	1.0	0.4	2.2	2.1	..	..
Universities	-	-	0.2	0.1	0.6	1.0	..	..
Undergraduates	-	-	0.2	0.1	0.6	0.8	..	..
Postgraduates	-	-	-	-	-	0.2	..	..
Other HE	-	-	0.8	0.3	1.6	1.0	..	..
Undergraduates	-	-	0.8	0.3	1.6	1.0	..	..
Postgraduates	-	-	-	-	-	-	..	..
Open University	-	-	-	-	-	0.1	..	..
Total part-time students	15.0	13.3	13.7	14.0	12.0	10.1	..	..
All full-time and part-time students	85.7	67.1	49.6	67.0	38.8	19.7	..	..

(5)   Includes former polytechnics and colleges which became universities as a result of the Further and Higher Education Act 1992.
(6)   Includes estimated age detail for 1,255,600 persons aged 16 years or more in adult education centres ((England and Wales) enrolments) and non-vocational further education students in Scotland and Northern Ireland.

19a(20)

POST-COMPULSORY EDUCATION
Numbers and percentages continuing their education aged 16 and over, by age, gender and type of course, 1993/94

(iii) FEMALES   Home students

	16	17	18	Total 16-18	19-20	21-24	25 and over(3)	All Ages (4)
NUMBERS (Thousands)								
Total population	316	329	342	986	735	1,704	.	.
FULL-TIME AND SANDWICH STUDENTS								
Schools	131	92	9	233	1	-	-	234
Further education	112	105	53	269	26	20	58	374
Higher education	-	5	67	73	176	126	94	469
Universities (5)	-	4	52	56	136	98	66	356
Undergraduates	-	4	52	56	136	81	53	326
Postgraduates	-	-	-	-	-	17	13	30
Other HE	-	2	15	17	40	28	28	113
Undergraduates	-	2	15	17	40	25	25	107
Postgraduates	-	-	-	-	-	3	3	6
Total full-time and sandwich students	243	203	129	575	203	147	153	1,077
PART-TIME STUDENTS								
Further education	49	34	36	118	90	261	1,303	1,773
Day students	26	18	17	62	40	107	579	788
Adult education centres (6)(7)	11	1	2	14	20	73	281	388
Other	16	17	15	48	20	34	298	400
Evening only students	22	16	18	57	50	155	724	985
Adult education centres (6)(7)	15	6	7	29	26	97	374	526
Other	7	10	11	28	24	58	349	459
Higher education (8)	-	-	2	2	8	29	193	233
Universities	-	-	-	-	3	15	88	106
Undergraduates	-	-	-	-	3	11	48	62
Postgraduates	-	-	-	-	-	4	39	43
Other HE	-	-	1	2	5	13	53	72
Undergraduates	-	-	1	2	5	12	46	64
Postgraduates	-	-	-	-	-	-	7	7
Open University	-	-	-	-	-	2	53	55
Total part-time students	49	34	37	120	98	291	1,496	2,006
All full-time and part-time students	292	237	166	695	301	438	1,649	3,083
AS PERCENTAGE OF THE POPULATION								
FULL-TIME AND SANDWICH STUDENTS								
Schools	41.4	28.1	2.7	23.6	0.2	-	..	..
Further education	35.4	31.8	15.5	27.3	3.5	1.2	..	..
Higher education	-	1.7	19.6	7.4	23.9	7.4	..	..
Universities (5)	-	1.2	15.1	5.7	18.5	5.8	..	..
Undergraduates	-	1.2	15.1	5.7	18.5	4.8	..	..
Postgraduates	-	-	-	-	-	1.0	..	..
Other HE	-	0.5	4.5	1.7	5.4	1.7	..	..
Undergraduates	-	0.5	4.5	1.7	5.4	1.5	..	..
Postgraduates	-	-	-	-	-	0.2	..	..
Total full-time and sandwich students	77.0	61.6	37.8	58.3	27.7	8.6	..	..
PART-TIME STUDENTS								
Further education	15.4	10.3	10.4	12.0	12.2	15.3	..	..
Day students	8.3	5.6	5.0	6.3	5.5	6.3	..	..
Adult education centres (6)(7)	3.4	0.4	0.7	1.4	2.7	4.3	..	..
Other	4.9	5.2	4.4	4.8	2.8	2.0	..	..
Evening only students	7.1	4.8	5.4	5.7	6.8	9.1	..	..
Adult education centres (6)(7)	4.9	1.9	2.0	2.9	3.6	5.7	..	..
Other	2.3	2.9	3.3	2.8	3.2	3.4	..	..
Higher education (8)	-	-	0.5	0.2	1.0	1.7	..	..
Universities	-	-	-	-	0.4	0.9	..	..
Undergraduates	-	-	-	-	0.4	0.6	..	..
Postgraduates	-	-	-	-	-	0.2	..	..
Other HE	-	-	0.4	0.2	0.6	0.7	..	..
Undergraduates	-	-	0.4	0.2	0.6	0.7	..	..
Postgraduates	-	-	-	-	-	-	..	..
Open University	-	-	-	-	-	0.1	..	..
Total part-time students	15.5	10.4	10.9	12.2	13.3	17.1	..	..
All full-time and part-time students	92.5	72.0	48.7	70.5	40.9	25.7	..	..

Age at 31 August 1994 (2)

(7) Excludes youth clubs and centres and an estimated 646,600 students on some courses of further education run by other bodies (see explanatory note 12.7) for whom age detail was not available.
(8) Excludes 85,100 (provisional) students enrolled on nursing and paramedic courses at Department of Health establishments.

19b(20)

POST-COMPULSORY EDUCATION

Numbers and percentages continuing their education aged 16 and over, by age, gender and type of course, 1994/95 (1)

								Home students
	(i) PERSONS (3)							
				Age at 31 August 1994 (2)				
	16	**17**	**18**	**Total 16-18**	**19-20**	**21-24**	**25 and over (4)**	**All Ages (5)**
NUMBERS (Thousands)								
Total population	669	654	682	2,004	1,443	3,377	.	.
FULL-TIME AND SANDWICH STUDENTS								
Schools	257	184	20	461	3	-	-	464
Further education	227	193	103	523	57	46	118	747
Higher education	1	11	138	150	369	293	204	1,021
Universities	-	7	113	121	299	239	153	814
Undergraduates	-	7	113	121	299	197	118	737
Postgraduates	-	-	-	-	-	42	35	77
Other HE estabs	1	4	25	30	70	54	51	206
Undergraduates	1	4	25	30	70	49	46	195
Postgraduates	-	-	-	-	-	5	6	11
Open University	-	-	-	-	-	-	-	-
Total full-time and sandwich students	485	388	261	1,135	430	340	322	2,232
PART-TIME STUDENTS								
Further education	98	72	72	241	157	417	1,908	2,733
Day students	63	50	48	161	81	174	832	1,253
Adult education centres (6)(7)	14	2	3	19	28	100	358	505
Other	49	48	45	142	53	75	474	748
Evening only students	35	22	24	81	76	243	1,076	1,480
Adult education centres (6)(7)	23	8	8	39	41	143	499	722
Other	12	14	16	42	35	100	577	758
Higher education (8)	-	1	5	6	21	67	417	525
Universities	-	-	1	1	7	34	199	248
Undergraduates	-	-	1	1	7	26	106	144
Postgraduates	-	-	-	-	-	9	93	104
Other HE estabs	-	1	4	5	14	29	108	162
Undergraduates	-	1	4	5	14	28	93	141
Postgraduates	-	-	-	-	-	1	14	20
Open University	-	-	-	-	-	4	111	114
Total part-time students	98	73	77	248	178	484	2,325	3,257
All full-time and part-time students	583	461	339	1,382	608	824	2,647	5,490
AS PERCENTAGE OF THE POPULATION								
FULL-TIME AND SANDWICH STUDENTS								
Schools	38.5	28.1	3.0	23.0	0.2	-	..	..
Further education	33.9	29.6	15.1	26.1	4.0	1.4	..	..
Higher education	0.2	1.7	20.3	7.5	25.6	8.7	..	..
Universities	-	1.1	16.6	6.0	20.7	7.1	..	..
Undergraduates	-	1.1	16.6	6.0	20.7	5.8	..	..
Postgraduates	-	-	-	-	-	1.3	..	..
Other HE estabs	0.1	0.6	3.7	1.5	4.8	1.6	..	..
Undergraduates	0.1	0.6	3.7	1.5	4.8	1.5	..	..
Postgraduates	-	-	-	-	-	0.1	..	..
Open University	-	-	-	-	-	-	..	..
Total full-time and sandwich students	72.5	59.4	38.4	56.6	29.8	10.1	..	..
PART-TIME STUDENTS								
Further education	14.6	11.0	10.6	12.0	10.9	12.4	..	..
Day students	9.5	7.6	7.0	8.0	5.6	5.2	..	..
Adult education centres (6)(7)	2.1	0.3	0.4	0.9	2.0	2.9	..	..
Other	7.3	7.3	6.6	7.1	3.7	2.2	..	..
Evening only students	5.2	3.4	3.5	4.0	5.2	7.2	..	..
Adult education centres (6)(7)	3.4	1.2	1.1	1.9	2.9	4.2	..	..
Other	1.8	2.2	2.4	2.1	2.4	2.9	..	..
Higher education (8)	-	0.1	0.8	0.3	1.5	2.0	..	..
Universities	-	-	0.2	0.1	0.5	1.0	..	..
Undergraduates	-	-	0.2	0.1	0.5	0.8	..	..
Postgraduates	-	-	-	-	-	0.3	..	..
Other HE estabs	-	0.1	0.6	0.3	1.0	0.9	..	..
Undergraduates	-	0.1	0.6	0.2	1.0	0.8	..	..
Postgraduates	-	-	-	-	-	-	..	..
Open University	-	-	-	-	-	0.1	..	..
Total part-time students	14.7	11.1	11.3	12.4	12.3	14.3	..	..
All full-time and part-time students	87.2	70.5	49.7	69.0	42.1	24.4	..	..

(1) Provisional.
(2) Includes gender unrecorded for England, Wales and Scotland.
(3) At 1 July for Northern Ireland schools and further education and 31 December for Northern Ireland higher education and Scotland schools.
(4) Includes ages unknown for Northern Ireland.
(5) Includes ages unknown for Wales, Scotland and Northern Ireland

19b(20) POST-COMPULSORY EDUCATION

Numbers and percentages continuing their education aged 16 and over, by age, gender and type of course, 1994/95 (1)

	(ii) MALES							Home students
	Age at 31 August 1994 (3)							
	16	17	18	Total 16-18	19-20	21-24	25 and over (4)	All Ages (5)
NUMBERS (Thousands)								
Total population	344	337	351	1,033	743	1,733	.	.
FULL-TIME AND SANDWICH STUDENTS								
Schools	128	90	11	229	2	-	-	230
Further education	112	93	52	257	31	24	50	362
Higher education	-	5	67	73	183	155	100	512
Universities	-	4	57	61	153	131	78	424
Undergraduates	-	4	57	61	153	107	58	381
Postgraduates	-	-	-	-	-	23	19	43
Other HE estabs	-	2	10	12	29	24	22	88
Undergraduates	-	2	10	12	29	22	20	83
Postgraduates	-	-	-	-	-	2	3	5
Open University	-	-	-	-	-	-	-	-
Total full-time and sandwich students	240	188	130	559	215	178	150	1,104
PART-TIME STUDENTS								
Further education	50	41	40	130	69	145	582	928
Day students	36	33	32	101	41	59	224	425
Adult education centres (6)(7)	6	-	1	7	8	25	69	110
Other	30	32	31	93	33	34	155	315
Evening only students	13	8	8	29	29	86	358	503
Adult education centres (6)(7)	9	3	2	14	16	51	139	220
Other	4	5	6	15	13	35	219	283
Higher education (8)	-	-	4	4	15	37	202	262
Universities	-	-	1	1	4	19	94	120
Undergraduates	-	-	1	1	4	15	45	66
Postgraduates	-	-	-	-	-	4	49	54
Other HE estabs	-	-	3	3	10	16	50	82
Undergraduates	-	-	3	3	10	16	45	75
Postgraduates	-	-	-	-	-	-	6	8
Open University	-	-	-	-	-	2	58	60
Total part-time students	50	41	43	134	84	182	784	1,190
All full-time and part-time students	290	229	174	693	299	360	934	2,294
AS PERCENTAGE OF THE POPULATION								
FULL-TIME AND SANDWICH STUDENTS								
Schools	37.1	26.6	3.2	22.1	0.2	-	..	..
Further education	32.6	27.6	14.8	24.9	4.2	1.4	..	..
Higher education	-	1.5	19.1	7.1	24.6	8.9	..	..
Universities	-	1.1	16.3	5.9	20.6	7.5	..	..
Undergraduates	-	1.1	16.3	5.9	20.6	6.2	..	..
Postgraduates	-	-	-	-	-	1.4	..	..
Other HE estabs	-	0.5	2.9	1.1	3.9	1.4	..	..
Undergraduates	-	0.5	2.8	1.1	3.9	1.3	..	..
Postgraduates	-	-	-	-	-	0.1	..	..
Open University	-	-	-	-	-	-	..	..
Total full-time and sandwich students	69.8	55.7	37.1	54.1	29.0	10.3	..	..
PART-TIME STUDENTS								
Further education	14.4	12.1	11.3	12.6	9.3	8.4	..	..
Day students	10.5	9.7	9.0	9.7	5.5	3.4	..	..
Adult education centres (6)(7)	1.8	-	0.2	0.7	1.1	1.5	..	..
Other	8.8	9.6	8.7	9.0	4.4	1.9	..	..
Evening only students	3.9	2.3	2.3	2.9	3.8	5.0	..	..
Adult education centres (6)(7)	2.6	0.8	0.7	1.4	2.1	2.9	..	..
Other	1.3	1.5	1.6	1.5	1.7	2.0	..	..
Higher education (8)	-	-	1.0	0.4	2.0	2.1	..	..
Universities	-	-	0.2	0.1	0.6	1.1	..	..
Undergraduates	-	-	0.2	0.1	0.6	0.8	..	..
Postgraduates	-	-	-	-	-	0.2	..	..
Other HE estabs	-	-	0.8	0.3	1.4	1.0	..	..
Undergraduates	-	-	0.8	0.3	1.4	0.9	..	..
Postgraduates	-	-	-	-	-	-	..	..
Open University	-	-	-	-	-	0.1	..	..
Total part-time students	14.5	12.2	12.3	13.0	11.3	10.5	..	..
All full-time and part-time students	84.3	68.0	49.5	67.1	40.3	20.8	..	..

(6) Includes estimated age detail for 1,226,900 persons aged 16 years or more in adult education centres ((England and Wales) enrolments) and non-vocational further education students in Scotland and Northern Ireland.

19b(20)

POST-COMPULSORY EDUCATION
Numbers and percentages continuing their education aged 16 and over, by age, gender and type of course, 1994/95 (1)

	(iii) FEMALES						Home students	
	Age at 31 August 1994 (3)							
	16	17	18	Total 16-18	19-20	21-24	25 and over(4)	All Ages (5)
NUMBERS (Thousands)								
Total population	325	317	330	971	701	1,644	.	.
FULL-TIME AND SANDWICH STUDENTS								
Schools	130	94	9	233	2	-	-	234
Further education	114	100	51	266	26	23	68	382
Higher education	1	6	71	78	187	138	104	509
Universities	-	4	56	60	146	109	75	391
Undergraduates	-	4	56	60	146	90	59	356
Postgraduates	-	-	-	-	-	19	16	35
Other HE estabs	1	2	15	18	41	30	29	118
Undergraduates	1	2	15	18	41	27	26	112
Postgraduates	-	-	-	-	-	3	3	6
Open University	-	-	-	-	-	-	-	-
Total full-time and sandwich students	245	200	131	576	215	161	172	1,125
PART-TIME STUDENTS								
Further education	48	31	32	111	88	272	1,325	1,799
Day students	27	17	16	60	41	115	608	825
Adult education centres (6) (7)	8	1	2	11	20	74	289	395
Other	19	15	14	49	20	41	319	430
Evening only students	21	14	16	51	47	157	718	974
Adult education centres (6) (7)	14	5	5	24	25	93	360	502
Other	7	9	11	27	22	64	358	472
Higher education (8)	-	-	2	2	7	30	215	262
Universities	-	-	-	-	3	16	105	128
Undergraduates	-	-	-	-	3	11	61	78
Postgraduates	-	-	-	-	-	4	44	50
Other HE estabs	-	-	1	2	4	13	57	80
Undergraduates	-	-	1	2	4	12	48	67
Postgraduates	-	-	-	-	-	1	9	13
Open University	-	-	-	-	-	2	53	55
Total part-time students	48	31	34	114	95	303	1,540	2,061
All full-time and part-time students	293	232	165	689	309	464	1,712	3,187
AS PERCENTAGE OF THE POPULATION								
FULL-TIME AND SANDWICH STUDENTS								
Schools	39.9	29.7	2.8	24.0	0.2	-	..	..
Further education	35.3	31.6	15.4	27.3	3.8	1.4	..	..
Higher education	0.2	1.9	21.5	8.0	26.6	8.4	..	..
Universities	-	1.2	16.9	6.2	20.8	6.6	..	..
Undergraduates	-	1.2	16.9	6.2	20.8	5.5	..	..
Postgraduates	-	-	-	-	-	1.1	..	..
Other HE estabs	0.2	0.7	4.6	1.8	5.8	1.8	..	..
Undergraduates	0.2	0.7	4.6	1.8	5.8	1.6	..	..
Postgraduates	-	-	-	-	-	0.2	..	..
Open University	-	-	-	-	-	-	..	..
Total full-time and sandwich students	75.4	63.2	39.6	59.3	30.6	9.8	..	..
PART-TIME STUDENTS								
Further education	14.8	9.8	9.7	11.5	12.5	16.6	..	..
Day students	8.3	5.3	4.9	6.2	5.8	7.0	..	..
Adult education centres (6)(7)	2.5	0.4	0.7	1.2	2.9	4.5	..	..
Other	5.8	4.9	4.3	5.0	2.9	2.5	..	..
Evening only students	6.5	4.5	4.8	5.3	6.7	9.5	..	..
Adult education centres (6)(7)	4.2	1.7	1.6	2.5	3.6	5.6	..	..
Other	2.3	2.8	3.2	2.8	3.1	3.9	..	..
Higher education (8)	-	-	0.5	0.2	1.0	1.8	..	..
Universities	-	-	-	-	0.4	0.9	..	..
Undergraduates	-	-	-	-	0.4	0.7	..	..
Postgraduates	-	-	-	-	-	0.3	..	..
Other HE estabs	-	-	0.4	0.2	0.6	0.8	..	..
Undergraduates	-	-	0.4	0.2	0.6	0.7	..	..
Postgraduates	-	-	-	-	-	-	..	..
Open University	-	-	-	-	-	0.1	..	..
Total part-time students	14.9	9.9	10.3	11.7	13.5	18.4	..	..
All full-time and part-time students	90.3	73.1	49.9	71.0	44.1	28.2	..	..

(7)   Excludes youth clubs and centres and an estimated 646,600 students on some courses of further education run by other bodies (see explanatory note 12.7) for whom age detail was not available.

(8)   Excludes 85,100 (provisional) students enrolled on nursing and paramedic courses at Department of Health establishments.

POST-COMPULSORY EDUCATION
Participation rates of pupils and students (1), (2) by gender, age (3) and type of education

Home students — Percentages of the population age group

		1980/81		1985/86		1990/91		1992/93		1993/94		1994/95 (4)	
		Full-time	Part-time	Full-time	Part-time	Full-time	Part-time	Full-time	Part-time	Full-time	Part-time	Full-time	Part-time
PERSONS													
Schools													
16-18	}	16.5	-	17.7	-	22.4	-	26.4	-	22.6	-	23.0	-
19-20	}			0.2	-	0.2	-	0.3	-	0.2	-	0.2	-
Further education (5)													
16-18 (6)		9.2	22.0	11.6	20.0	15.3	17.5	19.6	14.4	25.9	12.8	26.1	12.0
19-20		1.3	12.7	1.5	11.9	2.1	12.1	3.1	12.1	3.8	11.0	4.0	10.9
21-24		0.5	11.7	0.5	12.1	0.7	13.0	1.0	12.8	1.2	11.6	1.4	12.4
Higher education													
16-18		3.3	0.5	3.4	0.4	4.8	0.5	6.5	0.4	7.1	0.3	7.5	0.3
19-20		11.0	2.3	12.2	2.0	15.2	2.1	20.4	1.9	23.3	1.7	25.6	1.5
21-24		3.8	1.9	4.0	1.8	5.0	1.9	6.8	2.0	7.8	1.9	8.7	2.0
Total pupils and students													
16-18 (6)		28.9	22.5	32.7	20.4	42.5	18.0	52.5	14.7	55.6	13.1	56.6	12.4
19-20		12.4	15.0	13.9	14.0	17.5	14.2	23.7	14.0	27.2	12.6	29.8	12.3
21-24		4.3	13.6	4.5	13.8	5.6	14.9	6.8	14.8	9.1	13.5	10.1	14.3
MALES													
Schools													
16-18	}	16.0	-	17.2	-	21.4	-	25.3	-	21.7	-	22.1	-
19-20	}			0.2	-	0.2	-	0.3	-	0.2	-	0.2	-
Further education (5)													
16-18 (6)		7.2	26.7	9.8	21.2	13.6	20.0	18.2	15.5	24.5	13.6	24.9	12.6
19-20		1.4	14.2	1.5	11.4	2.1	11.2	3.2	11.0	4.0	9.8	4.2	9.3
21-24		0.5	8.5	0.4	8.6	0.6	9.0	1.0	8.9	1.3	8.0	1.4	8.4
Higher education													
16-18		3.5	0.8	3.5	0.6	4.7	0.6	6.2	0.5	6.8	0.4	7.1	0.4
19-20		12.3	3.6	12.9	3.1	15.4	2.9	20.0	2.5	22.6	2.2	24.6	2.0
21-24		4.7	2.8	4.6	2.4	5.4	2.3	7.2	2.3	8.3	2.1	8.9	2.1
Total pupils and students													
16-18 (6)		26.7	27.5	30.5	21.9	39.7	20.7	49.7	16.0	53.0	14.0	54.1	13.0
19-20		13.8	17.8	14.6	14.5	17.7	14.1	23.6	13.5	26.8	12.0	29.0	11.3
21-24		5.2	11.3	5.0	11.1	6.0	11.3	8.2	11.2	9.5	10.1	10.3	10.5
FEMALES													
Schools													
16-18	}	16.9	-	18.1	-	23.5	-	27.7	-	23.6	-	24.0	-
19-20	}			0.2	-	0.2	-	0.3	-	0.2	-	0.2	-
Further education (5)													
16-18 (6)		11.1	17.0	13.6	18.6	17.0	14.8	21.1	13.1	27.3	12.0	27.3	11.5
19-20		1.3	11.2	1.6	12.4	2.2	13.1	2.9	13.3	3.5	12.2	3.8	12.5
21-24		0.5	14.9	0.5	15.6	0.7	17.1	1.0	16.9	1.2	15.3	1.4	16.6
Higher education													
16-18		3.0	0.2	3.2	0.2	4.9	0.3	6.8	0.2	7.4	0.2	8.0	0.2
19-20		9.8	0.9	11.4	1.0	14.9	1.2	20.7	1.2	23.9	1.0	26.6	1.0
21-24		2.9	1.0	3.4	1.1	4.5	1.5	6.3	1.7	7.4	1.7	8.4	1.8
Total pupils and students													
16-18 (6)		31.2	17.2	34.9	18.8	45.4	15.1	55.5	13.4	58.3	12.2	59.3	11.7
19-20		11.0	12.1	13.1	13.4	17.3	14.3	24.0	14.4	27.7	13.3	30.6	13.5
21-24		3.4	15.9	3.9	16.7	5.2	18.6	7.3	18.6	8.6	17.1	9.8	18.4

Age at 31 August (3)

(1) Full-time includes sandwich course students.
(2) Part-time includes evening students.
(3) Age as at 31 August at the beginning of the academic year.
(4) Provisional.
(5) Includes estimated age detail for students in adult education centres in 1993/94 (see also Table 19a and 19b).
(6) Includes under-16s in Scotland for 1980/81.

FURTHER AND HIGHER EDUCATION

Enrolments in further and higher education by type of course, mode of study (1), gender and and subject group, 1993/94

	(i) Home Students										Thousands	
	Postgraduate level		First degree		Other Undergraduate		Total higher education		Further education (2)(3)		TOTAL FE/HE ENROLMENTS	
	Full-time	Part-time	Full-time	Part-time	Full-time	Part-time	Full-time	Part-time	Full-time	Part-time	Full-time	Part-time
PERSONS (4)												
Medicine & Dentistry	2.2	4.2	22.7	0.1	0.1	-	25.0	4.3	-	0.5	25.0	4.7
Allied Medicine (5)	2.5	5.5	27.7	9.6	15.0	98.1	45.2	113.1	49.2	34.1	94.4	147.2
Biological Sciences	4.9	3.2	36.7	2.2	1.8	1.0	43.5	6.4	0.1	0.8	43.6	7.1
Agriculture	0.9	0.5	7.8	0.1	4.1	0.9	12.9	1.4	14.1	30.7	27.0	32.1
Physical Sciences	7.5	2.5	43.1	2.3	2.5	2.8	53.1	7.6	0.6	2.0	53.7	9.6
Mathematical Science	5.2	3.7	43.7	2.8	13.3	8.5	62.2	15.0	27.1	87.2	89.2	102.3
Engineering & Tech.	7.4	6.2	68.4	7.3	18.2	37.5	94.0	50.9	56.2	162.2	150.2	213.2
Architecture	2.5	3.9	21.6	6.6	5.9	14.6	30.1	25.0	23.3	68.3	53.3	93.3
Social Sciences	9.9	11.2	85.2	9.7	12.5	11.7	107.6	32.6	16.9	55.7	124.5	88.3
Business & Financial	5.2	29.1	72.1	9.8	46.5	84.2	123.7	123.1	133.9	267.4	257.6	390.4
Documentation	1.3	1.2	7.5	0.4	1.5	0.8	10.4	2.4	7.8	17.0	18.2	19.4
Languages	2.6	2.9	49.0	2.1	0.7	4.8	52.3	9.8	6.4	162.3	58.7	172.1
Humanities	2.6	4.0	28.3	2.0	0.3	0.7	31.2	6.6	0.2	3.4	31.3	10.0
Creative arts	2.5	2.0	45.9	1.9	17.3	1.6	65.7	5.5	82.5	191.0	148.1	196.5
Education (6)	10.0	15.6	8.0	1.6	0.4	2.5	18.4	19.8	14.4	66.5	32.8	86.2
ITT and INSET (6)	10.9	9.1	45.6	2.6	0.5	15.6	57.1	27.4	-	-	57.1	27.4
Combined, gen (7)	1.2	2.1	116.4	12.8	4.9	3.7	122.5	18.6	270.2	557.8	392.7	576.4
Open University (8)	-	8.8	-	90.1	-	12.5	-	111.3	-	-	-	111.3
All subjects (9)	79.4	115.5	729.9	163.8	145.5	301.4	954.7	580.7	729.7	1,747.6	1,684.4	2,328.3
MALES												
Medicine & Dentistry	1.0	2.0	11.4	-	-	-	12.4	2.1	-	-	12.4	2.1
Allied Medicine (5)	1.0	1.7	7.0	1.3	2.2	14.0	10.1	16.9	3.3	5.8	13.3	22.7
Biological Sciences	2.5	1.5	15.0	0.7	0.9	0.4	18.4	2.6	0.1	0.2	18.4	2.8
Agriculture	0.5	0.3	3.9	-	2.6	0.5	7.0	0.8	8.2	15.1	15.2	15.9
Physical Sciences	5.6	1.7	28.5	1.4	1.7	1.6	35.8	4.7	0.4	1.4	36.2	6.2
Mathematical Science	4.1	2.8	32.9	2.3	10.2	6.0	47.2	11.0	20.4	39.2	67.6	50.2
Engineering & Tech.	6.2	5.6	58.1	6.9	16.0	35.3	80.3	47.8	52.4	148.8	132.7	196.6
Architecture	1.6	2.5	17.0	5.7	5.4	12.7	24.0	20.8	22.1	64.0	46.1	84.8
Social Sciences	4.6	5.0	39.5	4.6	4.1	3.1	48.3	12.7	3.0	10.0	51.3	22.7
Business & Financial	3.1	18.8	37.6	4.9	21.9	38.4	62.6	62.1	54.8	70.6	117.4	132.6
Documentation	0.6	0.4	2.9	0.1	0.8	0.2	4.3	0.7	4.5	7.9	8.8	8.7
Languages	1.2	1.2	14.9	0.6	0.2	1.9	16.2	3.6	2.9	64.0	19.2	67.5
Humanities	1.5	2.2	13.8	0.8	0.1	0.3	15.5	3.2	0.1	1.1	15.6	4.3
Creative arts	1.2	1.0	19.4	0.6	8.5	0.6	29.2	2.3	31.0	44.7	60.2	46.9
Education (6)	3.8	5.4	2.2	0.3	0.2	0.7	6.2	6.4	8.3	24.6	14.5	31.0
ITT and INSET (6)	3.7	2.9	9.1	0.6	0.2	4.1	13.0	7.6	-	-	13.0	7.6
Combined, gen (7)	0.7	1.0	52.0	4.9	2.7	1.6	55.5	7.5	130.2	200.0	185.7	207.4
Open University (8)	-	5.4	-	45.8	-	4.9	-	56.2	-	-	-	56.2
All subjects (9)	43.0	61.3	365.3	81.5	77.6	126.2	485.9	269.0	355.1	717.7	841.1	986.6
FEMALES												
Medicine & Dentistry	1.2	2.1	11.3	-	-	-	12.6	2.2	-	0.5	12.6	2.6
Allied Medicine (5)	1.6	3.8	20.8	8.3	12.8	84.1	35.2	96.2	45.9	28.3	81.1	124.5
Biological Sciences	2.4	1.7	21.8	1.5	1.0	0.7	25.1	3.8	-	0.6	25.2	4.4
Agriculture	0.4	0.2	3.9	-	1.5	0.3	5.9	0.6	5.9	15.6	11.8	16.2
Physical Sciences	1.9	0.7	14.6	0.9	0.8	1.1	17.4	2.8	0.2	0.6	17.6	3.4
Mathematical Science	1.1	1.0	10.8	0.5	3.1	2.5	15.0	4.0	6.6	48.0	21.6	52.0
Engineering & Tech.	1.1	0.6	10.3	0.4	2.3	2.1	13.7	3.2	3.8	13.4	17.4	16.6
Architecture	0.9	1.4	4.5	0.9	0.6	1.9	6.0	4.2	1.2	4.3	7.2	8.5
Social Sciences	5.2	6.1	45.7	5.2	8.4	8.6	59.3	19.9	14.0	45.7	73.2	65.6
Business & Financial	2.0	10.3	34.5	4.9	24.6	45.8	61.1	61.0	79.1	196.8	140.2	257.8
Documentation	0.8	0.8	4.6	0.3	0.7	0.6	6.1	1.6	3.3	9.1	9.5	10.7
Languages	1.4	1.7	34.2	1.5	0.5	3.0	36.1	6.2	3.5	98.4	39.5	104.6
Humanities	1.1	1.8	14.5	1.2	0.1	0.4	15.7	3.4	0.1	2.3	15.8	5.7
Creative arts	1.2	1.0	26.5	1.3	8.7	0.9	36.5	3.2	51.5	146.3	88.0	149.6
Education (6)	6.2	10.3	5.8	1.3	0.2	1.8	12.2	13.4	6.1	41.9	18.3	55.3
ITT and INSET (6)	7.2	6.2	36.6	2.0	0.3	11.6	44.0	19.8	-	-	44.0	19.8
Combined, gen (7)	0.5	1.1	64.3	7.9	2.2	2.1	67.1	11.1	140.0	357.8	207.0	368.9
Open University (8)	-	3.4	-	44.2	-	7.5	-	55.2	-	-	-	55.2
All subjects (9)	36.4	54.2	364.6	82.3	67.9	175.2	468.8	311.7	374.5	1,027.5	843.3	1,339.3

(1) Full-time includes sandwich, part-time comprises both day and evening.

(2) Includes 688 thousand students in all modes who are taking unspecified courses.

(3) Excludes SCOTVEC students in Scotland whose course outcome is not known and enrolments in adult education centres in England and Wales and non-vocational further education students in Scotland and Northern Ireland.

(4) Includes students in FE in Scotland whose gender is not recorded.

(5) Includes 85,100 enrolments on nursing and paramedical courses at Department of Health establishments.

21a (22) FURTHER AND HIGHER EDUCATION

Enrolments in further and higher education by type of course, mode of study (1), gender and and subject group, 1993/94

(ii) Overseas Students — Thousands

	Postgraduate level		First degree		Other Undergraduate		Total higher education		Further education (2)(3)		TOTAL FE/HE ENROLMENTS	
	Full-time	Part-time	Full-time	Part-time	Full-time	Part-time	Full-time	Part-time	Full-time	Part-time	Full-time	Part-time
PERSONS (4)												
Medicine & Dentistry	1.5	0.5	1.8	-	0.1	-	3.4	0.5	-	-	3.4	0.5
Allied Medicine (5)	1.0	0.4	2.1	0.1	0.7	0.2	3.7	0.7	0.2	0.1	3.9	0.7
Biological Sciences	1.9	0.4	1.8	-	0.3	-	4.0	0.5	-	-	4.0	0.5
Agriculture	1.1	0.1	0.6	-	0.3	-	1.9	0.1	0.2	0.1	2.1	0.2
Physical Sciences	2.3	0.4	1.7	-	0.4	-	4.5	0.4	-	-	4.5	0.4
Mathematical Science	2.2	0.5	3.2	0.1	0.5	0.1	5.9	0.6	0.3	0.2	6.2	0.9
Engineering & Tech.	6.1	1.4	11.9	0.1	1.9	0.2	19.9	1.6	1.3	0.6	21.3	2.2
Architecture	0.9	0.3	1.9	-	0.5	-	3.3	0.4	0.1	0.2	3.4	0.5
Social Sciences	6.2	1.5	7.9	1.8	1.3	0.1	15.4	3.4	0.1	0.1	15.5	3.5
Business & Financial	5.3	5.2	9.9	0.2	2.6	0.6	17.8	6.0	1.9	0.9	19.7	6.8
Documentation	0.5	0.1	0.4	-	0.1	-	1.0	0.1	0.1	0.1	1.1	0.2
Languages	2.1	0.8	2.2	-	1.8	0.8	6.1	1.6	1.8	4.6	7.9	6.2
Humanities	1.7	0.4	0.7	-	0.4	-	2.8	0.4	-	-	2.8	0.4
Creative arts	0.8	0.1	2.1	-	0.6	-	3.5	0.2	1.0	0.2	4.5	0.3
Education (6)	1.7	1.5	0.6	-	0.1	-	2.4	1.6	0.1	0.1	2.5	1.7
ITT and INSET (6)	0.2	0.2	0.5	0.7	0.1	0.1	0.8	1.0	-	-	0.8	1.0
Combined, gen (7)	0.6	0.1	5.5	0.1	6.4	0.3	12.6	0.6	1.5	1.2	14.1	1.8
Open University (8)	-	-	-	-	-	-	-	-	-	-	-	-
All subjects (9)	36.1	13.8	54.7	3.4	18.2	2.4	109.0	19.6	8.7	8.3	117.7	27.9
MALES												
Medicine & Dentistry	0.9	0.3	1.0	-	0.1	-	2.0	0.3	-	-	2.0	0.3
Allied Medicine (5)	0.5	0.2	0.6	0.1	0.1	-	1.3	0.3	-	-	1.3	0.3
Biological Sciences	1.1	0.2	0.6	-	0.1	-	1.8	0.3	-	-	1.8	0.3
Agriculture	0.8	0.1	0.3	-	0.2	-	1.3	0.1	0.2	-	1.4	0.1
Physical Sciences	1.7	0.3	1.1	-	0.3	-	3.1	0.3	-	-	3.1	0.3
Mathematical Science	1.7	0.3	2.2	0.1	0.4	-	4.2	0.5	0.2	0.1	4.4	0.6
Engineering & Tech.	5.4	1.2	10.5	0.1	1.6	0.2	17.5	1.4	1.2	0.5	18.7	1.9
Architecture	0.6	0.2	1.3	-	0.3	-	2.2	0.3	0.1	0.1	2.4	0.5
Social Sciences	3.8	0.9	4.0	1.4	0.6	-	8.4	2.3	-	-	8.4	2.4
Business & Financial	3.4	4.0	5.2	0.1	1.4	0.3	10.0	4.5	0.9	0.4	10.9	4.9
Documentation	0.2	0.1	0.1	-	-	-	0.4	0.1	-	-	0.4	0.1
Languages	0.9	0.3	0.6	-	0.4	0.4	1.9	0.7	0.8	0.9	2.6	1.7
Humanities	1.0	0.2	0.3	-	0.2	-	1.5	0.3	-	-	1.5	0.3
Creative arts	0.4	-	0.7	-	0.2	-	1.3	-	0.3	-	1.6	0.1
Education (6)	0.8	0.7	0.2	-	-	-	1.0	0.7	-	-	1.0	0.8
ITT and INSET (6)	0.2	0.1	0.1	0.2	-	-	0.2	0.3	-	-	0.2	0.3
Combined, gen (7)	0.4	0.1	2.7	-	2.6	0.2	5.7	0.3	0.9	0.5	6.6	0.8
Open University (8)	-	-	-	-	-	-	-	-	-	-	-	-
All subjects (9)	23.5	9.3	31.5	2.0	8.6	1.2	63.7	12.6	4.7	2.8	68.4	15.4
FEMALES												
Medicine & Dentistry	0.5	0.2	0.8	-	-	-	1.4	0.2	-	-	1.4	0.2
Allied Medicine (5)	0.4	0.2	1.4	0.1	0.6	0.1	2.4	0.4	0.2	-	2.6	0.4
Biological Sciences	0.8	0.2	1.2	-	0.2	-	2.2	0.2	-	-	2.2	0.2
Agriculture	0.3	-	0.2	-	0.1	-	0.6	-	0.1	-	0.7	0.1
Physical Sciences	0.6	0.1	0.6	-	0.2	-	1.4	0.1	-	-	1.4	0.1
Mathematical Science	0.5	0.1	1.0	-	0.2	-	1.7	0.1	0.1	0.1	1.8	0.3
Engineering & Tech.	0.7	0.2	1.4	-	0.2	-	2.4	0.2	0.1	0.1	2.5	0.3
Architecture	0.3	0.1	0.6	-	0.2	-	1.0	0.1	-	-	1.1	0.1
Social Sciences	2.4	0.6	3.9	0.5	0.7	0.1	7.0	1.1	0.1	-	7.0	1.1
Business & Financial	1.9	1.1	4.7	0.1	1.2	0.3	7.8	1.5	0.9	0.4	8.8	2.0
Documentation	0.3	0.1	0.3	-	-	-	0.7	0.1	-	0.1	0.7	0.1
Languages	1.3	0.5	1.6	-	1.4	0.4	4.2	0.9	1.1	3.7	5.3	4.5
Humanities	0.7	0.2	0.4	-	0.3	-	1.4	0.2	-	-	1.4	0.2
Creative arts	0.5	0.1	1.4	-	0.4	-	2.2	0.1	0.7	0.1	2.9	0.3
Education(6)	0.9	0.8	0.3	-	0.1	-	1.4	0.8	-	0.1	1.4	0.9
ITT and INSET (6)	0.1	0.1	0.4	0.5	-	0.1	0.6	0.7	-	-	0.6	0.7
Combined, gen (7)	0.2	0.1	2.8	0.1	3.8	0.2	6.9	0.3	0.7	0.8	7.6	1.1
Open University (8)	-	-	-	-	-	-	-	-	-	-	-	-
All subjects (9)	12.6	4.5	23.2	1.4	9.5	1.1	45.3	7.0	4.0	5.5	49.4	12.6

(6)   Students in Scotland on in-service teacher training courses are included in Education.
(7)   Includes GCSE, SCE, GCE and other combined and general courses.
(8)   Open University courses are not available by subject headings.
(9)   Further Education totals include students in Scotland who are taking National Certificate Modules (72,800 persons, 35,200 females).

21a (22)

FURTHER AND HIGHER EDUCATION
Enrolments in further and higher education by type of course, mode of study (1), gender and and subject group, 1993/94

(iii) Home and Overseas Students

Thousands

	Postgraduate level		First degree		Other Undergraduate		Total higher education		Further education (2)(3)		TOTAL FE/HE ENROLMENTS	
	Full-time	Part-time	Full-time	Part-time	Full-time	Part-time	Full-time	Part-time	Full-time	Part-time	Full-time	Part-time
PERSONS (4)												
Medicine & Dentistry	3.7	4.6	24.5	0.1	0.2	-	28.4	4.7	-	0.5	28.4	5.2
Allied Medicine (5)	3.5	5.8	29.8	9.7	15.6	98.2	49.0	113.8	49.4	34.2	98.4	147.9
Biological Sciences	6.8	3.6	38.6	2.2	2.2	1.0	47.5	6.8	0.1	0.8	47.6	7.6
Agriculture	2.0	0.6	8.4	0.1	4.4	0.9	14.8	1.6	14.3	30.8	29.1	32.3
Physical Sciences	9.8	2.8	44.8	2.3	2.9	2.8	57.6	7.9	0.6	2.0	58.2	10.0
Mathematical Science	7.4	4.2	46.9	2.9	13.8	8.6	68.1	15.7	27.4	87.5	95.5	103.1
Engineering & Tech.	13.5	7.6	80.3	7.3	20.1	37.6	113.9	52.6	57.5	162.8	171.4	215.4
Architecture	3.5	4.2	23.5	6.6	6.4	14.6	33.3	25.4	23.4	68.4	56.8	93.9
Social Sciences	16.1	12.7	93.1	11.6	13.8	11.8	123.0	36.0	17.0	55.8	140.0	91.8
Business & Financial	10.4	34.2	82.0	10.1	49.1	84.8	141.5	129.1	135.8	268.2	277.3	397.3
Documentation	1.8	1.4	8.0	0.4	1.6	0.8	11.4	2.5	7.9	17.1	19.3	19.6
Languages	4.7	3.7	51.2	2.1	2.4	5.6	58.4	11.4	8.2	166.9	66.6	178.3
Humanities	4.3	4.4	29.0	2.0	0.7	0.7	34.0	7.0	0.2	3.4	34.2	10.5
Creative arts	3.3	2.1	48.0	2.0	17.9	1.6	69.2	5.6	83.4	191.2	152.6	196.9
Education (6)	11.7	17.2	8.6	1.6	0.5	2.6	20.8	21.3	14.4	66.6	35.3	87.9
ITT and INSET (6)	11.1	9.3	46.1	3.3	0.6	15.7	57.8	28.3	-	-	57.8	28.3
Combined, gen (7)	1.9	2.3	121.9	12.9	11.4	4.0	135.1	19.2	271.7	559.0	406.8	578.2
Open University (8)	-	8.8	-	90.1	-	12.5	-	111.3	-	-	-	111.3
All subjects (9)	115.5	129.3	784.6	167.2	163.7	303.8	1,063.7	600.3	738.4	1,755.9	1,802.2	2,356.2
MALES												
Medicine & Dentistry	1.9	2.3	12.4	-	0.1	-	14.4	2.4	-	-	14.4	2.4
Allied Medicine (5)	1.5	1.8	7.6	1.3	2.3	14.0	11.3	17.2	3.3	5.9	14.7	23.0
Biological Sciences	3.6	1.8	15.6	0.7	1.0	0.4	20.2	2.8	0.1	0.2	20.2	3.0
Agriculture	1.3	0.3	4.2	-	2.8	0.6	8.3	0.9	8.4	15.1	16.7	16.0
Physical Sciences	7.3	2.0	29.6	1.4	1.9	1.6	38.9	5.0	0.4	1.4	39.3	6.4
Mathematical Science	5.8	3.1	35.1	2.3	10.5	6.0	51.4	11.5	20.6	39.4	72.0	50.8
Engineering & Tech.	11.6	6.7	68.6	7.0	17.6	35.5	97.8	49.2	53.6	149.3	151.5	198.5
Architecture	2.2	2.7	18.4	5.7	5.7	12.7	26.3	21.1	22.2	64.1	48.5	85.2
Social Sciences	8.5	6.0	43.5	5.9	4.8	3.2	56.7	15.1	3.0	10.0	59.7	25.1
Business & Financial	6.5	22.8	42.8	5.0	23.3	38.6	72.6	66.5	55.7	71.0	128.3	137.5
Documentation	0.8	0.5	3.0	0.1	0.8	0.2	4.6	0.8	4.5	7.9	9.2	8.7
Languages	2.1	1.5	15.4	0.6	0.6	2.3	18.1	4.3	3.7	64.9	21.8	69.2
Humanities	2.5	2.4	14.1	0.8	0.3	0.3	16.9	3.5	0.1	1.1	17.0	4.6
Creative arts	1.6	1.1	20.1	0.6	8.8	0.6	30.5	2.3	31.3	44.7	61.8	47.0
Education (6)	4.6	6.1	2.5	0.3	0.2	0.7	7.3	7.1	8.3	24.6	15.6	31.7
ITT and INSET (6)	3.8	3.0	9.2	0.8	0.2	4.1	13.2	7.9	-	-	13.2	7.9
Combined, gen (7)	1.1	1.1	54.7	4.9	5.3	1.7	61.1	7.8	131.1	200.4	192.2	208.2
Open University (8)	-	5.4	-	45.8	-	4.9	-	56.2	-	-	-	56.2
All subjects (9)	66.5	70.6	396.8	83.5	86.3	127.5	549.6	281.5	359.9	720.4	909.5	1,002.0
FEMALES												
Medicine & Dentistry	1.8	2.3	12.2	-	0.1	-	14.0	2.4	-	0.5	14.0	2.8
Allied Medicine (5)	2.0	4.0	22.2	8.4	13.3	84.2	37.6	96.6	46.1	28.3	83.7	124.9
Biological Sciences	3.2	1.8	23.0	1.5	1.2	0.7	27.3	4.0	-	0.6	27.4	4.6
Agriculture	0.7	0.2	4.2	-	1.6	0.3	6.5	0.6	6.0	15.7	12.4	16.3
Physical Sciences	2.5	0.9	15.2	0.9	1.0	1.1	18.7	2.9	0.2	0.6	18.9	3.5
Mathematical Science	1.6	1.1	11.8	0.5	3.3	2.6	16.7	4.2	6.8	48.1	23.4	52.3
Engineering & Tech.	1.9	0.8	11.7	0.4	2.5	2.1	16.1	3.4	3.9	13.5	20.0	16.9
Architecture	1.2	1.5	5.1	0.9	0.7	1.9	7.1	4.3	1.2	4.3	8.3	8.6
Social Sciences	7.6	6.7	49.6	5.6	9.1	8.6	66.2	21.0	14.0	45.8	80.3	66.7
Business & Financial	3.9	11.4	39.2	5.0	25.8	46.1	68.9	62.5	80.1	197.2	149.0	259.8
Documentation	1.1	0.9	4.9	0.3	0.8	0.6	6.8	1.7	3.4	9.2	10.1	10.9
Languages	2.7	2.2	35.8	1.5	1.8	3.3	40.3	7.0	4.5	102.0	44.8	109.1
Humanities	1.8	2.0	14.9	1.2	0.4	0.4	17.1	3.5	0.1	2.4	17.2	5.9
Creative arts	1.7	1.0	27.9	1.3	9.1	1.0	38.7	3.3	52.1	146.5	90.9	149.8
Education (6)	7.1	11.1	6.1	1.3	0.3	1.8	13.6	14.3	6.1	41.9	19.7	56.2
ITT and INSET (6)	7.3	6.3	36.9	2.5	0.3	11.6	44.6	20.5	-	-	44.6	20.5
Combined, gen (7)	0.8	1.2	67.2	8.0	6.1	2.3	74.0	11.4	140.6	358.6	214.6	370.0
Open University (8)	-	3.4	-	44.2	-	7.5	-	55.2	-	-	-	55.2
All subjects (9)	49.0	58.7	387.8	83.7	77.4	176.3	514.1	318.8	378.5	1,033.1	892.7	1,351.8

For footnotes see Table 21a(i) and (ii)

FURTHER AND HIGHER EDUCATION

21b (22) Enrolments in further and higher education by type of course, mode of study (1), gender and subject group, 1994/95 (2)

(i) Home Students | | | | | | | | | | | Thousands

	Postgraduate level		First degree		Other Undergraduate		Total higher education		Further education (3)(4)		TOTAL FE/HE ENROLMENTS	
	Full-time	Part-time	Full-time	Part-time	Full-time	Part-time	Full-time	Part-time	Full-time	Part-time	Full-time	Part-time
PERSONS (5)												
Medicine & Dentistry	2.5	4.5	24.1	0.1	0.1	0.1	26.6	4.6	-	0.1	26.6	4.7
Allied Medicine (6)	2.5	6.4	33.4	12.9	18.7	100.3	54.7	119.6	59.5	46.9	114.1	166.5
Biological Sciences	5.6	3.4	44.2	2.4	2.4	1.3	52.2	7.1	0.2	1.0	52.4	8.1
Agriculture	1.1	0.4	8.8	0.1	5.4	1.0	15.2	1.5	11.6	29.6	26.8	31.1
Physical Sciences	8.1	2.7	47.2	2.6	2.4	2.6	57.7	7.9	0.9	2.8	58.6	10.6
Mathematical Science	5.8	4.1	48.9	4.0	13.3	10.9	68.0	18.9	28.4	121.3	96.4	140.2
Engineering & Tech.	8.1	6.6	70.6	7.7	17.4	33.5	96.1	47.7	54.4	147.2	150.5	194.9
Architecture	3.2	4.1	22.4	6.2	5.1	11.9	30.7	22.2	23.3	62.1	53.9	84.2
Social Sciences	12.6	13.7	96.0	11.6	11.2	12.4	119.8	37.6	16.9	60.0	136.7	97.6
Business & Financial	5.5	31.5	80.5	10.9	44.6	80.2	130.6	122.6	126.8	272.0	257.4	394.5
Documentation	1.4	1.5	9.5	0.7	1.8	1.3	12.8	3.4	11.8	27.6	24.6	31.0
Languages	3.0	3.1	56.7	3.2	0.6	6.8	60.3	13.1	8.3	163.3	68.6	176.4
Humanities	2.7	4.2	31.4	2.2	0.2	3.6	34.3	10.0	0.4	3.1	34.7	13.1
Creative arts	2.9	2.3	53.7	2.5	20.3	4.1	76.9	8.9	73.1	195.1	150.0	204.0
Education (7)	2.3	11.8	8.8	1.0	1.0	5.5	12.1	18.3	13.3	70.9	25.4	89.2
ITT and INSET (7)	19.6	18.5	49.4	3.0	0.3	9.2	69.3	30.8	-	0.1	69.4	30.9
Combined, gen (8)	1.3	2.3	95.7	8.7	5.4	11.7	102.4	22.7	319.6	598.9	422.0	621.6
Open University (9)	0.4	25.2	-	81.0	-	8.3	0.4	114.5	-	-	0.4	114.5
All subjects	88.5	146.3	781.5	160.5	150.1	304.7	1,020.0	611.5	748.5	1,801.8	1,768.5	2,413.3
MALES												
Medicine & Dentistry	1.1	2.2	12.0	-	0.1	-	13.1	2.2	-	-	13.1	2.3
Allied Medicine (6)	1.0	1.9	8.2	1.8	2.7	14.0	11.9	17.6	4.1	7.5	16.1	25.2
Biological Sciences	2.7	1.5	17.8	0.8	1.2	0.5	21.7	2.8	0.1	0.3	21.8	3.1
Agriculture	0.6	0.3	4.2	-	3.4	0.6	8.2	0.9	6.8	14.2	15.0	15.1
Physical Sciences	5.8	1.8	30.8	1.5	1.5	1.5	38.1	4.8	0.5	1.9	38.7	6.7
Mathematical Science	4.6	3.0	36.8	3.2	10.4	7.6	51.8	13.8	20.7	52.4	72.5	66.2
Engineering & Tech.	6.8	5.8	59.5	7.3	15.2	31.0	81.5	44.1	51.0	134.5	132.5	178.5
Architecture	2.1	2.6	17.8	5.4	4.6	10.1	24.4	18.0	22.0	57.0	46.4	75.1
Social Sciences	5.9	6.1	43.1	5.4	3.4	3.1	52.3	14.5	3.8	11.4	56.1	25.9
Business & Financial	3.4	19.4	41.4	5.3	20.5	36.0	65.3	60.8	54.2	72.6	119.5	133.3
Documentation	0.6	0.6	3.7	0.2	0.9	0.4	5.2	1.1	6.7	13.2	11.9	14.3
Languages	1.4	1.2	17.0	0.9	0.2	2.6	18.5	4.7	3.8	64.1	22.3	68.8
Humanities	1.6	2.3	14.9	0.9	0.1	1.3	16.6	4.5	0.2	0.9	16.8	5.4
Creative arts	1.4	1.1	22.8	0.9	9.6	1.5	33.8	3.5	27.5	46.0	61.2	49.6
Education (7)	0.9	4.1	3.5	0.2	0.6	1.6	5.0	5.9	6.9	23.8	11.9	29.6
ITT and INSET (7)	7.0	5.4	10.3	0.7	0.1	2.4	17.4	8.6	-	-	17.4	8.6
Combined, gen (8)	0.8	1.2	42.7	3.2	3.0	4.7	46.4	9.1	155.0	220.4	201.4	229.5
Open University (9)	0.2	14.1	-	41.6	-	4.0	0.2	59.7	-	-	0.2	59.7
All subjects	47.7	74.6	386.4	79.1	77.4	123.0	511.5	276.7	363.3	720.2	874.8	996.9
FEMALES												
Medicine & Dentistry	1.4	2.3	12.1	-	-	0.1	13.5	2.4	-	0.1	13.5	2.5
Allied Medicine (6)	1.6	4.6	25.2	11.1	16.0	86.3	42.7	102.0	54.9	38.9	97.7	140.9
Biological Sciences	2.9	1.9	26.4	1.6	1.2	0.8	30.5	4.4	0.1	0.6	30.6	4.9
Agriculture	0.5	0.2	4.6	0.1	2.0	0.4	7.1	0.6	4.7	15.3	11.7	15.9
Physical Sciences	2.3	0.8	16.4	1.0	0.8	1.2	19.6	3.0	0.4	0.8	19.9	3.8
Mathematical Science	1.2	1.1	12.1	0.8	2.9	3.2	16.2	5.1	7.7	67.7	23.9	72.8
Engineering & Tech.	1.3	0.7	11.1	0.5	2.2	2.5	14.6	3.7	3.4	12.4	18.0	16.1
Architecture	1.1	1.5	4.7	0.9	0.5	1.8	6.2	4.1	1.2	4.7	7.5	8.8
Social Sciences	6.7	7.6	52.9	6.2	7.8	9.3	67.5	23.1	12.7	48.1	80.1	71.2
Business & Financial	2.1	12.1	39.1	5.5	24.1	44.2	65.3	61.8	72.3	197.5	137.6	259.3
Documentation	0.9	1.0	5.8	0.5	0.9	0.8	7.6	2.3	5.1	14.1	12.6	16.4
Languages	1.6	1.9	39.7	2.3	0.4	4.2	41.8	8.4	4.2	98.7	45.9	107.1
Humanities	1.1	1.9	16.5	1.3	0.1	2.3	17.7	5.5	0.2	2.1	17.9	7.6
Creative arts	1.5	1.2	31.0	1.6	10.7	2.6	43.1	5.4	45.6	148.9	88.7	154.2
Education (7)	1.4	7.7	5.3	0.8	0.4	3.9	7.1	12.4	5.5	47.0	12.6	59.4
ITT and INSET (7)	12.6	13.1	39.2	2.3	0.2	6.8	52.0	22.2	-	0.1	52.0	22.3
Combined, gen (8)	0.5	1.1	53.1	5.5	2.4	7.0	56.0	13.6	164.6	378.4	220.6	392.0
Open University (9)	0.2	11.1	-	39.4	-	4.3	0.2	54.8	-	-	0.2	54.8
All subjects	40.7	71.7	395.1	81.4	72.7	181.7	508.5	334.8	382.5	1,075.4	891.0	1,410.1

(1) Full-time includes sandwich, part-time comprises both day and evening.

(2) Provisional.

(3) Includes 710 thousand students in all modes who are taking unspecified courses.

(4) Excludes SCOTVEC students in Scotland whose course outcome is not known and enrolments in adult education centres in England and Wales and non-vocational further education students in Scotland and Northern Ireland.

(5) Includes students in FE in Scotland whose gender is not recorded.

(6) Includes 85,100 enrolments (1993/94 data) on nursing and paramedical courses at Department of Health establishments.

FURTHER AND HIGHER EDUCATION
Enrolments in further and higher education by type of course, mode of study (1), gender and subject group, 1994/95 (2)

(ii) Overseas Students   Thousands

	Postgraduate level		First degree		Other Undergraduate		Total higher education		Further education (3)(4)		TOTAL FE/HE ENROLMENTS	
	Full-time	Part-time	Full-time	Part-time	Full-time	Part-time	Full-time	Part-time	Full-time	Part-time	Full-time	Part-time
PERSONS (5)												
Medicine & Dentistry	1.7	0.4	2.0	-	0.1	-	3.8	0.4	-	-	3.8	0.4
Allied Medicine (6)	1.0	0.4	2.6	0.2	0.8	0.3	4.4	0.9	0.2	0.1	4.7	1.0
Biological Sciences	1.9	0.3	2.5	0.1	0.4	-	4.8	0.4	-	-	4.8	0.4
Agriculture	1.2	0.1	0.6	0.0	0.8	-	2.7	0.1	0.2	0.1	2.9	0.2
Physical Sciences	2.5	0.4	1.9	-	0.5	0.1	4.9	0.5	0.1	-	5.0	0.5
Mathematical Science	2.3	0.4	3.4	0.1	0.7	0.1	6.4	0.6	0.4	0.2	6.8	0.9
Engineering & Tech.	6.2	1.3	13.5	0.2	2.0	0.2	21.7	1.6	1.4	0.7	23.1	2.3
Architecture	1.1	0.4	2.3	0.1	0.5	-	3.9	0.5	0.1	0.1	4.0	0.6
Social Sciences	7.3	1.8	9.1	1.7	1.4	0.2	17.7	3.8	0.2	0.1	17.9	3.9
Business & Financial	6.3	7.3	12.0	0.4	2.9	1.2	21.2	9.0	1.6	0.8	22.9	9.7
Documentation	0.6	0.1	0.5	-	0.1	-	1.2	0.2	0.1	0.1	1.3	0.3
Languages	2.4	0.9	2.7	-	1.8	1.6	6.9	2.6	2.0	8.1	8.9	10.7
Humanities	1.8	0.4	0.8	-	0.3	0.1	2.9	0.4	-	-	2.9	0.5
Creative arts	1.1	0.1	2.6	0.0	0.9	0.1	4.6	0.2	0.9	0.3	5.5	0.5
Education (7)	1.6	1.1	0.6	-	0.1	0.1	2.2	1.2	0.1	0.2	2.3	1.4
ITT and INSET (7)	0.8	0.8	0.7	0.8	-	0.1	1.5	1.7	-	-	1.5	1.7
Combined, gen (8)	0.7	0.2	5.4	0.3	6.9	0.9	13.1	1.3	2.2	2.2	15.3	3.5
Open University (9)	-	1.9	-	2.4	-	0.4	-	4.6	-	-	-	4.6
All subjects	40.6	18.4	63.1	6.3	20.3	5.5	124.0	30.2	9.5	12.9	133.5	43.1
MALES												
Medicine & Dentistry	1.0	0.3	1.0	-	0.1	-	2.1	0.3	-	-	2.1	0.3
Allied Medicine (6)	0.5	0.2	0.7	0.1	0.1	0.1	1.4	0.3	-	-	1.4	0.3
Biological Sciences	1.1	0.2	0.8	-	0.1	-	2.1	0.2	-	-	2.1	0.2
Agriculture	0.9	0.1	0.3	0.0	0.4	-	1.6	0.1	0.1	-	1.7	0.1
Physical Sciences	1.8	0.3	1.2	-	0.3	-	3.3	0.3	0.1	-	3.3	0.3
Mathematical Science	1.8	0.3	2.3	0.1	0.5	0.1	4.6	0.5	0.3	0.1	4.9	0.6
Engineering & Tech.	5.4	1.1	11.7	0.2	1.8	0.2	18.9	1.4	1.2	0.5	20.1	2.0
Architecture	0.7	0.3	1.5	0.1	0.3	-	2.5	0.4	0.1	0.1	2.7	0.4
Social Sciences	4.3	1.2	4.5	1.2	0.6	0.1	9.4	2.5	0.1	-	9.5	2.5
Business & Financial	3.9	5.5	6.3	0.2	1.6	0.8	11.8	6.5	0.9	0.4	12.7	6.9
Documentation	0.3	-	0.2	-	-	-	0.5	0.1	-	-	0.5	0.1
Languages	1.0	0.4	0.7	-	0.5	0.2	2.2	0.7	0.8	2.0	3.0	2.7
Humanities	1.0	0.2	0.3	-	0.1	-	1.5	0.2	-	-	1.5	0.2
Creative arts	0.5	0.1	0.9	-	0.3	-	1.6	0.1	0.3	-	1.9	0.1
Education (7)	0.7	0.5	0.2	-	-	-	1.0	0.6	-	0.1	1.0	0.7
ITT and INSET (7)	0.3	0.3	0.2	0.2	-	-	0.5	0.6	-	-	0.5	0.6
Combined, gen (8)	0.4	0.1	2.6	0.1	2.7	0.3	5.7	0.5	1.1	0.7	6.9	1.3
Open University (9)	-	1.4	-	1.0	-	0.2	-	2.5	-	-	-	2.5
All subjects	25.7	12.5	35.5	3.1	9.5	2.2	70.8	17.8	5.0	4.0	75.8	21.8
FEMALES												
Medicine & Dentistry	0.7	0.1	0.9	-	-	-	1.6	0.1	-	-	1.6	0.1
Allied Medicine (6)	0.5	0.2	1.9	0.1	0.7	0.2	3.1	0.6	0.2	0.1	3.2	0.6
Biological Sciences	0.8	0.2	1.6	-	0.2	-	2.7	0.2	-	-	2.7	0.2
Agriculture	0.3	-	0.3	0.0	0.4	-	1.1	0.0	0.1	-	1.1	0.1
Physical Sciences	0.7	0.1	0.7	-	0.2	-	1.6	0.1	-	-	1.6	0.2
Mathematical Science	0.5	0.1	1.0	-	0.2	-	1.8	0.2	0.2	0.1	1.9	0.3
Engineering & Tech.	0.8	0.2	1.8	-	0.2	-	2.8	0.2	0.2	0.2	3.0	0.3
Architecture	0.4	0.1	0.8	-	0.2	-	1.3	0.1	-	-	1.3	0.1
Social Sciences	3.0	0.6	4.5	0.5	0.8	0.2	8.3	1.3	0.1	0.1	8.4	1.3
Business & Financial	2.3	1.8	5.8	0.2	1.4	0.5	9.4	2.5	0.8	0.4	10.2	2.9
Documentation	0.4	0.1	0.3	-	-	-	0.7	0.1	0.1	0.1	0.8	0.2
Languages	1.4	0.5	2.0	-	1.3	1.4	4.7	1.9	1.1	6.2	5.9	8.1
Humanities	0.8	0.1	0.4	-	0.2	-	1.4	0.2	-	-	1.4	0.2
Creative arts	0.6	0.1	1.7	0.0	0.6	-	3.0	0.2	0.6	0.2	3.6	0.4
Education (7)	0.9	0.6	0.4	-	0.1	0.1	1.3	0.6	0.1	0.1	1.3	0.8
ITT and INSET (7)	0.5	0.4	0.5	0.6	-	0.1	1.0	1.1	-	-	1.0	1.1
Combined, gen (8)	0.3	0.1	2.8	0.2	4.2	0.5	7.4	0.8	1.1	1.4	8.5	2.3
Open University (9)	-	0.5	-	1.4	-	0.2	-	2.1	-	-	-	2.1
All subjects	14.9	5.9	27.6	3.1	10.8	3.3	53.2	12.4	4.5	8.9	57.7	21.3

(7) Students in Scotland on in-service teacher training courses are included in Education.

(8) Includes GCSE, SCE, GCE and other combined and general courses and students whose course of study has not been recorded.

(9) Open University courses are not available by subject headings.

21b (22) FURTHER AND HIGHER EDUCATION

Enrolments in further and higher education by type of course, mode of study (1), gender and subject group, 1994/95 (2)

(iii) Home and Overseas Students — Thousands

	Postgraduate level		First degree		Other Undergraduate		Total higher education		Further education (3)(4)		TOTAL FE/HE ENROLMENTS	
	Full-time	Part-time	Full-time	Part-time	Full-time	Part-time	Full-time	Part-time	Full-time	Part-time	Full-time	Part-time
PERSONS (5)												
Medicine & Dentistry	4.2	4.9	26.0	0.1	0.2	0.1	30.4	5.0	-	0.1	30.4	5.1
Allied Medicine (6)	3.5	6.8	36.0	13.1	19.5	100.6	59.1	120.5	59.7	47.0	118.8	167.5
Biological Sciences	7.5	3.7	46.7	2.4	2.8	1.4	57.0	7.6	0.2	1.0	57.2	8.5
Agriculture	2.3	0.6	9.4	0.1	6.2	1.0	17.9	1.7	11.7	29.6	29.7	31.3
Physical Sciences	10.6	3.0	49.1	2.6	2.9	2.7	62.6	8.3	1.0	2.8	63.6	11.1
Mathematical Science	8.1	4.5	52.3	4.0	14.0	11.0	74.4	19.6	28.9	121.5	103.2	141.1
Engineering & Tech.	14.3	7.8	84.1	7.9	19.4	33.7	117.8	49.4	55.8	147.9	173.6	197.2
Architecture	4.3	4.4	24.7	6.3	5.5	11.9	34.5	22.7	23.4	62.1	57.9	84.8
Social Sciences	19.8	15.5	105.1	13.3	12.6	12.6	137.5	41.4	17.0	60.1	154.5	101.5
Business & Financial	11.8	38.9	92.5	11.2	47.6	81.4	151.9	131.5	128.4	272.8	280.3	404.3
Documentation	2.0	1.6	10.0	0.7	1.9	1.3	14.0	3.6	11.9	27.7	25.9	31.3
Languages	5.5	4.1	59.4	3.2	2.4	8.4	67.2	15.7	10.3	171.4	77.5	187.1
Humanities	4.5	4.5	32.2	2.2	0.5	3.7	37.3	10.4	0.4	3.1	37.7	13.5
Creative arts	4.0	2.5	56.3	2.5	21.2	4.1	81.5	9.1	74.0	195.4	155.5	204.5
Education (7)	3.9	12.9	9.4	1.0	1.1	5.6	14.3	19.4	13.4	71.1	27.8	90.6
ITT and INSET (7)	20.4	19.3	50.1	3.8	0.3	9.3	70.8	32.5	0.1	0.1	70.9	32.6
Combined, gen (8)	2.1	2.5	101.1	9.0	12.3	12.6	115.5	24.1	321.8	601.0	437.3	625.1
Open University (9)	0.4	27.1	-	83.3	-	8.7	0.4	119.1	-	-	0.4	119.1
All subjects	129.0	164.7	844.6	166.7	170.4	310.2	1,144.0	641.6	758.0	1,814.7	1,902.0	2,456.4
MALES												
Medicine & Dentistry	2.2	2.4	13.0	-	0.1	-	15.3	2.5	-	-	15.3	2.5
Allied Medicine (6)	1.5	2.0	9.0	1.8	2.9	14.1	13.3	17.9	4.2	7.5	17.5	25.5
Biological Sciences	3.8	1.6	18.6	0.8	1.3	0.5	23.8	3.0	0.1	0.3	23.9	3.3
Agriculture	1.5	0.3	4.5	0.0	3.8	0.6	9.8	1.0	7.0	14.2	16.7	15.2
Physical Sciences	7.6	2.1	32.0	1.6	1.8	1.5	41.4	5.2	0.6	1.9	42.0	7.0
Mathematical Science	6.4	3.4	39.1	3.2	10.9	7.7	56.4	14.3	21.0	52.5	77.3	66.8
Engineering & Tech.	12.2	6.9	71.3	7.4	17.0	31.2	100.4	45.5	52.1	135.0	152.6	180.5
Architecture	2.8	2.9	19.3	5.4	4.9	10.1	27.0	18.4	22.1	57.1	49.0	75.5
Social Sciences	10.2	7.3	47.6	6.6	4.0	3.2	61.8	17.1	3.8	11.4	65.6	28.5
Business & Financial	7.3	25.0	47.7	5.5	22.1	36.8	77.1	67.2	55.0	72.9	132.2	140.2
Documentation	0.8	0.6	3.9	0.2	0.9	0.4	5.7	1.2	6.7	13.2	12.4	14.4
Languages	2.4	1.7	17.7	0.9	0.6	2.8	20.7	5.3	4.6	66.1	25.4	71.4
Humanities	2.6	2.5	15.2	0.9	0.2	1.3	18.1	4.7	0.2	0.9	18.3	5.7
Creative arts	1.8	1.2	23.6	0.9	9.9	1.5	35.4	3.6	27.7	46.1	63.1	49.7
Education (7)	1.6	4.6	3.7	0.2	0.6	1.6	5.9	6.4	7.0	23.9	12.9	30.3
ITT and INSET (7)	7.3	5.8	10.4	0.9	0.1	2.5	17.9	9.2	-	-	17.9	9.2
Combined, gen (8)	1.2	1.2	45.2	3.3	5.7	5.1	52.1	9.6	156.1	221.1	208.3	230.7
Open University (9)	0.2	15.5	-	42.6	-	4.2	0.2	62.2	-	-	0.2	62.2
All subjects	73.4	87.1	421.9	82.2	86.9	125.1	582.3	294.5	368.3	724.2	950.6	1,018.7
FEMALES												
Medicine & Dentistry	2.0	2.4	13.0	-	0.1	0.1	15.1	2.5	-	0.1	15.1	2.6
Allied Medicine (6)	2.1	4.8	27.1	11.2	16.7	86.5	45.8	102.6	55.1	39.0	100.9	141.6
Biological Sciences	3.7	2.1	28.0	1.7	1.4	0.8	33.2	4.6	0.1	0.6	33.3	5.2
Agriculture	0.8	0.2	4.9	0.1	2.4	0.4	8.1	0.7	4.7	15.3	12.9	16.0
Physical Sciences	3.0	0.9	17.2	1.0	1.0	1.2	21.2	3.2	0.4	0.8	21.6	4.0
Mathematical Science	1.7	1.2	13.2	0.8	3.1	3.3	18.0	5.2	7.8	67.8	25.8	73.0
Engineering & Tech.	2.1	0.9	12.8	0.5	2.4	2.5	17.4	3.9	3.6	12.5	21.0	16.4
Architecture	1.5	1.6	5.5	0.9	0.7	1.8	7.6	4.3	1.2	4.7	8.8	9.0
Social Sciences	9.7	8.2	57.5	6.7	8.6	9.5	75.7	24.4	12.8	48.2	88.5	72.6
Business & Financial	4.4	13.9	44.8	5.7	25.5	44.6	74.8	64.3	73.1	198.0	147.8	262.2
Documentation	1.2	1.0	6.1	0.5	1.0	0.9	8.3	2.4	5.1	14.2	13.4	16.6
Languages	3.0	2.4	41.7	2.3	1.7	5.6	46.5	10.3	5.3	104.8	51.8	115.2
Humanities	1.9	2.0	17.0	1.3	0.3	2.4	19.2	5.7	0.2	2.1	19.4	7.8
Creative arts	2.1	1.3	32.7	1.6	11.3	2.6	46.1	5.5	46.2	149.1	92.3	154.6
Education (7)	2.3	8.3	5.6	0.8	0.5	4.0	8.4	13.0	5.5	47.2	13.9	60.2
ITT and INSET (7)	13.1	13.5	39.7	2.9	0.2	6.9	53.0	23.3	-	0.1	53.0	23.4
Combined, gen (8)	0.9	1.2	55.9	5.7	6.6	7.5	63.4	14.5	165.7	379.8	229.0	394.3
Open University (9)	0.2	11.6	-	40.8	-	4.5	0.2	56.9	-	-	0.2	56.9
All subjects	55.6	77.6	422.6	84.5	83.5	185.1	561.7	347.2	387.0	1,084.3	948.8	1,431.4

For footnotes see Table 21b(i) and (ii)

FURTHER AND HIGHER EDUCATION

First year enrolments in further and higher education by age, gender and mode of study (1), 1993/94

| Home and Overseas Students | | | | | | | | | | | Thousands |
| | Postgraduate level | | First degree | | Other Undergraduate | | All higher education | | Further education | | TOTAL FE/HE ENROLMENTS | |
	Full-time	Part-time	Full-time	Part-time	Full-time	Part-time	Full-time	Part-time	Full-time	Part-time	Full-time	Part-time
Ages as at 31 August 1993 (2)												
PERSONS												
<16	-	-	-	-	-	-	-	0.1	2.6	7.0	2.7	7.1
16	-	-	0.3	-	0.4	0.1	0.7	0.1	213.8	70.3	214.5	70.4
17	-	-	8.3	0.1	2.7	0.6	11.0	0.7	107.3	68.4	118.2	69.2
18	-	-	109.1	0.4	19.4	4.9	128.6	5.3	60.4	62.9	189.0	68.1
19	0.1	-	59.3	0.6	17.7	7.4	77.0	8.0	22.1	49.7	99.0	57.7
20	0.7	0.1	24.8	1.2	11.5	7.6	37.1	8.9	13.7	39.8	50.8	48.7
21	10.4	0.6	16.7	1.6	8.6	7.5	35.7	9.7	10.4	37.5	46.2	47.2
22	14.4	1.4	11.8	1.9	7.2	7.9	33.4	11.2	9.2	37.8	42.5	49.0
23	10.5	1.7	8.0	2.0	5.3	7.4	23.8	11.2	7.5	35.1	31.4	46.2
24	7.8	2.1	6.2	2.2	3.9	7.3	17.9	11.6	6.6	33.5	24.6	45.1
25	6.0	2.3	5.1	2.3	3.1	6.9	14.3	11.6	6.0	31.8	20.3	43.4
26	4.8	2.6	4.5	2.4	2.6	6.7	11.9	11.6	5.6	31.7	17.6	43.4
27	4.0	2.7	3.9	2.5	2.2	6.5	10.0	11.7	5.0	30.4	15.1	42.0
28	3.2	2.8	3.3	2.5	1.9	6.0	8.5	11.2	4.9	29.5	13.4	40.7
29	2.9	2.8	2.9	2.5	1.8	5.7	7.6	11.0	4.6	28.6	12.2	39.6
30 +	20.7	41.2	25.5	34.0	17.6	70.3	63.8	145.5	50.0	479.9	113.8	625.4
Unknown	0.2	0.6	0.7	0.3	0.9	3.0	1.7	3.9	4.5	121.4	6.2	125.3
ALL AGES	85.7	60.8	290.5	56.5	106.8	156.0	483.0	273.3	519.2	1,146.3	1,017.3	1,468.6
MALES												
<16	-	-	-	-	-	-	-	-	1.5	3.8	1.6	3.9
16	-	-	0.2	-	0.2	0.1	0.4	0.1	104.2	39.0	104.5	39.1
17	-	-	3.9	0.1	1.3	0.3	5.2	0.4	56.8	38.2	62.1	38.6
18	-	-	54.0	0.2	10.3	3.4	64.3	3.7	30.5	34.7	94.9	38.3
19	-	-	30.0	0.4	10.0	5.3	40.0	5.7	12.1	27.0	52.1	32.7
20	0.3	-	13.4	0.7	6.4	5.2	20.2	5.9	7.6	19.1	27.7	25.1
21	5.2	0.3	9.7	0.9	4.6	4.7	19.5	5.9	5.6	16.5	25.0	22.4
22	7.4	0.7	7.1	1.0	3.8	4.5	18.3	6.2	4.9	15.8	23.2	21.9
23	5.6	0.9	4.9	1.1	3.0	3.9	13.5	5.8	3.9	14.6	17.4	20.4
24	4.3	1.0	3.8	1.1	2.2	3.7	10.3	5.7	3.4	13.8	13.7	19.6
25	3.3	1.2	3.0	1.1	1.8	3.6	8.1	5.8	3.0	13.4	11.1	19.2
26	2.7	1.3	2.6	1.1	1.5	3.4	6.9	5.8	2.8	13.4	9.7	19.2
27	2.3	1.5	2.2	1.2	1.3	3.2	5.8	5.9	2.5	12.8	8.2	18.7
28	1.9	1.5	1.8	1.1	1.1	3.0	4.8	5.6	2.3	12.3	7.2	17.9
29	1.8	1.5	1.6	1.1	1.0	3.0	4.3	5.6	2.1	11.8	6.4	17.4
30 +	12.2	21.6	11.6	15.1	8.8	32.4	32.7	69.1	20.0	174.5	52.6	243.6
Unknown	0.1	0.2	0.3	0.2	0.6	1.4	1.0	1.8	0.9	34.2	1.9	36.0
ALL AGES	47.3	31.7	150.2	26.4	57.9	81.0	255.3	139.0	264.0	494.9	519.4	633.9
FEMALES												
<16	-	-	-	-	-	-	-	-	1.1	3.2	1.1	3.2
16	-	-	0.2	-	0.2	0.1	0.3	0.1	109.6	31.3	110.0	31.3
17	-	-	4.3	-	1.4	0.3	5.7	0.4	50.4	30.2	56.2	30.6
18	-	-	55.2	0.1	9.1	1.5	64.2	1.6	29.9	28.2	94.1	29.8
19	-	-	29.3	0.3	7.7	2.0	37.0	2.3	9.9	22.7	46.9	25.0
20	0.4	-	11.4	0.5	5.2	2.5	16.9	3.0	6.1	20.7	23.0	23.7
21	5.2	0.3	7.1	0.7	4.0	2.8	16.3	3.8	4.9	20.9	21.1	24.8
22	7.0	0.7	4.7	0.9	3.4	3.5	15.1	5.1	4.2	22.0	19.3	27.1
23	4.9	0.9	3.1	1.0	2.3	3.5	10.3	5.4	3.6	20.5	13.9	25.8
24	3.5	1.1	2.5	1.1	1.7	3.7	7.6	5.8	3.2	19.7	10.9	25.6
25	2.7	1.2	2.1	1.2	1.3	3.4	6.1	5.8	3.0	18.4	9.2	24.2
26	2.1	1.3	1.8	1.2	1.1	3.3	5.0	5.9	2.9	18.3	7.9	24.2
27	1.7	1.2	1.7	1.3	0.9	3.2	4.2	5.8	2.6	17.6	6.8	23.4
28	1.3	1.3	1.5	1.3	0.9	3.0	3.6	5.6	2.6	17.2	6.2	22.8
29	1.1	1.3	1.4	1.3	0.8	2.7	3.3	5.3	2.5	16.8	5.8	22.2
30 +	8.5	19.6	13.9	19.0	8.7	37.9	31.1	76.4	30.0	305.4	61.1	381.8
Unknown	0.1	0.3	0.3	0.2	0.3	1.6	0.7	2.1	0.9	81.3	1.6	83.4
ALL AGES	38.5	29.2	140.3	30.1	48.9	75.0	227.7	134.3	267.5	694.4	495.2	828.6

(1) Full-time includes sandwich, part-time comprises both day only and evening only.
(2) Ages as at 1 July 1993 for Northern Ireland and 31 December for Scotland.

FURTHER AND HIGHER EDUCATION

22b (-)

First year enrolments in further and higher education by age, gender and mode of study (1), 1994/95 (2)

	Home and Overseas Students										Thousands	
	Postgraduate level		First degree		Other Undergraduate		All higher education		Further education		TOTAL FE/HE ENROLMENTS	
	Full-time	Part-time	Full-time	Part-time	Full-time	Part-time	Full-time	Part-time	Full-time	Part-time	Full-time	Part-time
Ages as at 31 August 1994 (3)												
PERSONS												
Age												
<16	-	-	-	-	-	-	-	-	2.6	8.0	2.7	8.1
16	-	-	0.3	-	0.9	0.2	1.2	0.3	222.7	90.9	223.9	91.2
17	-	-	8.3	0.1	3.3	0.7	11.7	0.8	107.8	77.5	119.5	78.3
18	-	0.1	115.0	0.4	19.8	4.9	134.9	5.4	62.5	69.8	197.4	75.2
19	0.1	0.1	63.1	0.5	17.3	6.3	80.4	7.0	24.1	53.9	104.5	60.8
20	0.7	0.2	28.8	1.1	11.5	6.6	41.0	7.9	14.8	44.2	55.8	52.1
21	10.6	0.8	19.8	1.6	8.3	7.1	38.7	9.5	13.0	59.4	51.7	68.9
22	14.8	1.6	13.1	1.9	6.7	7.5	34.6	11.0	10.6	45.8	45.2	56.8
23	11.7	2.3	9.4	2.1	5.2	7.7	26.2	12.1	9.3	47.1	35.5	59.2
24	8.3	2.4	6.8	2.1	3.9	7.2	19.0	11.8	7.9	44.9	26.9	56.7
25	6.6	2.9	5.4	2.3	3.0	7.0	15.0	12.2	7.5	43.8	22.5	56.1
26	5.1	3.1	4.6	2.4	2.3	6.8	12.0	12.3	7.0	43.7	19.0	56.0
27	4.0	3.2	4.1	2.4	2.1	6.4	10.2	12.0	6.5	43.4	16.6	55.4
28	3.4	3.5	3.5	2.4	1.8	5.9	8.7	11.8	6.0	42.7	14.7	54.4
29	3.0	3.4	3.2	2.5	1.6	5.7	7.9	11.5	5.9	42.2	13.8	53.7
30 +	21.8	51.2	27.2	32.9	16.7	77.5	65.8	161.6	72.4	841.2	138.2	1002.8
Unknown	0.5	1.0	1.1	0.5	0.8	3.9	2.3	5.4	7.0	118.8	9.3	124.2
ALL AGES	90.6	75.7	313.8	55.2	105.3	161.5	509.7	292.4	587.4	1717.3	1097.1	2009.7
MALES												
Age												
<16	-	-	-	-	-	-	-	-	1.6	4.2	1.6	4.2
16	-	-	0.2	-	0.3	0.1	0.5	0.2	110.1	48.9	110.6	49.1
17	-	-	3.9	0.1	1.6	0.4	5.5	0.5	57.2	42.3	62.6	42.7
18	-	0.1	55.8	0.3	10.2	3.3	66.1	3.6	32.1	37.3	98.2	40.9
19	-	0.1	31.6	0.3	9.7	4.4	41.3	4.8	13.2	27.2	54.5	31.9
20	0.3	0.1	15.5	0.6	6.2	4.2	22.1	4.9	8.1	19.7	30.1	24.6
21	5.3	0.4	11.3	0.9	4.2	4.2	20.8	5.5	6.7	23.2	27.5	28.6
22	7.5	0.7	7.8	1.0	3.5	4.0	18.8	5.7	5.4	17.8	24.2	23.4
23	6.1	1.0	5.7	1.1	2.8	3.9	14.6	6.1	4.7	18.0	19.3	24.0
24	4.5	1.2	4.0	1.1	2.2	3.5	10.7	5.8	4.0	17.3	14.6	23.1
25	3.6	1.4	3.2	1.1	1.7	3.4	8.5	5.9	3.8	17.2	12.3	23.2
26	2.9	1.6	2.7	1.1	1.3	3.4	6.9	6.1	3.3	16.9	10.2	23.0
27	2.3	1.6	2.3	1.2	1.1	3.1	5.8	5.9	3.1	17.3	8.9	23.2
28	2.0	1.9	1.9	1.1	1.0	3.0	4.8	6.0	2.8	16.3	7.7	22.2
29	1.8	1.9	1.7	1.2	0.9	2.8	4.4	5.9	2.7	16.3	7.1	22.2
30 +	12.6	27.1	12.3	14.6	7.8	35.2	32.6	77.0	29.7	294.1	62.3	371.1
Unknown	0.2	0.3	0.6	0.2	0.3	1.6	1.2	2.2	1.9	32.9	3.1	35.0
ALL AGES	49.2	39.5	160.5	25.7	54.7	80.6	264.4	145.8	290.3	666.8	554.7	812.6
FEMALES												
Age												
<16	-	-	-	-	-	-	-	-	1.1	3.8	1.1	3.8
16	-	-	0.2	-	0.6	0.1	0.8	0.1	112.6	42.0	113.4	42.1
17	-	-	4.5	-	1.8	0.3	6.2	0.3	50.6	35.3	56.8	35.6
18	-	-	59.2	0.1	9.6	1.6	68.9	1.8	30.4	32.5	99.2	34.2
19	-	-	31.5	0.2	7.6	1.9	39.1	2.2	10.9	26.7	50.0	28.9
20	0.4	0.1	13.2	0.5	5.4	2.4	18.9	3.0	6.7	24.5	25.6	27.5
21	5.4	0.4	8.5	0.7	4.0	2.9	17.9	4.0	6.3	36.2	24.2	40.2
22	7.3	0.8	5.3	0.9	3.2	3.5	15.8	5.3	5.2	28.0	21.0	33.3
23	5.5	1.2	3.7	1.0	2.4	3.8	11.6	6.0	4.6	29.1	16.2	35.1
24	3.8	1.2	2.8	1.0	1.8	3.7	8.3	6.0	3.9	27.7	12.3	33.7
25	3.0	1.5	2.2	1.2	1.3	3.6	6.5	6.3	3.7	26.6	10.2	32.9
26	2.2	1.5	1.9	1.3	1.0	3.5	5.1	6.2	3.7	26.8	8.8	33.0
27	1.7	1.5	1.8	1.2	0.9	3.3	4.4	6.1	3.4	26.1	7.8	32.2
28	1.4	1.6	1.6	1.3	0.8	2.9	3.9	5.8	3.1	26.4	7.0	32.2
29	1.2	1.5	1.5	1.3	0.8	2.8	3.5	5.6	3.2	25.9	6.7	31.5
30 +	9.3	24.0	15.0	18.4	8.9	42.3	33.2	84.7	42.7	547.0	75.8	631.7
Unknown	0.2	0.6	0.5	0.3	0.4	2.3	1.2	3.2	2.4	80.0	3.5	83.2
ALL AGES	41.4	36.2	153.3	29.5	50.6	80.9	245.4	146.5	294.4	1044.6	539.8	1191.1

(1) Full-time includes sandwich, part-time comprises both day only and evening only.
(2) Provisional.
(3) Ages as at 1 July 1994 for Northern Ireland and 31 December for Scotland.

FURTHER AND HIGHER EDUCATION
23a(23)
Enrolments in further and higher education by level, mode of study (1), gender and age (2), 1993/94

(i) Home Students — Thousands

	Postgraduate level		First degree		Other Undergraduate		All higher education		Further education (3)(4)(5)		TOTAL FE/HE ENROLMENTS	
	Full-time	Part-time (6)	Full-time	Part-time (6)	Full-time	Part-time (6)	Full-time	Part-time (6)	Full-time	Part-time	Full-time	Part-time
PERSONS (7)												
AGE												
<16	-	-	-	-	0.4	0.1	0.1	0.1	2.4	4.6	2.4	4.7
16	-	-	0.3	-	0.4	0.1	0.7	0.1	218.7	79.6	219.4	79.7
17	-	-	7.7	0.1	2.8	0.7	10.4	0.8	200.0	95.6	210.4	96.4
18	-	-	112.5	0.4	20.3	5.3	132.9	5.7	106.0	88.7	238.9	94.4
19	-	-	151.0	1.1	28.6	11.2	179.6	12.3	37.2	68.2	216.9	80.5
20	0.4	0.1	150.2	2.2	21.1	12.6	171.7	14.9	19.7	53.0	191.4	67.9
21	9.3	0.6	105.9	3.5	12.9	12.0	128.1	16.1	13.8	49.4	141.9	65.4
22	14.2	1.7	50.5	4.5	8.5	11.9	73.2	18.1	11.7	50.3	84.9	68.5
23	11.7	2.7	25.3	4.5	5.8	10.9	42.7	18.0	9.5	47.1	52.3	65.1
24	8.6	3.7	16.5	5.0	4.4	10.6	29.5	19.3	8.2	45.7	37.8	65.0
25	5.8	4.4	12.5	5.2	3.7	9.9	22.1	19.4	7.5	44.2	29.6	63.7
26	4.3	4.7	10.5	5.4	3.4	9.3	18.1	19.4	7.0	44.3	25.1	63.6
27	3.4	4.9	9.1	5.8	2.8	8.9	15.4	19.6	6.3	43.1	21.7	62.7
28	2.7	5.2	7.7	5.9	2.7	8.3	13.0	19.4	6.1	42.1	19.1	61.5
29	2.3	5.2	6.8	6.2	2.4	7.8	11.5	19.1	5.8	41.1	17.3	60.3
30 +	16.6	81.3	61.0	113.6	24.7	92.5	102.4	287.4	66.6	788.6	169.0	1,076.0
Unknown (8)	0.1	1.0	2.1	0.5	1.0	89.4	3.3	90.9	3.1	162.1	6.5	253.0
ALL AGES (9)	79.4	115.5	729.9	163.8	145.5	301.4	954.7	580.7	729.7	1,747.6	1,684.4	2,328.3
MALES												
AGE												
<16	-	-	-	-	-	-	-	-	1.4	2.5	1.5	2.6
16	-	-	0.2	-	0.2	0.1	0.4	0.1	107.6	45.0	107.9	45.1
17	-	-	3.6	0.1	1.3	0.4	4.9	0.4	95.4	55.9	100.3	56.3
18	-	-	55.4	0.3	10.7	3.6	66.1	3.9	53.0	52.3	119.1	56.2
19	-	-	74.0	0.7	15.5	8.1	89.5	8.8	20.1	38.8	109.6	47.6
20	0.2	-	74.6	1.4	11.7	8.8	86.5	10.2	10.8	26.3	97.4	36.5
21	4.7	0.3	53.6	2.1	7.4	7.8	65.7	10.2	7.4	22.0	73.1	32.2
22	7.5	0.8	27.8	2.7	4.8	7.0	40.2	10.6	6.3	20.9	46.5	31.5
23	6.7	1.4	14.7	2.7	3.4	5.9	24.8	9.9	5.0	19.4	29.8	29.3
24	4.9	1.9	9.7	2.8	2.5	5.4	17.1	10.1	4.2	18.6	21.3	28.7
25	3.2	2.2	7.2	2.8	2.1	5.0	12.5	10.0	3.7	18.3	16.2	28.4
26	2.3	2.5	6.0	2.7	1.9	4.7	10.2	9.9	3.4	18.4	13.6	28.3
27	1.9	2.7	5.1	3.0	1.6	4.5	8.5	10.2	3.1	17.8	11.6	28.0
28	1.5	2.8	4.2	3.0	1.4	4.3	7.1	10.1	2.9	17.4	10.0	27.5
29	1.3	2.8	3.7	3.1	1.3	4.1	6.3	10.1	2.6	16.9	8.9	26.9
30 +	8.5	43.5	24.9	53.8	11.3	42.7	44.7	140.0	26.8	278.6	71.5	418.5
Unknown (8)	0.1	0.4	0.7	0.3	0.6	13.8	1.4	14.5	1.4	48.5	2.8	63.0
ALL AGES (9)	43.0	61.3	365.3	81.5	77.6	126.2	485.9	269.0	355.1	717.7	841.1	986.6
FEMALES												
AGE												
<16	-	-	-	-	-	-	-	-	0.9	2.1	1.0	2.1
16	-	-	0.2	-	0.2	0.1	0.3	0.1	111.2	34.5	111.5	34.6
17	-	-	4.0	-	1.4	0.4	5.5	0.4	104.6	39.7	110.0	40.1
18	-	-	57.2	0.2	9.7	1.6	66.8	1.8	53.0	36.4	119.8	38.2
19	-	-	77.1	0.4	13.0	3.1	90.1	3.5	17.1	29.4	107.2	32.9
20	0.2	-	75.6	0.8	9.4	3.8	85.2	4.7	8.9	26.7	94.0	31.4
21	4.6	0.3	52.3	1.3	5.5	4.2	62.4	5.8	6.4	27.4	68.8	33.2
22	6.6	0.9	22.7	1.8	3.6	4.9	32.9	7.6	5.4	29.4	38.4	37.0
23	5.0	1.3	10.6	1.8	2.4	5.0	17.9	8.1	4.6	27.7	22.5	35.8
24	3.7	1.9	6.8	2.1	1.9	5.2	12.4	9.2	4.0	27.1	16.4	36.3
25	2.6	2.1	5.3	2.4	1.7	4.9	9.6	9.4	3.8	25.9	13.4	35.3
26	1.9	2.3	4.5	2.6	1.5	4.6	7.9	9.5	3.6	25.9	11.5	35.3
27	1.5	2.2	4.1	2.8	1.3	4.4	6.9	9.4	3.3	25.3	10.1	34.7
28	1.2	2.4	3.5	2.9	1.2	4.0	5.9	9.3	3.2	24.7	9.1	34.0
29	1.0	2.4	3.2	3.1	1.1	3.7	5.3	9.1	3.1	24.3	8.4	33.4
30 +	8.1	37.8	36.1	59.8	13.5	49.8	57.6	147.5	39.8	510.0	97.5	657.5
Unknown (8)	0.1	0.6	1.5	0.2	0.4	75.6	1.9	76.4	1.7	111.2	3.6	187.6
ALL AGES (9)	36.4	54.2	364.6	82.3	67.9	175.2	468.8	311.7	374.5	1,027.5	843.3	1,339.3

(1) Full-time includes sandwich, part-time comprises both day only and evening only.
(2) Ages as at 31 August 1993.
(3) Includes 690 thousand students in all modes who are taking unspecified courses.
(4) Excludes SCOTVEC students in Scotland whose course outcome is not known and enrolments in adult education centres in England and Wales and non-vocational further educational students in Scotland and Northern Ireland.
(5) Includes sixth form colleges in England and Wales which were reclassified as further education colleges.
(6) Home students data include 111,300 Open University enrolments (8,800 postgraduate, 90,100 first degree and 12,500 other undergraduate).
(7) Includes students in FE in Scotland whose gender is not recorded.
(8) Includes 85,100 enrolments on nursing and paramedical courses at Department of Health establishments.
(9) Further Education totals include students in Scotland who are taking National Certificate Modules (72,800 persons).
(10) Includes part-time overseas students in universities, formerly recorded with the home students.

23a (23) FURTHER AND HIGHER EDUCATION

Enrolments in further and higher education by level, mode of study (1), gender and age (2), 1993/94

(ii) Overseas Students — Thousands

AGE	Postgraduate level Full-time	Part-time (10)	First degree Full-time	Part-time (10)	Other Undergraduate Full-time	Part-time (10)	All higher education Full-time	Part-time (10)	Further education (3)(4)(5) Full-time	Part-time	TOTAL FE/HE ENROLMENTS Full-time	Part-time
PERSONS (7)												
AGE												
<16	-	-	-	-	-	-	-	-	-	-	-	-
16	-	-	-	-	-	-	-	-	0.4	0.2	0.4	0.2
17	-	-	1.0	-	0.1	-	1.1	-	0.9	0.3	2.0	0.3
18	-	-	4.1	-	0.5	-	4.5	0.1	1.4	0.7	5.9	0.8
19	-	-	7.2	0.1	1.4	0.1	8.7	0.2	1.2	0.9	9.8	1.1
20	0.3	-	9.4	0.1	3.2	0.2	12.9	0.4	0.9	0.8	13.8	1.2
21	1.3	0.1	9.6	0.2	3.1	0.2	14.1	0.5	0.7	0.8	14.8	1.2
22	2.7	0.2	7.5	0.2	2.9	0.2	13.0	0.6	0.6	0.6	13.6	1.2
23	3.2	0.3	4.8	0.1	2.1	0.2	10.1	0.6	0.4	0.6	10.6	1.2
24	3.3	0.4	3.1	0.2	1.4	0.2	7.8	0.7	0.4	0.4	8.2	1.1
25	3.0	0.5	2.1	0.2	0.9	0.1	6.0	0.9	0.3	0.4	6.3	1.2
26	2.6	0.6	1.4	0.2	0.6	0.1	4.6	0.9	0.2	0.3	4.8	1.2
27	2.4	0.7	0.9	0.2	0.4	0.1	3.6	1.0	0.2	0.2	3.8	1.2
28	2.1	0.7	0.7	0.2	0.2	0.1	3.0	0.9	0.1	0.2	3.2	1.1
29	2.0	0.8	0.5	0.1	0.2	0.1	2.7	1.0	0.1	0.2	2.8	1.1
30 +	13.1	9.5	2.2	1.7	1.1	0.6	16.4	11.9	0.6	1.5	17.1	13.3
Unknown (8)	0.1	-	0.2	0.1	0.1	-	0.4	0.1	0.3	0.3	0.7	0.5
ALL AGES (9)	36.1	13.8	54.7	3.4	18.2	2.4	109.0	19.6	8.7	8.3	117.7	27.9
MALES												
AGE												
<16	-	-	-	-	-	-	-	-	-	-	-	-
16	-	-	-	-	-	-	-	-	0.2	0.1	0.2	0.1
17	-	-	0.5	-	0.1	-	0.6	-	0.4	0.1	1.0	0.1
18	-	-	2.1	-	0.2	-	2.3	-	0.7	0.2	3.0	0.2
19	-	-	3.7	-	0.6	-	4.3	0.1	0.6	0.2	4.9	0.3
20	0.1	-	4.9	-	1.2	0.1	6.3	0.2	0.5	0.2	6.8	0.4
21	0.6	0.1	5.4	0.1	1.2	0.1	7.2	0.3	0.4	0.2	7.6	0.5
22	1.4	0.1	4.5	0.1	1.2	0.1	7.1	0.3	0.3	0.2	7.4	0.5
23	1.8	0.1	3.1	0.1	1.1	0.1	6.0	0.3	0.2	0.2	6.2	0.4
24	1.9	0.2	2.1	0.1	0.8	0.1	4.8	0.4	0.2	0.2	5.0	0.5
25	1.8	0.3	1.4	0.1	0.5	0.1	3.8	0.5	0.2	0.1	3.9	0.6
26	1.6	0.4	0.9	0.1	0.3	0.1	2.9	0.5	0.1	0.1	3.0	0.6
27	1.6	0.4	0.6	0.1	0.2	-	2.4	0.5	0.1	0.1	2.5	0.6
28	1.4	0.5	0.5	0.1	0.2	-	2.0	0.6	0.1	0.1	2.1	0.6
29	1.4	0.5	0.3	0.1	0.1	-	1.8	0.6	0.1	0.1	1.9	0.7
30 +	9.7	6.8	1.5	1.2	0.8	0.3	11.9	8.3	0.4	0.6	12.3	8.9
Unknown (8)	-	-	0.1	-	0.1	-	0.2	0.1	0.2	0.2	0.4	0.3
ALL AGES (9)	23.5	9.3	31.5	2.0	8.6	1.2	63.7	12.6	4.7	2.8	68.4	15.4
FEMALES												
AGE												
<16	-	-	-	-	-	-	-	-	-	-	-	-
16	-	-	-	-	-	-	-	-	0.2	0.1	0.2	0.1
17	-	-	0.5	-	0.1	-	0.5	-	0.5	0.2	1.0	0.2
18	-	-	2.0	-	0.2	-	2.2	-	0.7	0.5	2.9	0.5
19	-	-	3.6	-	0.9	0.1	4.4	0.1	0.5	0.7	5.0	0.8
20	0.2	-	4.5	-	1.9	0.1	6.6	0.2	0.4	0.6	7.0	0.8
21	0.7	-	4.3	0.1	1.9	0.1	6.9	0.2	0.3	0.5	7.2	0.8
22	1.3	0.1	3.0	0.1	1.7	0.1	5.9	0.3	0.3	0.5	6.2	0.8
23	1.4	0.1	1.7	0.1	1.0	0.1	4.1	0.3	0.2	0.4	4.3	0.7
24	1.3	0.2	1.0	0.1	0.6	0.1	3.0	0.3	0.2	0.2	3.2	0.6
25	1.2	0.2	0.7	0.1	0.4	0.1	2.2	0.4	0.1	0.3	2.4	0.7
26	1.0	0.2	0.4	0.1	0.2	0.1	1.7	0.4	0.1	0.2	1.8	0.6
27	0.8	0.3	0.3	0.1	0.1	0.1	1.2	0.4	0.1	0.2	1.3	0.6
28	0.6	0.3	0.2	0.1	0.1	-	1.0	0.4	0.1	0.1	1.0	0.5
29	0.6	0.3	0.2	0.1	0.1	-	0.8	0.4	-	0.1	0.9	0.5
30 +	3.4	2.8	0.8	0.5	0.3	0.3	4.5	3.6	0.2	0.9	4.8	4.4
Unknown (8)	-	-	0.1	-	-	-	0.2	0.1	0.1	0.1	0.3	0.2
ALL AGES (9)	12.6	4.5	23.2	1.4	9.5	1.1	45.3	7.0	4.0	5.5	49.4	12.6

For footnotes see Table 23a (i).

FURTHER AND HIGHER EDUCATION

Enrolments in further and higher education by level, mode of study (1), gender and age (2), 1993/94

(iii) Home and Overseas Students
Thousands

	Postgraduate level		First degree		Other Undergraduate		All higher education		Further education (3)(4)(5)		TOTAL FE/HE ENROLMENTS	
	Full-time	Part-time (6)	Full-time	Part-time (6)	Full-time	Part-time (6)	Full-time	Part-time (6)	Full-time	Part-time	Full-time	Part-time
PERSONS (7)												
AGE												
<16	-	-	.	.	.	.	0.1	0.1	2.4	4.6	2.4	4.7
16	-	-	0.4	-	0.4	0.1	0.7	0.1	219.2	79.7	219.9	79.9
17	-	-	8.6	0.1	2.9	0.7	11.5	0.8	200.8	95.8	212.4	96.7
18	-	-	116.6	0.4	20.8	5.3	137.4	5.8	107.4	89.4	244.8	95.1
19	0.1	-	158.3	1.2	30.0	11.3	188.3	12.5	38.4	69.1	226.7	81.6
20	0.7	0.1	159.6	2.3	24.2	12.8	184.6	15.3	20.6	53.8	205.2	69.1
21	10.6	0.7	115.5	3.7	16.1	12.2	142.2	16.6	14.5	50.1	156.7	66.7
22	16.9	1.9	58.0	4.7	11.3	12.1	86.2	18.7	12.3	51.0	98.5	69.7
23	15.0	2.9	30.1	4.6	7.9	11.1	52.9	18.6	10.0	47.6	62.9	66.2
24	11.9	4.1	19.7	5.1	5.8	10.8	37.3	20.0	8.6	46.1	45.9	66.1
25	8.9	4.9	14.6	5.3	4.6	10.0	28.1	20.3	7.8	44.6	35.9	64.9
26	6.9	5.3	11.9	5.5	3.9	9.4	22.7	20.3	7.2	44.6	29.9	64.9
27	5.7	5.6	10.1	6.0	3.2	9.0	19.0	20.6	6.5	43.3	25.5	63.9
28	4.7	5.9	8.4	6.1	2.9	8.4	16.0	20.3	6.3	42.3	22.3	62.7
29	4.2	5.9	7.4	6.3	2.6	7.9	14.2	20.1	5.9	41.3	20.1	61.4
30 +	29.7	90.9	63.2	115.3	25.9	93.1	118.8	299.3	67.3	790.0	186.1	1,089.3
Unknown (8)	0.2	1.0	2.4	0.6	1.1	89.4	3.7	91.0	3.4	162.4	7.1	253.4
ALL AGES (9)	115.5	129.3	784.6	167.2	163.7	303.8	1,063.7	600.3	738.4	1,755.9	1,802.2	2,356.2
MALES												
AGE												
<16	-	-	.	.	.	.	-	-	1.4	2.5	1.5	2.6
16	-	-	0.2	-	0.2	0.1	0.4	0.1	107.8	45.1	108.1	45.2
17	-	-	4.1	0.1	1.4	0.4	5.5	0.4	95.8	56.0	101.3	56.4
18	-	-	57.4	0.3	10.9	3.7	68.4	3.9	53.7	52.5	122.1	56.5
19	-	-	77.7	0.7	16.1	8.2	93.8	8.9	20.7	39.0	114.5	47.9
20	0.3	-	79.6	1.4	12.9	8.9	92.8	10.4	11.3	26.5	104.2	36.9
21	5.3	0.3	59.0	2.2	8.6	7.9	72.9	10.5	7.8	22.2	80.6	32.7
22	9.0	1.0	32.3	2.8	6.1	7.1	47.3	10.9	6.6	21.1	53.9	32.0
23	8.6	1.5	17.8	2.7	4.4	6.0	30.8	10.2	5.2	19.5	36.0	29.7
24	6.9	2.1	11.8	2.9	3.3	5.5	21.9	10.5	4.4	18.8	26.3	29.3
25	5.1	2.5	8.6	2.9	2.6	5.1	16.3	10.5	3.9	18.5	20.1	29.0
26	4.0	2.8	6.9	2.8	2.2	4.8	13.1	10.4	3.5	18.5	16.6	28.9
27	3.4	3.1	5.7	3.1	1.8	4.5	10.9	10.7	3.2	17.9	14.1	28.6
28	2.9	3.2	4.6	3.1	1.6	4.3	9.2	10.6	3.0	17.5	12.1	28.1
29	2.6	3.3	4.0	3.2	1.5	4.2	8.1	10.7	2.7	16.9	10.7	27.6
30 +	18.2	50.2	26.4	55.0	12.1	43.0	56.6	148.2	27.2	279.2	83.8	427.4
Unknown (8)	0.1	0.5	0.8	0.3	0.7	13.8	1.6	14.5	1.6	48.7	3.2	63.3
ALL AGES (9)	66.5	70.6	396.8	83.5	86.3	127.5	549.6	281.5	359.9	720.4	909.5	1,002.0
FEMALES												
AGE												
<16	-	-	.	.	.	.	-	-	0.9	2.1	1.0	2.1
16	-	-	0.2	-	0.2	0.1	0.3	0.1	111.4	34.6	111.7	34.7
17	-	-	4.5	-	1.5	0.4	6.0	0.4	105.0	39.8	111.0	40.3
18	-	-	59.2	0.2	9.9	1.7	69.1	1.8	53.7	36.9	122.7	38.7
19	-	-	80.6	0.4	13.9	3.1	94.5	3.6	17.6	30.1	112.2	33.7
20	0.4	0.1	80.1	0.9	11.3	3.9	91.8	4.9	9.3	27.3	101.0	32.1
21	5.3	0.3	56.6	1.4	7.5	4.3	69.3	6.0	6.7	28.0	76.0	34.0
22	7.9	0.9	25.7	1.9	5.3	5.0	38.9	7.8	5.7	29.9	44.6	37.7
23	6.4	1.4	12.3	1.9	3.4	5.1	22.1	8.4	4.7	28.1	26.8	36.5
24	5.0	2.0	7.9	2.2	2.5	5.3	15.4	9.5	4.1	27.3	19.6	36.8
25	3.8	2.4	6.0	2.5	2.1	4.9	11.8	9.8	3.9	26.2	15.8	36.0
26	2.9	2.5	5.0	2.7	1.7	4.6	9.6	9.8	3.7	26.1	13.3	35.9
27	2.3	2.5	4.4	2.9	1.4	4.5	8.1	9.9	3.3	25.4	11.4	35.3
28	1.8	2.7	3.7	3.0	1.3	4.1	6.8	9.7	3.3	24.8	10.1	34.5
29	1.6	2.7	3.4	3.1	1.2	3.7	6.1	9.5	3.2	24.4	9.3	33.8
30 +	11.5	40.6	36.9	60.3	13.8	50.1	62.1	151.0	40.1	510.9	102.2	661.9
Unknown (8)	0.1	0.6	1.6	0.3	0.4	75.6	2.1	76.5	1.8	111.3	3.9	187.8
ALL AGES (9)	49.0	58.7	387.8	83.7	77.4	176.3	514.1	318.8	378.5	1,033.1	892.7	1,351.8

For footnotes see Table 23a (i).

FURTHER AND HIGHER EDUCATION
Enrolments in further and higher education by level, mode of study (1), gender and age (2), 1994/95 (3)

23b (23)

	(i) Home Students											Thousands
	Postgraduate level		First degree		Other Undergraduate		All higher education		Further education (4)(5)		TOTAL FE/HE ENROLMENTS	
	Full-time	Part-time (6)	Full-time	Part-time (6)	Full-time	Part-time (6)	Full-time	Part-time (6)	Full-time	Part-time	Full-time	Part-time
PERSONS (7)												
AGE												
<16	-	-	-	-	-	-	-	-	2.9	8.2	2.9	8.2
16	-	-	0.3	-	0.9	0.2	1.2	0.3	223.3	91.6	224.5	91.8
17	-	-	7.7	0.1	3.5	0.8	11.2	0.9	193.5	93.1	204.7	94.0
18	-	0.1	117.4	0.4	20.8	5.2	138.2	5.7	103.3	82.4	241.5	88.1
19	0.1	0.1	156.8	1.0	29.6	8.9	186.4	10.0	38.0	61.0	224.4	71.0
20	0.4	0.1	160.3	2.1	22.2	10.1	183.0	12.3	19.8	48.2	202.8	60.5
21	9.6	0.8	112.2	3.3	13.2	10.3	135.0	14.4	15.3	62.0	150.3	76.4
22	14.5	1.9	54.7	4.4	8.0	10.3	77.2	16.6	11.9	47.8	89.1	64.4
23	13.6	3.3	28.9	5.1	5.8	10.5	48.3	18.9	10.4	48.8	58.8	67.8
24	9.4	4.1	19.1	4.9	4.5	9.8	33.0	18.8	8.7	46.6	41.7	65.4
25	6.7	5.1	13.9	5.3	3.7	9.5	24.3	19.9	8.2	45.5	32.4	65.4
26	4.7	5.5	11.6	5.5	3.2	9.2	19.6	20.2	7.5	45.2	27.1	65.5
27	3.7	5.8	10.2	5.8	2.9	8.6	16.9	20.3	7.0	45.2	23.9	65.4
28	3.1	6.2	9.0	6.0	2.7	8.1	14.9	20.4	6.5	44.4	21.3	64.9
29	2.6	6.3	7.9	6.3	2.5	7.9	13.1	20.5	6.5	44.0	19.5	64.4
30 +	19.7	103.2	70.1	109.5	25.7	106.0	115.5	318.7	79.3	868.4	194.8	1,187.1
Unknown (8)	0.3	3.5	1.4	0.8	0.9	89.3	2.6	93.5	6.4	119.4	9.0	212.9
ALL AGES	88.5	146.3	781.5	160.5	150.1	304.7	1,020.0	611.5	748.5	1,801.8	1,768.5	2,413.3
MALES												
AGE												
<16	-	-	-	-	-	-	-	-	1.7	4.3	1.7	4.3
16	-	-	0.2	-	0.3	0.1	0.5	0.1	110.7	49.5	111.1	49.7
17	-	-	3.6	0.1	1.6	0.5	5.2	0.5	93.4	52.8	98.6	53.4
18	-	0.1	56.6	0.3	10.6	3.4	67.3	3.8	52.2	47.2	119.5	51.0
19	-	0.1	76.3	0.6	15.9	6.3	92.2	7.0	20.4	33.2	112.6	40.2
20	0.2	0.1	78.2	1.3	12.1	6.9	90.5	8.2	10.8	22.8	101.3	31.1
21	4.8	0.4	55.6	2.0	7.3	6.6	67.6	8.9	8.0	25.2	75.6	34.1
22	7.6	0.9	29.1	2.6	4.5	5.9	41.3	9.4	6.1	19.2	47.4	28.6
23	7.6	1.5	16.6	2.9	3.2	5.7	27.4	10.1	5.3	19.2	32.7	29.4
24	5.4	2.0	10.8	2.8	2.5	4.8	18.6	9.6	4.4	18.5	23.0	28.1
25	3.7	2.5	7.9	2.8	2.0	4.7	13.6	10.0	4.1	18.3	17.8	28.3
26	2.7	2.8	6.6	2.7	1.7	4.5	10.9	10.0	3.6	17.9	14.5	28.0
27	2.1	2.9	5.7	3.0	1.5	4.2	9.3	10.1	3.3	18.3	12.7	28.4
28	1.8	3.4	4.8	3.1	1.4	4.1	8.0	10.5	3.0	17.3	11.1	27.8
29	1.5	3.4	4.2	3.2	1.3	4.0	7.0	10.6	2.9	17.3	9.9	28.0
30 +	10.2	53.4	29.5	51.5	11.3	47.7	51.0	152.6	31.7	305.9	82.7	458.5
Unknown (8)	0.2	1.2	0.7	0.4	0.3	13.6	1.2	15.1	1.7	33.0	2.9	48.2
ALL AGES	47.7	74.6	386.4	79.1	77.4	123.0	511.5	276.7	363.3	720.2	874.8	996.9
FEMALES												
AGE												
<16	-	-	-	-	-	-	-	-	1.2	3.9	1.2	3.9
16	-	-	0.2	-	0.6	0.1	0.8	0.1	113.3	42.4	114.0	42.5
17	-	-	4.1	-	1.9	0.3	6.0	0.3	100.0	40.3	106.0	40.6
18	-	-	60.7	0.1	10.2	1.8	71.0	1.9	51.0	35.2	122.0	37.1
19	-	-	80.5	0.4	13.7	2.5	94.2	3.0	17.6	27.8	111.8	30.8
20	0.2	0.1	82.1	0.8	10.2	3.2	92.5	4.1	9.0	25.3	101.5	29.4
21	4.8	0.4	56.6	1.3	6.0	3.7	67.4	5.4	7.3	36.8	74.7	42.2
22	6.9	1.1	25.5	1.8	3.5	4.5	35.9	7.3	5.9	28.5	41.8	35.8
23	6.0	1.8	12.3	2.1	2.6	4.9	20.9	8.8	5.1	29.6	26.1	38.4
24	4.0	2.1	8.2	2.2	2.1	4.9	14.4	9.2	4.3	28.1	18.7	37.3
25	3.0	2.6	5.9	2.5	1.7	4.8	10.6	9.9	4.0	27.2	14.7	37.1
26	2.1	2.8	5.1	2.8	1.5	4.7	8.7	10.2	4.0	27.3	12.6	37.5
27	1.6	2.9	4.5	2.9	1.4	4.4	7.5	10.2	3.7	26.9	11.2	37.0
28	1.3	2.9	4.2	3.0	1.3	4.1	6.8	9.9	3.4	27.1	10.3	37.1
29	1.1	2.9	3.7	3.1	1.2	3.8	6.1	9.8	3.6	26.6	9.7	36.5
30 +	9.5	49.8	40.6	58.0	14.4	58.4	64.6	166.1	47.6	562.5	112.2	728.6
Unknown (8)	0.2	2.3	0.7	0.5	0.5	75.6	1.4	78.4	2.0	80.1	3.4	158.5
ALL AGES	40.7	71.7	395.1	81.4	72.7	181.7	508.5	334.8	382.5	1,075.4	891.0	1,410.1

(1) Full-time includes sandwich, part-time comprises both day only and evening only.
(2) Ages as at 31 August 1994.
(3) Provisional.
(4) Includes 710 thousand students in all modes who are taking unspecified courses.
(5) Excludes SCOTVEC students in Scotland whose course outcome is not known and enrolments in adult education centres in England and Wales and non-vocational further education students in Scotland and Northern Ireland.
(6) Home students data include 114,900 Open University enrolments (25,600 postgraduate, 81,000 first degree and 8,300 other undergraduate).
(7) Includes students in FE in Scotland whose gender is not recorded.
(8) Includes 85,100 enrolments (1993/94 data) on nursing and paramedical courses at Department of Health establishments.
(9) Includes part-time overseas students in universities, formerly recorded with the home students.

23b (23) FURTHER AND HIGHER EDUCATION

Enrolments in further and higher education by level, mode of study (1), gender and age (2), 1994/95 (3)

(ii) Overseas Students — Thousands

PERSONS (7) AGE	Postgraduate level Full-time	Postgraduate level Part-time (9)	First degree Full-time	First degree Part-time (9)	Other Undergraduate Full-time	Other Undergraduate Part-time (9)	All higher education Full-time	All higher education Part-time (9)	Further education (4)(5) Full-time	Further education (4)(5) Part-time	TOTAL FE/HE ENROLMENTS Full-time	TOTAL FE/HE ENROLMENTS Part-time
<16	-	-	-	-	-	-	-	-	0.4	0.1	0.4	0.1
16	-	-	-	-	-	-	-	-	0.7	0.3	1.8	0.4
17	-	-	1.0	-	0.2	-	1.2	-	0.7	0.3	1.8	0.4
18	-	-	5.0	-	0.7	-	5.8	0.1	1.0	0.8	6.7	0.8
19	-	-	8.6	0.1	1.5	0.2	10.1	0.3	1.0	1.2	11.2	1.4
20	0.4	0.1	10.8	0.1	3.3	0.5	14.5	0.7	0.9	1.0	15.4	1.7
21	1.5	0.1	10.7	0.2	3.3	0.5	15.5	0.8	0.8	1.0	16.4	1.8
22	3.2	0.2	8.6	0.2	3.0	0.4	14.8	0.9	0.7	1.0	15.5	1.9
23	3.9	0.3	5.7	0.2	2.3	0.3	11.9	0.9	0.6	1.0	12.5	1.9
24	3.9	0.5	3.5	0.3	1.6	0.3	9.0	1.1	0.4	0.9	9.4	2.0
25	3.6	0.6	2.2	0.3	1.0	0.2	6.8	1.2	0.3	0.7	7.1	1.8
26	3.1	0.8	1.5	0.3	0.6	0.2	5.2	1.3	0.3	0.7	5.5	2.0
27	2.5	0.8	1.0	0.2	0.4	0.2	4.0	1.2	0.2	0.5	4.2	1.7
28	2.2	1.0	0.7	0.3	0.3	0.2	3.2	1.4	0.1	0.3	3.3	1.7
29	2.0	1.0	0.6	0.3	0.2	0.1	2.8	1.4	0.1	0.4	2.9	1.7
30 +	14.1	12.8	2.5	3.7	1.2	1.5	17.9	18.1	0.8	2.3	18.6	20.4
Unknown (8)	0.2	-	0.5	0.1	0.5	0.1	1.2	0.3	1.1	0.7	2.3	1.0
ALL AGES	40.6	18.4	63.1	6.3	20.3	5.5	124.0	30.2	9.5	12.9	133.5	43.1
MALES AGE												
<16	-	-	-	-	-	-	-	-	0.2	0.1	0.3	0.1
16	-	-	-	-	-	-	-	-	0.3	0.1	0.9	0.2
17	-	-	0.5	-	0.1	-	0.6	-	0.3	0.1	0.9	0.2
18	-	-	2.6	-	0.4	-	2.9	-	0.5	0.2	3.5	0.2
19	-	-	4.4	-	0.7	0.1	5.1	0.1	0.6	0.3	5.7	0.4
20	0.1	-	5.6	0.1	1.2	0.2	6.9	0.3	0.5	0.2	7.5	0.5
21	0.7	0.1	5.8	0.1	1.3	0.2	7.8	0.3	0.4	0.3	8.2	0.6
22	1.6	0.1	5.1	0.1	1.4	0.2	8.1	0.4	0.4	0.3	8.5	0.7
23	2.1	0.2	3.6	0.1	1.2	0.1	6.8	0.4	0.3	0.3	7.2	0.8
24	2.3	0.3	2.3	0.1	0.9	0.1	5.4	0.6	0.2	0.3	5.6	0.8
25	2.1	0.4	1.5	0.1	0.5	0.1	4.1	0.6	0.2	0.2	4.3	0.8
26	2.0	0.5	1.0	0.1	0.4	0.1	3.3	0.7	0.1	0.2	3.4	1.0
27	1.6	0.5	0.7	0.1	0.2	0.1	2.5	0.7	0.1	0.2	2.7	0.9
28	1.4	0.6	0.5	0.1	0.2	0.1	2.1	0.8	0.1	0.1	2.1	0.9
29	1.4	0.6	0.4	0.1	0.1	0.1	1.9	0.8	0.1	0.1	1.9	1.0
30 +	10.2	9.1	1.6	1.9	0.8	0.9	12.5	11.8	0.4	0.8	12.9	12.6
Unknown (8)	0.1	-	0.2	0.1	0.2	-	0.6	0.1	0.4	0.2	1.0	0.4
ALL AGES	25.7	12.5	35.5	3.1	9.5	2.2	70.8	17.8	5.0	4.0	75.8	21.8
FEMALES AGE												
<16	-	-	-	-	-	-	-	-	0.2	0.1	0.2	0.1
16	-	-	-	-	-	-	-	-	0.3	0.2	0.9	0.2
17	-	-	0.5	-	0.1	-	0.6	-	0.3	0.2	0.9	0.2
18	-	-	2.5	-	0.3	-	2.8	-	0.5	0.6	3.3	0.6
19	-	-	4.1	-	0.9	0.1	5.0	0.2	0.5	0.9	5.5	1.1
20	0.2	0.1	5.2	0.1	2.1	0.3	7.5	0.5	0.4	0.7	7.9	1.2
21	0.8	0.1	4.9	0.1	2.0	0.3	7.7	0.5	0.4	0.8	8.1	1.2
22	1.5	0.1	3.5	0.1	1.7	0.3	6.8	0.5	0.3	0.7	7.1	1.2
23	1.8	0.1	2.1	0.1	1.1	0.2	5.0	0.4	0.3	0.7	5.3	1.1
24	1.6	0.2	1.2	0.1	0.7	0.2	3.6	0.5	0.2	0.7	3.8	1.2
25	1.4	0.3	0.8	0.1	0.4	0.1	2.6	0.5	0.1	0.5	2.8	1.0
26	1.2	0.3	0.5	0.1	0.2	0.1	2.0	0.6	0.1	0.5	2.1	1.0
27	0.9	0.3	0.3	0.1	0.2	0.1	1.4	0.5	0.1	0.3	1.5	0.8
28	0.7	0.4	0.3	0.1	0.1	0.1	1.1	0.6	0.1	0.2	1.2	0.8
29	0.6	0.3	0.2	0.1	0.1	0.1	0.9	0.5	0.1	0.2	1.0	0.8
30 +	3.9	3.8	1.0	1.8	0.5	0.7	5.3	6.2	0.4	1.5	5.7	7.8
Unknown (8)	0.1	-	0.2	0.1	0.3	-	0.6	0.1	-	0.4	1.2	0.6
ALL AGES	14.9	5.9	27.6	3.1	10.8	3.3	53.2	12.4	4.5	8.9	57.7	21.3

For footnotes see Table 23b (i).

CONTINUED

23b (23) FURTHER AND HIGHER EDUCATION

Enrolments in further and higher education by level, mode of study (1), gender and age (2), 1994/95 (3)

	(iii) Home and Overseas Students											Thousands	
	Postgraduate level		First degree		Other Undergraduate		All higher education		Further education (4)(5)		TOTAL FE/HE ENROLMENTS	
	Full-time	Part-time (6)(9)	Full-time	Part-time (6)(9)	Full-time	Part-time (6)(9)	Full-time	Part-time (6)(9)	Full-time	Part-time	Full-time	Part-time
PERSONS (7)												
AGE												
<16	-	-	-	-	-	-	-	-	2.9	8.2	2.9	8.2
16	-	-	0.3	-	0.9	0.2	1.3	0.3	223.7	91.7	225.0	92.0
17	-	-	8.7	0.1	3.7	0.8	12.4	0.9	194.1	93.5	206.5	94.3
18	-	0.1	122.4	0.5	21.6	5.2	144.0	5.8	104.2	83.2	248.2	88.9
19	0.1	0.2	165.3	1.1	31.1	9.1	196.6	10.3	39.0	62.2	235.6	72.5
20	0.7	0.2	171.2	2.2	25.5	10.6	197.4	13.0	20.8	49.2	218.2	62.2
21	11.1	0.9	122.9	3.5	16.6	10.7	150.5	15.2	16.2	63.1	166.7	78.2
22	17.7	2.2	63.3	4.6	11.0	10.8	92.1	17.5	12.6	48.8	104.7	66.3
23	17.5	3.7	34.6	5.3	8.1	10.9	60.2	19.8	11.0	49.8	71.2	69.6
24	13.3	4.7	22.6	5.2	6.1	10.1	41.9	19.9	9.1	47.5	51.0	67.4
25	10.2	5.7	16.1	5.6	4.7	9.7	31.0	21.0	8.5	46.2	39.5	67.2
26	7.9	6.4	13.1	5.7	3.8	9.4	24.8	21.5	7.8	45.9	32.6	67.5
27	6.2	6.7	11.3	6.1	3.4	8.8	20.8	21.5	7.2	45.6	28.1	67.1
28	5.3	7.2	9.7	6.3	3.0	8.3	18.0	21.8	6.6	44.8	24.6	66.6
29	4.6	7.3	8.5	6.5	2.7	8.0	15.8	21.8	6.6	44.3	22.4	66.2
30 +	33.8	116.0	72.7	113.2	27.0	107.6	133.4	336.8	80.1	870.7	213.5	1,207.5
Unknown (8)	0.5	3.5	1.9	0.9	1.4	89.4	3.8	93.8	7.5	120.1	11.3	213.9
ALL AGES	129.0	164.7	844.6	166.7	170.4	310.2	1,144.0	641.6	758.0	1,814.7	1,902.0	2,456.4
MALES												
AGE												
<16	-	-	-	-	-	-	-	-	1.7	4.3	1.7	4.3
16	-	-	0.2	-	0.3	0.1	0.5	0.1	110.9	49.6	111.4	49.7
17	-	-	4.0	0.1	1.7	0.5	5.8	0.5	93.8	53.0	99.5	53.5
18	-	0.1	59.2	0.3	11.0	3.5	70.2	3.8	52.7	47.3	123.0	51.2
19	-	0.1	80.7	0.6	16.6	6.4	97.3	7.1	21.0	33.5	118.3	40.6
20	0.4	0.1	83.8	1.3	13.3	7.1	97.4	8.5	11.3	23.1	108.7	31.6
21	5.5	0.4	61.4	2.1	8.6	6.7	75.4	9.3	8.4	25.5	83.8	34.7
22	9.3	1.0	34.2	2.7	5.9	6.0	49.4	9.8	6.4	19.5	55.8	29.3
23	9.7	1.7	20.2	3.0	4.4	5.8	34.3	10.5	5.6	19.6	39.9	30.1
24	7.6	2.3	13.1	2.9	3.3	5.0	24.0	10.2	4.6	18.7	28.6	28.9
25	5.8	2.9	9.4	3.0	2.5	4.8	17.8	10.6	4.3	18.5	22.1	29.1
26	4.6	3.3	7.5	2.8	2.1	4.6	14.2	10.7	3.7	18.2	17.9	28.9
27	3.7	3.4	6.4	3.1	1.8	4.3	11.9	10.8	3.5	18.5	15.4	29.3
28	3.2	4.0	5.3	3.2	1.6	4.1	10.1	11.3	3.1	17.4	13.2	28.7
29	2.9	4.1	4.5	3.3	1.4	4.1	8.8	11.5	3.0	17.5	11.8	28.9
30 +	20.4	62.5	31.1	53.4	12.1	48.5	63.5	164.4	32.1	306.7	95.6	471.1
Unknown (8)	0.3	1.2	0.9	0.4	0.6	13.7	1.8	15.3	2.2	33.3	4.0	48.6
ALL AGES	73.4	87.1	421.9	82.2	86.9	125.1	582.3	294.5	368.3	724.2	950.6	1,018.7
FEMALES												
AGE												
<16	-	-	-	-	-	-	-	-	1.2	3.9	1.2	3.9
16	-	-	0.2	-	0.6	0.1	0.8	0.1	113.4	42.5	114.2	42.6
17	-	-	4.7	-	2.0	0.3	6.6	0.3	100.3	40.5	107.0	40.8
18	-	-	63.2	0.1	10.5	1.8	73.8	1.9	51.5	35.8	125.3	37.8
19	0.1	0.1	84.6	0.5	14.6	2.7	99.2	3.2	18.1	28.7	117.3	31.9
20	0.4	0.1	87.4	0.9	12.2	3.6	100.0	4.5	9.4	26.1	109.4	30.6
21	5.6	0.5	61.5	1.4	8.0	4.0	75.1	5.9	7.8	37.6	82.9	43.5
22	8.4	1.1	29.1	1.9	5.2	4.7	42.7	7.8	6.2	29.3	48.9	37.0
23	7.8	2.0	14.4	2.2	3.8	5.1	26.0	9.3	5.4	30.3	31.4	39.5
24	5.6	2.3	9.5	2.3	2.8	5.1	17.9	9.7	4.5	28.7	22.4	38.5
25	4.4	2.9	6.7	2.6	2.1	5.0	13.3	10.4	4.2	27.6	17.5	38.1
26	3.2	3.1	5.6	2.9	1.8	4.8	10.6	10.8	4.1	27.8	14.7	38.5
27	2.6	3.2	4.8	3.0	1.6	4.5	8.9	10.7	3.8	27.1	12.7	37.8
28	2.1	3.2	4.5	3.1	1.4	4.2	7.9	10.5	3.5	27.3	11.4	37.9
29	1.7	3.3	3.9	3.2	1.3	3.9	7.0	10.4	3.7	26.9	10.6	37.2
30 +	13.4	53.5	41.6	59.8	14.9	59.0	69.9	172.4	48.0	564.0	117.9	736.3
Unknown (8)	0.3	2.3	0.9	0.5	0.8	75.7	2.0	78.5	2.6	80.6	4.6	159.1
ALL AGES	55.6	77.6	422.6	84.5	83.5	185.1	561.7	347.2	387.0	1,084.3	948.8	1,431.4

For footnotes see Table 23b (i).

FURTHER AND HIGHER EDUCATION

Enrolments on further education courses by age (1), gender and mode of attendance, 1993/94

24a(24)

Thousands

	COURSES LEADING TO SPECIFIED QUALIFICATIONS										All Courses leading to Unspecified Quals	All FE Courses
	National Vocational Qualifications (NVQs)(2)			General National Vocational Qualifications (GNVQs)(2)			Other Vocational Qualifications(2)(3)	GCE A Level/AS Exam (4)	GCSE (5)	All Courses leading to Specified Quals		
	Level 1	Level 2	Level 3	Found-ation	Inter-mediate	Ad-vanced						
Students aged 16-18 (6)												
Full-time and sandwich												
Persons	13.6	34.7	16.4	1.3	19.3	19.9	215.8	161.5	30.4	513.0	16.1	529.1
Males	10.0	13.2	7.0	0.7	9.1	9.0	110.6	72.9	16.4	248.9	9.5	258.4
Females	3.6	21.5	9.4	0.6	10.2	10.9	105.1	88.7	14.0	264.1	6.6	270.7
Part-time day												
Persons	17.8	33.9	14.3	0.1	0.6	0.7	73.2	12.0	15.1	167.7	26.5	194.2
Males	14.3	22.0	11.8	-	0.3	0.4	49.3	5.0	7.3	110.5	14.5	125.0
Females	3.5	11.9	2.4	-	0.3	0.3	23.9	7.0	7.8	57.2	12.0	69.2
Evening only												
Persons	1.7	2.5	1.2	-	-	0.1	16.9	16.4	22.7	61.5	12.0	73.5
Males	1.2	1.4	0.8	-	-	-	6.1	6.2	9.5	25.3	4.7	30.0
Females	0.5	1.1	0.4	-	-	-	10.8	10.2	13.2	36.2	7.2	43.5
All modes												
Persons	33.2	71.1	31.9	1.4	20.0	20.7	305.9	189.9	68.2	742.2	54.5	796.7
Males	25.6	36.6	19.6	0.7	9.5	9.4	166.1	84.0	33.2	384.7	28.7	413.4
Females	7.6	34.6	12.3	0.7	10.5	11.3	139.8	105.8	34.9	357.5	25.8	383.4
Students aged 19 and over												
Full-time and sandwich												
Persons	7.5	19.6	8.3	0.1	1.9	3.9	120.1	15.6	4.3	181.4	27.2	208.6
Males	4.8	7.5	3.8	0.1	0.9	1.9	57.5	8.3	2.0	86.8	14.2	101.1
Females	2.7	12.1	4.5	0.1	1.0	2.0	62.6	7.3	2.3	94.6	12.9	107.5
Part-time day												
Persons	27.5	44.8	28.1	-	0.3	0.7	246.3	27.2	29.9	404.7	267.7	672.4
Males	14.7	22.0	16.6	-	0.1	0.3	99.2	11.2	9.6	173.8	80.6	254.4
Females	12.7	22.8	11.4	-	0.2	0.4	147.0	15.9	20.3	230.8	187.1	418.0
Evening only												
Persons	25.8	27.5	11.3	-	0.1	0.5	244.8	73.0	88.9	472.0	337.9	809.9
Males	17.3	16.1	6.5	-	-	0.3	93.0	28.3	30.5	192.0	117.2	309.2
Females	8.5	11.5	4.8	-	0.1	0.2	151.8	44.8	58.4	280.0	220.7	500.7
All modes												
Persons	60.7	91.9	47.6	0.2	2.3	5.1	611.2	115.8	123.1	1,058.1	632.8	1,690.8
Males	36.8	45.6	27.0	0.1	1.1	2.5	249.8	47.8	42.1	452.6	212.1	664.7
Females	23.9	46.4	20.7	0.1	1.2	2.6	361.5	68.0	81.0	605.4	420.7	1,026.1
Students all ages (6)(7)												
Full-time and sandwich												
Persons	21.1	54.4	24.7	1.5	21.2	23.9	335.9	177.2	34.7	694.5	43.3	737.7
Males	14.8	20.7	10.8	0.7	10.1	11.0	168.1	81.2	18.4	335.7	23.7	359.5
Females	6.3	33.7	13.9	0.7	11.2	12.9	167.8	96.0	16.3	358.7	19.5	378.2
Part-time day												
Persons	45.3	78.7	42.4	0.1	0.9	1.4	319.6	39.1	45.0	572.6	294.5	867.1
Males	29.1	44.0	28.5	0.1	0.4	0.6	148.6	16.2	16.9	284.4	95.2	379.6
Females	16.2	34.7	13.9	-	0.5	0.7	171.0	22.9	28.1	288.2	199.3	487.5
Evening only												
Persons	27.5	30.0	12.5	-	0.1	0.6	262.0	89.4	111.7	533.9	350.6	884.5
Males	18.6	17.5	7.4	-	-	0.3	99.2	34.5	40.1	217.5	122.2	339.7
Females	9.0	12.6	5.2	-	0.1	0.3	162.8	55.0	71.6	316.5	228.4	544.9
All modes												
Persons	94.0	163.1	79.6	1.6	22.3	25.8	917.5	305.7	191.4	1,801.0	688.4	2,489.4
Males	62.4	82.2	46.6	0.8	10.5	11.9	416.0	131.9	75.3	837.6	241.1	1,078.8
Females	31.5	80.9	32.9	0.8	11.7	13.9	501.5	173.9	116.1	963.3	447.3	1,410.6

(1)　Ages as at 31 August 1993.
(2)　GNVQ/NVQ split is not available for Northern Ireland. Figures are included in Other Vocational Qualifications.
(3　Includes Scottish Vocational Qualifications (SVQs) for Scotland.
(4)　Includes SCE Higher Grades.
(5)　Includes SCE Standard Grades.
(6)　Includes students aged under 16 in England, Wales and Scotland.
(7)　Includes students in Wales whose age is unknown.

FURTHER AND HIGHER EDUCATION

24b(24)

Enrolments on further education courses by age (1), gender and mode of attendance, 1994/95 (2)

Thousands

	COURSES LEADING TO SPECIFIED QUALIFICATIONS										All Courses leading to Specified Quals	All Courses leading to Unspecified Quals	All FE Courses
	National Vocational Qualifications (NVQs)(3)			General National Vocational Qualifications (GNVQs)(3)			Other Vocational Qualifications (3)(4)	GCE A Level/AS Exam (5)	GCSE (6)				
	Level 1	Level 2	Level 3	Found-ation	Inter-mediate	Ad-vanced							
Students aged 16-18 (7)													
Full-time and sandwich													
Persons	11.8	35.9	12.9	4.9	39.3	60.0	161.6	154.0	21.2	501.7	23.4	525.0
Males	8.6	16.1	5.6	1.9	20.0	27.9	84.0	69.3	11.6	245.1	13.2	258.3
Females	3.2	19.8	7.3	3.0	19.4	32.1	77.6	84.7	9.7	256.6	10.2	266.8
Part-time day													
Persons	12.3	35.1	12.9	0.5	2.4	2.8	66.5	17.0	18.0	167.6	38.4	206.0
Males	9.7	22.1	10.5	0.2	1.2	1.4	43.3	7.7	8.8	104.9	20.7	125.5
Females	2.6	13.1	2.4	0.3	1.3	1.4	23.3	9.3	9.2	62.7	17.8	80.5
Evening only													
Persons	1.3	2.6	1.0	-	-	0.1	16.9	15.1	18.2	55.2	11.5	66.7
Males	0.8	1.3	0.4	-	-	0.1	6.0	5.8	7.5	22.0	4.8	26.8
Females	0.5	1.3	0.5	-	-	0.1	10.9	9.3	10.6	33.3	6.6	39.9
All modes													
Persons	25.4	73.7	26.7	5.4	41.8	63.0	245.0	186.1	57.4	724.5	73.2	797.8
Males	19.1	39.5	16.6	2.1	21.2	29.4	133.3	82.8	27.9	371.9	38.7	410.6
Females	6.3	34.2	10.2	3.3	20.6	33.6	111.7	103.3	29.5	352.6	34.6	387.2
Students aged 19 and over													
Full-time and sandwich													
Persons	9.1	24.1	9.8	0.7	5.4	13.6	117.7	13.2	3.7	197.3	34.1	231.4
Males	5.3	9.6	4.3	0.2	2.5	6.7	55.8	6.9	1.6	92.9	17.1	110.0
Females	3.8	14.6	5.5	0.4	2.9	6.9	61.9	6.3	2.2	104.4	17.0	121.4
Part-time day													
Persons	26.6	47.2	31.9	0.7	1.2	2.9	268.1	28.1	27.5	434.3	269.1	703.5
Males	13.9	22.2	16.5	0.1	0.4	1.4	103.4	10.9	8.6	177.4	81.2	258.6
Females	12.7	25.1	15.4	0.6	0.8	1.6	164.7	17.1	18.9	256.9	187.9	444.8
Evening only													
Persons	26.5	31.4	17.1	-	0.5	1.0	275.5	66.6	75.7	494.3	332.2	826.6
Males	16.3	16.9	7.6	-	0.2	0.5	103.4	25.7	25.8	196.4	115.0	311.4
Females	10.2	14.5	9.5	-	0.3	0.5	172.0	40.9	50.0	298.0	217.2	515.2
All modes													
Persons	62.2	102.8	58.7	1.4	7.0	17.5	661.3	107.9	107.0	1,125.9	635.5	1,761.6
Males	35.5	48.6	28.4	0.4	3.1	8.6	262.6	43.5	36.0	466.7	213.3	680.0
Females	26.7	54.2	30.3	1.0	4.0	8.9	398.7	64.4	71.1	659.3	422.2	1,081.5
Students all ages (7)(8)													
Full-time and sandwich													
Persons	20.8	60.1	22.7	5.6	44.7	73.6	279.3	167.3	25.0	699.0	57.5	756.6
Males	13.9	25.7	10.0	2.2	22.4	34.6	139.8	76.3	13.1	338.0	30.3	368.3
Females	6.9	34.4	12.7	3.4	22.3	39.0	139.5	91.0	11.8	361.0	27.2	388.3
Part-time day													
Persons	38.9	82.4	44.8	1.2	3.6	5.8	334.7	45.0	45.6	602.1	308.0	910.1
Males	23.6	44.2	27.0	0.3	1.6	2.8	146.7	18.7	17.4	282.4	102.0	384.4
Females	15.3	38.2	17.8	0.9	2.0	3.0	188.0	26.4	28.2	319.8	206.0	525.8
Evening only													
Persons	27.8	34.1	18.0	-	0.5	1.2	292.6	81.7	94.0	549.9	344.5	894.4
Males	17.1	18.2	8.0	-	0.2	0.6	109.5	31.5	33.3	218.4	120.1	338.6
Females	10.7	15.9	10.0	-	0.3	0.6	183.1	50.3	60.6	331.5	224.4	555.9
All modes													
Persons	87.5	176.6	85.5	6.8	48.9	80.5	906.6	294.1	164.5	1,851.1	710.1	2,561.1
Males	54.6	88.1	45.0	2.5	24.2	38.0	396.0	126.4	63.9	838.8	252.5	1,091.2
Females	32.9	88.4	40.5	4.3	24.6	42.6	510.6	167.7	100.6	1,012.3	457.6	1,469.9

(1) Ages as at 31 August 1994.
(2) Provisional figures.
(3) GNVQ/NVQ split is not available for Northern Ireland. Figures are included in Other Vocational Qualifications.
(4) Includes Scottish Vocational Qualifications (SVQs) for Scotland.
(5) Includes SCE Higher Grades.
(6) Includes SCE Standard Grades.
(7) Includes students aged under 16 in England, Wales and Scotland.
(8) Includes students in Wales whose age is unknown.

(i) First year enrolments (Home and Overseas)

Thousands

| | Universities (1) | | | | | | Open Univer-sity (3) | Other higher education (2) | | | | | | All students |
| | Full-time | | | Part-time | | | | Full-time | | | Part-time | | | |
	Under-graduate	Post graduate	Total	Under-graduate	Post graduate	Total		Under-graduate	Post graduate	Total	Under-graduate	Post graduate	Total	
1975/76														
Persons	77	31	108	2	7	9	12	..	..	106	..	..	87	322
Males	49	22	71	1	5	6	7	..	..	58	..	..	72	214
Females	27	9	37	1	2	3	5	..	..	48	..	..	14	107
1980/81 (4)														
Persons	86	31	116	2	8	11	14	91	12	103	108	7	115	361 (5)
Males	52	20	72	1	6	7	8	52	6	58	80	5	85	230
Females	34	11	45	1	3	4	7	39	6	45	28	2	30	131
1985/86														
Persons	84	37	121	5	13	17	26	116	12	127	131	9	141	433 (5)
Males	49	24	73	2	8	10	14	63	6	68	87	6	93	258
Females	35	12	48	2	5	7	12	53	6	59	45	3	48	174
1990/91														
Persons	107	45	152	6	20	26	34	158 (6)	16 (6)	174 (6)	156 (6)	17 (6)	173 (6)	560 (5)(6)
Males	58	27	85	2	11	14	17	80	8	89	90	9	100	304
Females	49	18	67	3	9	12	18	77	8	85	65	7	73	254
1992/93														
Persons (7)	131	55	186	7	26	33	37	238	22	260	167	26	192	708 (5)
Males	69	32	101	3	14	17	18	123	11	133	91	13	104	373
Females (7)	62	23	85	4	12	16	20	115	11	126	76	13	88	335
1993/94 (8)														
Persons	298	76	374	68	50	118	40	99	10	109	108	7	115	756 (5)
Males	161	43	204	32	26	58	19	48	4	52	59	3	62	394
Females	138	33	170	36	24	60	21	51	6	57	49	4	53	362
1994/95 (9)														
Persons	321	80	401	83	53	136	38	99	10	109	109	9	118	802 (5)(6)
Males	169	44	214	37	27	64	20	46	5	51	57	4	61	410
Females	151	36	187	46	26	72	17	52	6	58	52	5	57	392

(ii) All enrolments (Home and Overseas)

| | Universities (1) | | | | | | Open Univer-sity (3) | Other higher education (2) | | | | | | All students |
| | Full-time | | | Part-time | | | | Full-time | | | Part-time | | | |
	Under-graduate	Post graduate	Total	Under-graduate	Post graduate	Total		Under-graduate	Post graduate	Total	Under-graduate	Post graduate	Total	
1975/76														
Persons	218	51	269	4	23	26	56	..	..	246	..	..	137	734
Males	141	37	178	2	17	19	34	..	..	123	..	..	115	470
Females	77	13	91	2	5	7	22	..	..	123	..	..	21	264
1980/81														
Persons	258	48	307	5	29	33	68	215	13	228	180	12	191	827 (5)
Males	157	34	191	2	20	23	38	120	7	127	138	9	146	524
Females	101	15	116	2	8	11	29	95	6	101	42	3	45	303
1985/86														
Persons	256	54	310	9	33	42	78	275	14	289	199	17	216	937 (5)
Males	148	37	185	5	22	26	43	146	7	154	134	12	146	553
Females	108	17	125	5	11	16	36	129	7	136	65	5	70	384
1990/91														
Persons	305	65	370	12	47	59	95	358 (6)	19 (6)	377 (6)	243 (6)	32 (6)	274 (6)	1,175 (5)(6)
Males	167	41	208	5	27	32	49	177	9	186	143	18	161	637
Females	138	24	162	7	19	26	46	180	9	190	99	13	112	536
1992/93														
Persons	357	78	436	14	61	76	105	496	26	522	260	46	306	1,444 (5)
Males	191	48	238	6	35	40	53	245	13	258	144	24	168	759
Females	166	31	197	9	26	35	52	250	13	264	116	21	137	685
1993/94 (8)														
Persons	753	104	857	128	106	234	111	196	11	207	156	14	170	1,580 (5)
Males	398	62	459	62	59	121	56	85	5	90	86	7	92	819
Females	355	43	398	65	48	113	55	110	6	117	70	8	78	760
1994/95 (9)														
Persons	812	116	928	150	119	269	120	203	12	215	151	18	169	1,701 (5)(6)
Males	422	68	489	69	64	134	62	87	6	93	80	7	87	866
Females	390	49	439	80	55	135	57	115	7	122	71	11	82	835

(1) 'Undergraduate' includes first diplomas and certificates.
(2) Excludes students in university departments of education, included under 'Universities'.
(3) Includes associate and postgraduate students.
(4) The split between undergraduates and postgraduates for Other Higher Education is estimated.
(5) In addition there were the following numbers of students in the United Kingdom enrolled on nursing and paramedical courses at Department of Health establishments :

| | Entrants | | | | | | Enrolments | | | | | |
	1980/81	1985/86	1990/91	1992/93	1993/94	1994/95	1980/81 (est)	1985/86	1990/91	1992/93	1993/94	1994/95
Basic nursing courses	46	39	33	33	29	..	91	86	71	72	72	..
Paramedical courses	3	3	4	5	4	..	10	9	11	13	13	..
All courses	49	42	37	38	33	..	101	95	82	85	85	..

(6) Includes students in Scotland whose gender is not recorded.
(7) Includes revised universities figures.
(8) From 1993/94 universities figures include former polytechnics and colleges which became universities as a result of the Further and Higher Education Act 1992.
(9) Provisional.

THIS PAGE HAS BEEN LEFT BLANK

FURTHER AND HIGHER EDUCATION

Countries of domicile and study of full-time and sandwich student enrolments in higher education, 1993/94

Thousands

| | COUNTRY OF STUDY | | | | | | | | | | | | | | |
| | Postgraduates | | | | | First degree and other undergraduates | | | | | All higher education | | | | |
	England	Wales	Scotland	N Ireland	UK	England	Wales	Scotland	N Ireland	UK	England	Wales	Scotland	N Ireland	UK
COUNTRY OF DOMICILE															
Home enrolments															
Universities	56.3	3.6	7.4	2.1	69.4	567.2	24.9	78.0	17.3	687.5	623.5	28.6	85.4	19.4	756.9
Other HE	7.0	0.7	2.2	-	10.0	130.8	23.0	31.5	2.7	187.9	137.8	23.7	33.7	2.7	197.9
Total	63.3	4.3	9.6	2.1	79.4	698.0	47.9	109.5	20.0	875.4	761.3	52.2	119.1	22.1	954.7
Enrolments from overseas (1)															
Universities	28.8	1.7	3.9	0.5	34.8	52.9	2.6	7.2	2.8	65.5	81.7	4.3	11.1	3.3	100.3
Other HE	0.9	0.1	0.2	-	1.3	4.4	2.1	0.7	0.2	7.4	5.3	2.2	0.9	0.2	8.7
Total	29.7	1.8	4.1	0.6	36.1	57.3	4.7	7.9	3.0	72.9	87.0	6.5	12.0	3.5	109.0
Grand total all students	93.0	6.1	13.7	2.7	115.5	755.2	52.6	117.4	23.0	948.2	848.2	58.7	131.1	25.7	1063.7
Country of domicile of home enrolments															
England	59.1	2.0	1.9	0.1	63.1	662.8	23.9	16.3	0.5	703.6	721.9	26.0	18.2	0.6	766.7
Wales	1.7	2.2	0.1	-	3.9	20.2	23.1	0.4	-	43.8	21.9	25.3	0.5	-	47.7
Scotland	1.4	0.1	7.2	-	8.7	5.5	0.2	86.3	0.1	92.1	6.9	0.3	93.5	0.1	100.8
Northern Ireland	0.6	-	0.2	2.0	2.9	6.7	0.5	3.6	19.4	30.2	7.4	0.6	3.8	21.4	33.1
UK not known	0.5	-	0.3	-	0.8	2.7	0.1	2.8	-	5.6	3.2	0.2	3.1	-	6.4
UK Total	63.3	4.3	9.6	2.1	79.4	698.0	47.9	109.5	20.0	875.4	761.3	52.2	119.1	22.1	954.7
Domicile of enrolments from overseas (1)															
European Community (2)	8.1	0.4	1.2	0.4	10.1	23.8	2.6	3.8	2.6	32.8	31.9	3.0	5.0	3.0	42.9
Other Europe (3)(4)	1.9	0.1	0.2	-	2.2	4.6	0.2	0.9	-	5.7	6.5	0.2	1.1	-	7.9
Commonwealth (2)(3)	8.5	0.6	1.1	0.1	10.3	21.0	1.4	2.0	0.3	24.7	29.4	2.0	3.1	0.4	34.9
Other Countries (4)	11.6	0.7	1.6	0.1	14.0	9.1	0.6	1.2	0.1	11.0	20.7	1.3	2.8	0.1	25.0
All students from overseas (2)(3)(4)	29.7	1.8	4.1	0.6	36.1	57.3	4.7	7.9	3.0	72.9	87.0	6.5	12.0	3.5	109.0

(1) See paragraph 12.10 of the explanatory notes.
(2) Gibraltar is included in both EC and Commonwealth figures.
(3) Cyprus and Malta are included in both Other Europe and Commonwealth.
(4) Russia Federation is included in both Other Europe and Other Countries.

FURTHER AND HIGHER EDUCATION
Countries of domicile and study of full-time and sandwich student enrolments in higher education, 1994/95 (1)

26b(26)

Thousands

| | COUNTRY OF STUDY | | | | | | | | | | | | | | |
| | Postgraduates | | | | | First degree and other undergraduates | | | | | All higher education | | | | |
	England	Wales	Scotland	N Ireland	UK	England	Wales	Scotland	N Ireland	UK	England	Wales	Scotland	N Ireland	UK
COUNTRY OF DOMICILE															
Home enrolments															
Universities	63.3	4.1	8.3	2.1	77.8	599.8	35.0	83.6	18.0	736.3	663.2	39.1	91.9	20.1	814.2
Other HE	8.2	0.7	1.7	0.1	10.6	141.0	15.6	35.4	3.3	195.2	149.2	16.3	37.0	3.3	205.8
Total	71.6	4.8	9.9	2.2	88.5	740.8	50.5	119.0	21.3	931.6	812.4	55.3	128.9	23.4	1020.0
Enrolments from overseas (2)															
Universities	32.5	1.8	4.0	0.6	38.9	60.4	4.5	7.5	3.0	75.5	92.9	6.3	11.6	3.6	114.4
Other HE	1.4	-	0.2	-	1.7	5.8	1.0	0.8	0.3	8.0	7.3	1.0	1.0	0.3	9.7
Total	34.0	1.8	4.2	0.6	40.6	66.3	5.5	8.3	3.3	83.5	100.2	7.3	12.6	3.9	124.0
Grand total all students	105.5	6.6	14.2	2.7	129.0	807.1	56.0	127.3	24.6	1015.0	912.6	62.6	141.5	27.3	1144.0
Country of domicile of home enrolments															
England	63.2	2.0	1.8	0.1	67.0	669.6	24.0	16.8	0.4	710.8	732.7	26.0	18.6	0.5	777.8
Wales	1.7	2.6	0.1	-	4.5	19.9	25.0	0.5	-	45.4	21.6	27.7	0.6	-	49.9
Scotland	1.4	0.1	7.7	-	9.2	5.5	0.2	96.4	0.1	102.2	6.9	0.3	104.1	0.1	111.3
Northern Ireland	0.7	-	0.3	2.1	3.0	6.3	0.6	4.2	20.7	31.8	6.9	0.6	4.4	22.8	34.8
UK not known	4.6	0.1	0.2	-	4.8	39.7	0.6	1.0	0.1	41.4	44.3	0.7	1.2	0.1	46.2
UK Total	71.6	4.8	9.9	2.1	88.5	740.8	50.5	119.0	21.3	931.6	812.4	55.3	128.9	23.4	1020.0
Domicile of enrolments from overseas (2)															
European Community (3)	9.8	0.4	1.3	0.4	11.9	29.2	3.5	4.1	3.0	39.8	39.0	3.9	5.4	3.4	51.7
Other Europe (4)(5)	1.9	-	0.1	-	2.1	3.7	0.2	0.4	-	4.3	5.6	0.2	0.5	-	6.4
Commonwealth (3)(4)	9.6	0.7	1.2	0.1	11.5	21.2	1.4	2.1	0.3	25.0	30.9	2.1	3.3	0.4	36.5
Other Countries (5)	13.3	0.7	1.6	0.1	15.6	13.5	0.5	1.8	-	15.8	26.7	1.2	3.4	0.1	31.4
All students from overseas (3)(4)(5)	34.0	1.8	4.2	0.6	40.6	66.3	5.5	8.3	3.3	83.5	100.2	7.3	12.6	3.9	124.0

(1) Provisional.
(2) See paragraph 12.10 of the explanatory notes.
(3) Gibraltar is included in both EC and Commonwealth figures.
(4) Cyprus and Malta are included in both Other Europe and Commonwealth.
(5) Russia Federation is included in both Other Europe and Other Countries.

FURTHER AND HIGHER EDUCATION
Full-time students from overseas, 1993/94

27

(i) Enrolments by type of course, gender and country, in higher and further education Thousands

1993 RANK	1992 RANK	TOP FIFTY NAMED COUNTRIES	Higher Education Post graduate	Higher Education First degree	Higher Education Other	Higher Education Total	Further Education	Higher and Further Education 1993/94 Persons	1993/94 Males	1993/94 Females	1992/93 Persons	1992/93 Males	1992/93 Females	1980/81 Persons
1	(1)	Malaysia	2.0	7.9	0.3	10.2	0.5	10.7	6.4	4.3	8.8	5.2	3.6	13.3
2	(2)	Irish Republic	1.0	5.7	1.2	7.9	1.2	9.1	4.6	4.5	7.8	4.0	3.9	0.5
3	(4)	Germany (1)	1.8	3.4	3.5	8.7	0.3	9.0	4.8	4.2	7.4	4.0	3.4	1.3
4	(6)	Greece	3.1	4.5	0.4	8.0	0.3	8.3	5.4	2.9	6.3	4.1	2.1	2.5
5	(5)	France	1.5	3.6	2.2	7.3	0.5	7.8	3.7	4.1	6.8	3.3	3.5	0.7
6	(3)	Hong Kong	1.2	4.7	0.3	6.2	0.8	7.0	4.2	2.8	7.4	4.6	2.8	7.2
7	(7)	USA	1.8	0.8	2.9	5.6	0.1	5.6	2.5	3.1	5.2	2.3	2.9	2.9
8	(8)	Singapore	0.6	3.1	-	3.8	-	3.8	2.5	1.4	3.4	2.1	1.2	1.6
9	(9)	Spain	0.7	1.4	1.2	3.3	0.4	3.8	1.8	2.0	3.3	1.6	1.7	..
10	(10)	Japan	1.0	0.8	0.5	2.2	0.5	2.7	1.1	1.7	2.5	1.0	1.5	..
11	(11)	Italy	0.7	1.0	0.8	2.5	0.1	2.7	1.3	1.4	2.3	1.1	1.2	..
12	(13)	Norway	0.3	1.5	0.2	2.0	-	2.1	1.1	1.0	1.9	1.1	0.8	0.5
13	(12)	Cyprus	0.4	1.5	0.1	1.9	0.1	2.0	1.2	0.8	2.0	1.2	0.8	1.5
14	(15)	Netherlands	0.4	0.9	0.4	1.6	0.1	1.7	0.9	0.8	1.4	0.7	0.7	..
15	(14)	China	1.4	0.2	0.1	1.6	0.1	1.7	1.2	0.5	1.5	1.1	0.4	0.2
16	(21)	Taiwan	1.0	0.3	0.1	1.4	0.2	1.6	0.8	0.8	1.2	0.6	0.5	..
17	(17)	Canada	0.9	0.3	0.2	1.4	-	1.4	0.8	0.7	1.3	0.7	0.6	0.7
18	(18)	Belgium	0.3	0.7	0.3	1.3	0.1	1.3	0.7	0.6	1.2	0.7	0.6	..
19	(16)	Kenya	0.3	0.9	0.1	1.2	0.1	1.3	0.8	0.5	1.4	0.8	0.5	1.1
20	(19)	Pakistan	0.7	0.4	0.1	1.2	0.1	1.3	1.1	0.2	1.2	1.0	0.2	0.8
21	(20)	India	0.8	0.3	0.1	1.2	0.1	1.3	0.9	0.3	1.2	0.9	0.3	0.9
22	(24)	Turkey	0.7	0.3	-	1.1	0.1	1.2	0.9	0.4	0.9	0.7	0.3	..
23	(22)	Israel	0.2	0.9	-	1.1	-	1.1	0.8	0.3	1.0	0.7	0.3	..
24	(26)	Portugal	0.4	0.4	0.1	0.9	0.1	1.0	0.6	0.4	0.8	0.5	0.3	..
25	(31)	Iran	0.8	0.1	-	0.9	-	1.0	0.8	0.1	0.7	0.6	0.1	6.6
26	(23)	Nigeria	0.5	0.3	0.1	0.9	0.1	0.9	0.6	0.3	0.9	0.6	0.3	5.2
27	(27)	Denmark	0.2	0.4	0.2	0.8	-	0.9	0.4	0.5	0.8	0.4	0.4	..
28	(28)	Thailand	0.5	0.2	-	0.7	0.1	0.9	0.4	0.4	0.7	0.4	0.4	..
29	(25)	Brazil	0.8	-	-	0.8	-	0.9	0.5	0.4	0.9	0.5	0.3	0.5
30	(33)	Sweden	0.1	0.3	0.3	0.7	0.1	0.8	0.3	0.5	0.7	0.3	0.4	0.1
31	(36)	South Korea	0.5	0.1	-	0.7	0.1	0.8	0.6	0.2	0.6	0.5	0.1	..
32	(32)	Oman	0.1	0.3	0.1	0.5	0.2	0.7	0.6	0.1	0.7	0.6	0.1	..
33	(29)	Brunei	0.1	0.5	0.1	0.7	-	0.7	0.5	0.3	0.7	0.4	0.3	1
34	(40)	Switzerland	0.2	0.4	0.1	0.7	-	0.7	0.4	0.4	0.6	0.3	0.3	..
35	(30)	Sri Lanka	0.2	0.4	-	0.6	-	0.7	0.5	0.2	0.7	0.5	0.2	1.2
36	(41)	Indonesia	0.5	0.1	-	0.6	0.1	0.7	0.5	0.2	0.5	0.4	0.1	..
37	(38)	Botswana	0.2	0.4	0.1	0.7	-	0.7	0.5	0.2	0.6	0.4	0.2	..
38	(35)	Saudi Arabia	0.4	0.1	-	0.6	0.1	0.7	0.6	0.1	0.6	0.6	0.1	0.4
39	(39)	South Africa	0.3	0.2	-	0.5	-	0.6	0.4	0.2	0.6	0.4	0.2	..
40	(34)	Zambia	0.2	0.3	-	0.5	-	0.6	0.5	0.2	0.6	0.5	0.1	0.8
41	(37)	Australia	0.4	0.2	-	0.5	-	0.6	0.3	0.3	0.6	0.4	0.3	..
42	(42)	Libya	0.5	-	0.1	0.5	-	0.6	0.6	-	0.5	0.5	-	0.7
43	(43)	Tanzania	0.3	0.2	-	0.4	-	0.5	0.4	0.2	0.5	0.4	0.1	0.7
44	(-)	Gibraltar	-	0.3	-	0.3	0.2	0.5	0.3	0.2	..	..	..	..
45	(50)	Kuwait	0.1	0.2	-	0.4	0.1	0.5	0.4	0.1	0.4	0.3	0.1	0.2
46	(48)	Mexico	0.5	-	-	0.5	-	0.5	0.3	0.2	0.4	0.3	0.1	..
47	(45)	Mauritius	0.1	0.3	0.1	0.5	-	0.5	0.3	0.2	0.5	0.3	0.2	..
48	(44)	Zimbabwe	0.2	0.2	0.1	0.4	0.1	0.5	0.3	0.2	0.5	0.4	0.1	..
49	(49)	Bahrain	0.1	0.1	-	0.2	0.2	0.4	0.3	0.1	0.4	0.3	0.1	..
50	(-)	Finland	0.1	0.1	0.1	0.4	-	0.4	0.2	0.2	..	..	..	..
		Other/unknown	5.1	3.4	1.3	9.8	1.2	11.0	7.0	3.9	10.7	6.8	3.9	22.5
		TOTAL	36.1	54.7	18.2	109.0	8.7	117.7	68.4	49.4	103.6	61.1	42.6	75.6

(1) Includes the former East Germany

27

FURTHER AND HIGHER EDUCATION
Full-time students from overseas, 1993/94

(ii) First Year Students and Enrolments by grouped country of domicile and gender, in higher and further education (1)

PERSONS   Thousands

	First Year Students					All Enrolments				
	1980/81 (2)	1985/86 (3)	1990/91	1992/93	1993/94	1980/81 (2)	1985/86 (3)	1990/91	1992/93	1993/94
European Community (4)(5)	3.0	5.6	16.3	24.6	29.4	5.4	8.9	26.5	38.6	46.3
Other Europe (5)	1.1	2.1	3.1	4.2	4.8	3.1	3.8	5.7	7.3	8.2
Commonwealth (4)	18.1	16.9	17.3	19.2	18.6	39.6	30.2	34.7	36.3	35.6
Other Countries	13.4	13.9	13.5	14.4	18.2	27.4	20.8	20.8	21.7	27.6
All countries	35.6	38.5	50.2	62.3	70.9	75.6	63.7	87.6	103.7	117.7
of which										
Higher education	23.8	31.0	44.2	55.9	63.7	55.5	53.7	80.2	95.9	109.0
Further education	11.8	7.5	6.0	6.4	7.2	20.2	10.0	7.3	7.7	8.7

MALES

	First Year Students					All Enrolments				
	1980/81 (2)	1985/86 (3)	1990/91	1992/93	1993/94	1980/81 (2)	1985/86 (3)	1990/91	1992/93	1993/94
European Community (4)(5)	1.7	3.2	8.6	13.0	15.3	3.4	5.1	14.3	20.7	24.6
Other Europe (5)	0.7	1.2	1.7	2.3	2.4	1.8	2.6	3.3	4.0	4.4
Commonwealth (4)	13.4	12.0	11.3	12.1	11.7	29.5	21.6	22.7	23.0	22.4
Other Countries	10.1	10.3	8.2	8.4	10.7	21.8	15.8	13.5	13.5	17.1
All countries	25.9	26.7	29.7	35.7	40.2	56.5	45.1	53.6	61.1	68.4
of which										
Higher education	17.5	21.8	26.6	32.4	36.3	41.9	38.4	49.7	57.0	63.7
Further education	8.4	4.9	3.1	3.3	3.8	14.7	6.7	3.9	4.1	4.7

FEMALES

	First Year Students					All Enrolments				
	1980/81 (2)	1985/86 (3)	1990/91	1992/93	1993/94	1980/81 (2)	1985/86 (3)	1990/91	1992/93	1993/94
European Community (4)(5)	1.3	2.4	7.7	11.6	14.1	2.0	3.7	12.2	17.9	21.7
Other Europe (5)	0.5	0.8	1.4	1.9	2.4	1.1	1.3	2.4	3.3	3.9
Commonwealth (4)	4.8	4.9	6.0	7.1	6.8	10.1	8.6	12.1	13.4	13.2
Other Countries	3.1	3.8	5.3	6.0	7.4	5.7	5.0	7.3	8.2	10.6
All countries	9.7	11.9	20.5	26.6	30.8	19.0	18.6	33.9	42.6	49.4
of which										
Higher education	6.3	9.2	17.6	23.5	27.4	13.5	15.3	30.5	39.0	45.3
Further education	3.4	2.6	2.9	3.1	3.4	5.5	3.3	3.5	3.6	4.0

(1) Figures for Scotland are Autumn counts for vocational further education.

(2) Estimated.

(3) For 1985/86 and subsequent years, figures have been adjusted to take account of the change of definition of a 'student from overseas'. See paragraph 12.10 of explanatory notes.

(4) From 1990/91 Gibraltar is included in both EC and Commonwealth figures. Numbers in grouped countries do not sum to overall student numbers due to overlap.

(5) From 1992/93 Russia Federation is included in both EC and Other Europe figures. Numbers in grouped countries do not sum to overall student numbers due to overlap.

QUALIFICATIONS AND DESTINATIONS
GCE, GCSE and SCE Qualifications obtained by pupils and students of any age

United Kingdom — Thousands

	1992/93					1993/94				
	Schools (1)		All Schools	Further Education (3)(4)	All Schools and FE	Schools (1)		All Schools	Further Education (3)(4)	All Schools and FE
	Maintained (2)	Non-maintained				Maintained (2)	Non-maintained			
PERSONS										
Pupils with GCE A levels or equivalent (5)										
2 or more passes (6)	102	34	136	58	193	105	34	139	59	198
1 pass (7)	45	6	52	48	99	44	6	51	48	98
1 or more passes	147	40	187	105	293	150	40	190	107	297
Pupils with GCSEs or equivalent										
5 or more A-C/1-3 grades (8)	220	41	262	1	262	246	42	288	1	288
1-4 A-C/1-3 grades (8)(9)	261	32	293	115	408	244	28	272	110	383
5 or more D-G/4-7 grades (10)(11)(12)	99	1	100	1	100	118	1	118	-	119
1-4 D-G/4-7 grades (10)(11)(12)	95	4	99	52	152	80	3	83	51	135
1 or more grades	675	78	754	169	922	670	74	743	163	906
No graded results (13)	46	3	49	21	70	33	1	35	25	59
MALES (14)										
Pupils with GCE A levels or equivalent (5)										
2 or more passes (6)	48	19	66	25	92	49	18	67	26	93
1 pass (7)	21	3	24	19	43	20	3	23	19	43
1 or more passes	68	22	90	45	135	69	21	90	45	136
Pupils with GCSEs or equivalent										
5 or more A-C/1-3 grades (8)	99	21	120	-	120	111	22	133	-	133
1-4 A-C/1-3 grades (8)(9)	127	19	145	44	190	119	17	135	44	179
5 or more D-G/4-7 grades (10)(11)(12)	59	1	60	-	60	71	-	72	-	72
1-4 D-G/4-7 grades (10)(11)(12)	52	3	54	22	76	44	2	46	22	67
1 or more grades	336	43	379	67	447	335	41	375	66	441
No graded results (13)	26	2	28	9	37	18	1	19	11	30
FEMALES (14)										
Pupils with GCE A levels or equivalent (5)										
2 or more passes (6)	54	16	69	32	102	57	16	72	33	105
1 pass (7)	25	3	28	29	56	24	3	27	29	56
1 or more passes	79	19	97	61	158	81	19	99	62	161
Pupils with GCSEs or equivalent										
5 or more A-C/1-3 grades (8)	122	20	142	-	142	135	20	155	-	155
1-4 A-C/1-3 grades (8)(9)	134	13	148	71	218	126	12	137	67	204
5 or more D-G/4-7 grades (10)(11)(12)	40	-	40	-	40	46	-	47	-	47
1-4 D-G/4-7 grades (10)(11)(12)	43	2	45	30	75	36	1	38	30	67
1 or more grades	339	35	374	102	476	335	33	368	97	465
No graded results (13)	20	1	21	11	33	15	1	16	14	30

(1) School pupils of any age in Great Britain; school leavers only in Northern Ireland.
(2) Sixth form colleges in England which were reclassified as further education colleges from 1 April 1993 are included in FE figures for 'A' levels and GCSEs.
(3) Excludes Scotland.
(4) From 1 April 1993 includes sixth form colleges in England which were reclassified as further education colleges.
(5) 2 AS levels count as 1 A level pass.
(6) 3 or more SCE Higher grades in Scotland.
(7) 1 or 2 SCE Higher grades in Scotland.
(8) Grades A-C at GCSE and Scottish SCE Standard grades 1-3. From 1993/94 grades A*-C at GCSE (see paragraph 13.2a of explanatory notes).
(9) Includes pupils with 1 AS level for England and Wales.
(10) Pupils in Northern Ireland with GCSE grades D-G may also have GCSE grades A*-C (see paragraph 13.2a of explanatory notes).
(11) Grades D-G at GCSE and Scottish SCE Standard grades 4-7.
(12) No split available for 'other grades' for Wales. Figures are included in '1-4 grades D-G/4-7'.
(13) 1992/93 figures for Scotland include pupils who did not sit SCE examinations. 1993/94 figures include only those who sat and failed.
(14) 1993/94 males and females figures are estimated for Northern Ireland.

29 QUALIFICATIONS AND DESTINATIONS
GCSE/SCE (S grade) attempts and achievements (1) for all ages in all schools by subject and gender by the end of 1993/94 (2)

Great Britain

SUBJECT GROUP	Number of attempts (000s)			Percentage Achieving grade A-C			Percentage Achieving grade D-G		
	Persons	Males	Females	Persons	Males	Females	Persons	Males	Females
Biological Science	68.5	33.7	34.8	72	73	72	25	24	26
Chemistry	64.2	37.9	26.4	79	78	81	19	20	18
Physics	62.7	42.1	20.7	81	80	82	18	18	17
Science Single Award	107.6	52.2	55.4	38	36	41	53	54	51
Science Double Award	425.7	213.7	212.0	49	49	49	48	47	48
Other Science	28.3	17.2	11.1	35	35	35	54	54	54
Mathematics	626.7	315.0	311.7	45	46	45	50	49	50
Computer Studies	69.7	44.3	25.4	51	49	55	44	45	40
Craft, Design and Technology	211.4	162.4	49.1	41	38	52	51	54	42
Business Studies (3)	131.6	58.2	73.4	51	47	55	43	47	40
Home Economics	103.3	15.2	88.1	41	21	44	54	70	51
Art and Design	220.3	106.1	114.2	55	45	64	42	50	33
Geography	277.5	159.0	118.4	51	48	55	45	48	42
History	243.9	116.6	127.2	54	51	57	42	44	39
Area Studies (4)	2.7	1.5	1.2	33	30	38	58	60	56
Economics	14.7	9.7	5.0	56	57	55	39	38	40
Humanities (4)	48.5	23.4	25.0	41	33	49	55	62	48
Religious Studies	94.8	36.7	58.2	55	48	59	41	46	38
Social Studies	32.8	11.3	21.5	47	37	51	45	52	42
English	602.9	306.4	296.5	57	49	66	39	47	32
English Literature (4)	419.9	200.6	219.3	61	54	67	37	43	31
Drama	69.0	26.0	43.0	67	57	73	29	37	24
Communication Studies (4)	32.9	15.4	17.5	48	38	56	47	55	40
Modern Languages	581.4	265.9	315.5	51	43	57	44	50	38
French	375.4	174.0	201.5	47	40	54	47	53	41
German	138.3	63.6	74.7	56	48	63	39	46	33
Spanish	34.2	13.7	20.5	53	45	58	42	49	38
Other languages	33.5	14.7	18.9	65	60	70	30	35	26
Classical Studies	17.3	8.9	8.4	87	86	88	12	13	11
Creative Arts (4)	44.2	18.8	25.4	60	52	66	36	42	31
Physical Education	71.4	46.2	25.3	46	45	46	49	49	49
Vocational Studies	49.6	16.9	32.7	47	38	52	47	53	43
General Studies (4)	9.5	4.9	4.6	55	50	61	37	41	33
Modern Studies (5)	12.9	5.9	7.0	51	45	56	43	48	38
Music (5)	7.4	2.6	4.8	73	65	78	19	25	16
English and Mathematics (6)	551.0	278.6	272.3	42	39	44	53	55	52
English, Maths and Science (6)	531.0	267.8	263.2	38	37	39	56	57	55
English, Maths, Science and Modern Languages (6)	431.4	205.3	226.1	36	32	39	59	62	56
Mathematics and Science (6)	542.2	275.0	267.1	41	41	40	54	53	54
Any Subject	734.4	370.3	364.1	73	69	77	24	28	21

(1)   For each subject, only one attempt is counted, that which achieved the highest grade.

(2)   Excludes sixth form colleges in England and Wales which were reclassified as Further Education colleges.

(3)   Includes Business and Information Studies for Wales.

(4)   England and Wales only.

(5)   Scotland only.

(6)   England and Scotland only.

QUALIFICATIONS AND DESTINATIONS

30

GCE A level (1) /SCE H grade (2) entries and achievements for all ages in all Schools and Further Education Sector Colleges by subject and gender,1993/94

Great Britain

Subject group	Number of entries (000s)			Percentage Achieved grades A-C			Percentage Achieved grades D-E			Percentage with No graded result		
	Persons	Males	Females	Persons	Males	Females	Persons	Males	Females	Persons	Males	Females
Biological Sciences	60.2	22.4	37.7	48.5	47.6	49.1	30.1	30.7	29.7	21.4	21.7	21.2
Chemistry	50.6	28.3	22.4	56.6	56.6	56.7	26.1	25.6	26.7	17.3	17.7	16.7
Physics	46.0	35.0	11.0	54.3	53.3	57.8	28.9	29.3	27.7	16.7	17.4	14.6
Other Science	7.6	4.2	3.4	44.5	43.7	45.5	34.3	33.6	35.2	21.2	22.7	19.3
Mathematics	82.4	51.4	31.1	59.3	58.3	61.0	22.8	22.8	22.9	17.8	18.8	16.1
Computer Studies	12.4	10.1	2.3	44.3	45.4	39.5	32.0	31.5	34.0	23.7	23.1	26.4
Craft, Design and Technology	14.5	12.1	2.4	49.0	48.3	52.9	33.7	33.9	32.9	17.2	17.8	14.2
Business Studies	31.0	15.7	15.4	44.5	44.8	44.3	34.4	34.7	34.2	21.0	20.6	21.5
Home Economics	3.2	0.1	3.1	43.7	34.3	44.1	37.2	36.5	37.2	19.1	29.2	18.7
Art and Design	39.4	15.4	24.0	61.3	57.5	63.9	28.5	29.8	27.6	10.2	12.7	8.5
Geography	51.1	28.3	22.9	50.4	48.3	53.0	31.1	32.4	29.6	18.5	19.3	17.4
History	50.0	22.2	27.8	51.3	52.4	50.4	30.8	30.4	31.1	17.9	17.2	18.5
Economics	32.3	21.1	11.2	46.8	47.4	45.8	31.0	31.0	31.0	22.1	21.5	23.2
Religious Studies	8.2	2.0	6.2	50.7	52.6	50.1	34.5	32.3	35.2	14.8	15.2	14.6
Social Studies (3)	79.3	27.4	51.9	38.5	36.8	39.4	29.7	29.2	30.0	31.7	34.0	30.5
English	55.3	21.1	34.2	58.5	57.5	59.0	27.3	27.0	27.6	14.2	15.5	13.4
English Literature (3)	62.4	19.1	43.3	55.7	55.8	55.6	34.0	32.9	34.5	10.3	11.4	9.8
Communication studies (3)	19.2	6.9	12.3	44.9	40.8	47.1	36.2	35.7	36.4	19.0	23.5	16.4
Modern Languages	55.9	16.9	39.0	60.1	61.8	59.3	27.6	25.8	28.4	12.3	12.4	12.3
French	32.9	9.6	23.3	58.1	60.0	57.3	28.9	27.3	29.6	13.0	12.8	13.1
German	12.6	3.8	8.8	59.9	61.8	59.1	28.8	27.1	29.5	11.3	11.1	11.4
Spanish	4.9	1.4	3.5	64.2	66.5	63.2	23.4	22.1	23.9	12.4	11.4	12.9
Other Languages	5.5	2.1	3.4	68.7	67.2	69.6	20.8	19.0	21.8	10.5	13.8	8.6
Classical Studies	8.1	3.5	4.6	65.2	63.1	66.9	24.6	25.4	23.9	10.2	11.5	9.2
Creative Arts (3)	5.6	2.1	3.5	60.2	60.8	59.9	30.8	28.9	31.8	9.0	10.3	8.3
Physical Education	8.0	5.0	3.1	45.5	43.7	48.3	39.4	40.7	37.2	15.1	15.5	14.5
Vocational Studies (3)	7.2	3.6	3.6	36.3	36.7	35.8	25.7	25.2	26.3	38.0	38.1	37.9
General Studies (3)	54.5	27.2	27.3	45.6	50.8	40.4	33.9	32.4	35.5	20.5	16.8	24.2

(1) Includes AS equivalent.
(2) See paragraph 13.2 of the explanatory notes.
(3) England and Wales only.

31

QUALIFICATIONS AND DESTINATIONS

(i) Students achieving GCE A-level qualifications at school by gender

ENGLAND, WALES & NORTHERN IRELAND (1)

| | Numbers in thousands | | | | | | | | As a percentage of total population aged 17 (2) | | | | | | | |
| | 1985/86 | | 1990/91 | | 1992/93 | | 1993/94 (3) | | 1985/86 | | 1990/91 | | 1992/93 | | 1993/94 (3) | |
	Male	Female	Male	Female	Male	Female	Male	Female	Male	Female	Male	Female	Male	Female	Male	Female
Total population aged 17 (2)	417	398	358	339	328	309	318	298	100	100	100	100	100	100	100	100
From schools only																
3 or more A-level passes	43	36	48	47	51	53	44	46	10.2	9.0	13.5	14.0	15.5	17.1	13.9	15.5
2 A-level passes	15	16	16	19	19	22	15	16	3.5	4.0	4.4	5.7	5.8	7.1	4.6	5.5
1 A-level pass	11	13	11	12	17	18	12	13	2.7	3.2	3.0	3.6	5.2	5.9	3.9	4.5
Total	70	64	75	79	87	93	71	76	16.7	16.2	21.0	23.3	26.5	30.1	22.5	25.5

(ii) School leavers achieving SCE Higher grade qualifications (A-C), by gender

SCOTLAND

| | Numbers in thousands | | | | | | | | As a percentage of total population aged 16 (2) | | | | | | | |
| | 1985/86 | | 1990/91 | | 1992/93 | | 1993/94 | | 1985/86 | | 1990/91 | | 1992/93 | | 1993/94 | |
	Male	Female	Male	Female	Male	Female	Male	Female	Male	Female	Male	Female	Male	Female	Male	Female
Total population aged 16 (2)	43	41	34	32	32	31	30	28	100	100	100	100	100	100	100	100
School leavers																
4 or more passes	6	7	6	7	6	7	6	8	14.5	15.9	17.6	20.9	18.3	23.1	21.3	27.0
3 passes	2	2	2	2	2	2	2	2	4.0	5.5	4.7	6.5	4.9	6.3	5.1	6.5
2 passes	2	3	2	2	2	2	2	2	4.2	6.1	4.6	6.1	4.8	6.6	5.2	7.1
1 pass	2	3	2	3	2	3	2	3	5.5	7.3	5.8	7.9	6.5	8.5	7.1	9.1
Total leavers with Higher Grade passes	12	15	11	13	11	14	12	14	28.2	34.8	32.8	41.5	34.6	44.5	38.7	49.6

(iii) Students achieving GCE A-level qualifications at school and through further education (4) by gender

ENGLAND & WALES

| | Numbers in thousands | | | | | | | | As a percentage of total population aged 17 (2) | | | | | | | |
| | 1985/86 (5) | | 1990/91 (5) | | 1992/93 (6) | | 1993/94 (6) | | 1985/86 (5) | | 1990/91 (5) | | 1992/93 (6) | | 1993/94 (3) (6) | |
	Male	Female	Male	Female	Male	Female	Male	Female	Male	Female	Male	Female	Male	Female	Male	Female
Total population aged 17 (2)	381	363	326	308	315	297	305	286	100	100	100	100	100	100	100	100
From schools and home students from FE colleges aged 18 or less at 31 August (7)	74	71	82	88	93	102	107	122	19.3	19.5	25.1	28.6	29.4	34.5	35.2	42.5
From schools and all students from FE colleges	76	73	94	102	114	132	140	162	..	..	..	..	..	..	..	..

(1) Schools data for Northern Ireland are based upon the School Leavers Survey for Northern Ireland.

(2) Age at the previous 31 August.

(3) From 1 April 1993, schools figures exclude sixth form colleges in England and Wales, which transferred to the FE sector, and are included with FE from that date.

(4) Includes full-time, sandwich and part-time students at FE colleges.

(5) England only.

(6) Changes in source data from 1991/92 mean data may not be directly comparable with earlier years.

(7) Wales data for 1992/93 include FE students aged 19 or less.

Foundation Target 1 For 2000: 'By age 19, 85% of young people to achieve 5 GCSEs at grade C or above, an Intermediate GNVQ or an NVQ level 2'

Percentage of 19-21 year olds qualified to NVQ level 2 or equivalent by region (2)(3)(4)

	1985	1986	1987	1988	1989	1990	1991	1992	1993	1994	1995	(% point difference 1994-1995)
United Kingdom	45	45	47	48	50	52	54	59	62	65	64	-
North	38	42	42	38	48	44	50	54	58	63	64	1
Yorkshire & Humberside	42	42	46	44	46	46	50	56	63	63	63	-
North West	43	42	45	47	48	48	52	55	59	63	62	-1
East Midlands	39	40	43	45	47	53	50	57	59	62	70	8
West Midlands	40	43	40	38	46	47	53	57	57	58	59	1
East Anglia	44	46	42	46	49	44	51	54	62	62	57	-5
South East												
Greater London	52	50	52	53	56	56	57	59	61	68	63	-5
Other South East	49	47	49	51	52	54	55	61	64	67	66	-
South West	46	44	49	49	49	54	56	62	63	66	66	-
Great Britain	45	45	47	48	50	52	54	59	62	65	64	-
England	45	44	46	47	50	51	53	58	61	64	64	-
Wales	40	39	39	40	43	48	52	56	58	61	56	-5
Scotland	53	56	54	58	61	63	65	71	70	70	70	-
Northern Ireland	42	45	45	45	48	50	53	59	63	67	69	2

Foundation Target 3 (5) For 2000: 'By age 21, 60% of young people to achieve 2 GCE A levels, an Advanced GNVQ or NVQ level 3'

Percentage of 21-23 (4) year olds qualified to NVQ level 3 or equivalent by region (2)(3)(4)

	1985	1986	1987	1988	1989	1990	1991	1992	1993	1994	1995	(% point difference 1994-1995)
United Kingdom	26	26	27	26	28	30	30	35	37	41	44	4
North	21	20	21	19	26	27	29	29	33	38	45	7
Yorkshire & Humberside	21	20	23	26	23	23	24	32	36	39	45	6
North West	27	24	23	23	23	29	27	30	35	38	38	-
East Midlands	21	24	22	21	26	29	30	29	37	38	47	9
West Midlands	24	23	23	21	25	28	25	31	36	39	41	2
East Anglia	29	26	23	26	23	23	24	29	35	36	41	5
South East												
Greater London	31	33	36	34	39	39	37	42	42	47	52	5
Other South East	29	27	29	27	28	30	29	33	35	38	44	7
South West	25	24	31	28	25	29	30	32	38	41	43	2
Great Britain	27	26	27	26	28	30	30	35	38	41	44	3
England	26	25	27	26	27	30	29	33	37	40	44	5
Wales	19	20	23	23	24	23	24	30	32	39	39	1
Scotland	34	33	35	34	40	40	42	52	49	50	51	1
Northern Ireland	23	25	27	27	25	27	30	34	34	40	37	-3

Source: Labour Force Survey (LFS) Spring Quarter

(1)   Updated National Targets were launched in 1995. The aim is to help set an agenda for education and training as the 21st century approaches and focus on the improvements that will be necessary to achieve a better educated and more highly qualified society at all levels.

(2)   Regional estimates are not very precise due to the small sample sizes, which are below 200 in the smallest region.

(3)   Data prior to 1993 uses assumptions for the number of GCSEs and GCE levels achieved and are thus not directly comparable with subsequent data.

(4)   Because of the limited number of sample cases available, the estimates for FT1 are based on all respondents aged 19-21 and those for FT3 on all respondents aged 21-23.

Lifetime Target 1 (3)   For 2000: '60% of the workforce to be qualified to NVQ level 3, Advanced GNVQ or 2 GCE A level standard'

Percentage of the employed workforce (6)
qualified to NVQ level 3
or equivalent by region

	1985	1986	1987	1988	1989	1990	1991	1992	1993	1994	1995	(% point difference 1994-1995)
United Kingdom	27	27	27	27	28	30	31	33	38	40	40	-
North	24	26	26	25	25	26	29	30	35	37	38	1
Yorkshire & Humberside	24	25	25	25	27	26	28	30	34	37	38	-
North West	27	25	28	27	28	28	29	32	38	39	39	-
East Midlands	25	24	23	25	25	27	29	29	34	37	37	-
West Midlands	24	25	24	24	23	25	25	28	33	36	36	-
East Anglia	24	25	25	24	27	27	27	29	34	37	39	2
South East												
Greater London	32	32	32	32	35	36	36	40	44	47	47	-
Other South East	29	29	29	28	29	31	32	35	40	41	41	-
South West	27	27	27	26	26	28	29	33	39	39	39	-
Great Britain	27	27	27	27	28	30	31	33	38	40	40	-
England	27	27	27	27	28	29	30	33	38	40	40	-
Wales	25	27	24	25	24	27	27	31	34	38	38	1
Scotland	31	30	31	33	36	36	37	42	46	48	47	-1
Northern Ireland	26	27	27	28	29	30	30	32	34	36	37	1

Lifetime Target 2 (7)   For 2000: '30% of the workforce to have a vocational, professional, management or academic qualification at NVQ level 4 or above'

Percentage of the employed workforce (6)
qualified to NVQ level 4
or equivalent by region

	1985	1986	1987	1988	1989	1990	1991	1992	1993	1994	1995	(% point difference 1994-1995)
United Kingdom	15	16	16	16	16	17	17	20	22	23	23	-
North	12	14	14	13	12	13	14	17	19	20	21	1
Yorkshire & Humberside	13	14	14	14	15	14	15	17	18	20	21	1
North West	15	14	16	15	15	15	16	19	21	21	22	1
East Midlands	14	14	13	14	13	15	16	17	19	21	20	-1
West Midlands	13	14	14	14	12	14	13	16	19	20	21	-
East Anglia	13	14	14	14	15	14	15	17	18	20	21	1
South East												
Greater London	21	20	21	20	23	22	23	28	30	31	32	1
Other South East	17	18	17	17	16	19	19	21	24	24	24	-
South West	15	15	15	15	14	16	16	20	22	22	21	-
Great Britain	15	16	16	16	16	17	17	20	22	23	24	-
England	16	16	16	16	16	17	17	20	22	23	23	-
Wales	14	17	14	15	14	15	15	18	19	22	23	1
Scotland	14	14	15	15	17	17	17	22	24	25	26	1
Northern Ireland	14	14	14	15	16	16	16	18	20	21	21	-

Source: Labour Force Survey (LFS) Spring Quarter

(5) Foundation target 2 is about young people achieving the core skills of communication, numeracy and IT which employers have consistently identified as the foundation for effective transition to work.

(6) The employed workforce includes employees, the self employed, unpaid family workers and those on government employment and training programmes.

(7) Young people can improve their core skills throughout life and make them more transferable through a range of opportunities to apply these skills in work related settings.

QUALIFICATIONS AND DESTINATIONS
Students obtaining higher education qualifications by subject of study (1)(2), gender and type of awarding body in year ending 31 December 1993 (3)

Thousands

	Medicine and Dentistry	Allied Medicine	Biological Sciences	Agri-culture and related	Physical Sciences	Mathematical and Computing Sciences	Engineering and Technology	Archi-tecture building, planning	Social Studies
PERSONS									
Higher degree Level									
University (4)	2.1	1.4	2.6	0.9	3.2	2.7	5.4	0.9	7.4
Other HE	-	-	-	-	-	-	-	-	-
Open University (5)	..	..	..	..	..	..	..	..	..
Professional quals (6)	-	0.3	-	-	-	-	0.4	0.4	0.1
Total Higher Degree Level	2.1	1.7	2.6	0.9	3.2	2.8	5.8	1.3	7.5
Higher diplomas and certificates									
University (4)(7)	0.5	0.5	0.2	0.1	0.2	0.7	0.8	0.4	2.1
Other HE (7)	-	-	0.1	-	0.1	0.1	-	-	0.1
Total Higher Diplomas and Certificates	0.5	0.5	0.3	0.1	0.3	0.9	0.8	0.4	2.2
First degree Level									
University (4)	5.6	5.2	8.2	1.6	10.4	10.0	17.6	5.2	21.6
Other HE	-	0.5	0.1	0.1	0.3	0.3	0.2	0.1	0.7
Open University (5)	..	..	..	..	..	..	..	..	..
Professional quals (6)	-	-	0.1	-	0.1	0.7	1.6	0.9	1.6
Total First Degree Level	5.6	5.7	8.4	1.8	10.8	10.9	19.4	6.2	23.9
Sub-degree Level									
First university diplomas and certificates (4)(8)	0.1	2.1	0.7	0.3	0.7	2.6	2.7	1.1	2.6
Other HE	-	0.3	-	0.3	-	0.4	0.9	0.2	0.3
Professional quals (6)	-	5.7	0.1	0.4	0.1	1.1	2.6	1.9	6.6
BTEC higher diploma	-	0.1	0.4	0.9	0.5	3.4	3.9	1.2	0.5
BTEC higher certificate	-	0.4	0.3	0.1	0.8	1.6	10.6	4.0	0.6
SCOTVEC higher diploma/certificate	-	-	0.1	0.2	0.1	0.8	0.9	0.2	0.3
Total Sub-degree Level	0.2	8.7	1.7	2.1	2.3	9.9	21.6	8.6	11.0
Nursing and Paramedical courses	.	30.3	.	.	.	.	.	.	.
TOTAL HIGHER EDUCATION 1993	8.3	46.9	12.9	4.9	16.6	24.4	47.5	16.5	44.6
TOTAL HIGHER EDUCATION 1992 (9)	8.2	43.3	12.5	3.6	15.9	20.2	43.6	15.4	40.8
TOTAL HIGHER EDUCATION 1979 (2)(10)	..	..	..	..	..	..	..	..	..
MALES	4.5	6.5	5.7	2.9	11.4	17.1	38.8	12.5	20.3
Higher degree Level (5)	1.1	0.7	1.4	0.6	2.4	2.1	5.1	0.9	4.2
Higher diplomas and certificates (7)	0.3	0.1	0.1	-	0.2	0.6	0.7	0.2	1.1
First degree Level (5)	3.0	1.5	3.4	0.9	7.2	7.7	16.8	4.8	11.1
Sub-degree Level	0.1	1.5	0.8	1.3	1.6	6.7	16.3	6.5	4.0
Nursing and Paramedical courses	.	2.7	.	.	.	.	.	.	.
FEMALES	3.8	40.5	7.2	2.0	5.3	7.3	8.7	3.9	24.3
Higher degree Level (5)	0.9	1.0	1.2	0.3	0.7	0.6	0.7	0.3	3.3
Higher diplomas and certificates (7)	0.2	0.4	0.1	-	-	0.3	0.1	0.1	1.1
First degree Level (5)	2.6	4.2	5.0	0.8	3.6	3.2	2.5	1.4	12.8
Sub-degree Level	0.1	7.2	0.8	0.8	0.8	3.2	5.3	2.1	7.0
Nursing and Paramedical courses	.	27.6	.	.	.	.	.	.	.

(1) Teacher training results are shown in Table 8. However, these overlap with results shown here.
(2) Due to changes in subject classification in 1987/88, a comparable subject split of the qualifications for earlier years is not available.
(3) Excludes qualifications from the private sector. University diplomas and certificates relate to the calendar year 1993.
(4) Includes former polytechnics and colleges which became universites as a result of the Further and Higher Education Act 1992.
(5) Open University degrees subject detail is not available in this format. Included only in 'All students', 'Males' and 'Females' totals.
(6) Public sector only. DfEE estimates based on final year of course data.
(7) Includes Postgraduate Certificates in Education (PGCEs).
(8 Excludes students who successfully completed courses for which formal qualifications are not awarded.
(9) Includes revised data.
(10) Excludes degrees validated by universities (but taught in other institutions) and nursing and paramedic qualifiers.

33a(33) QUALIFICATIONS AND DESTINATIONS

Students obtaining higher education qualifications by subject of study (1)(2), gender and type of awarding body in year ending 31 December 1993 (3)

Thousands

	Business and admin studies	Communi-cation and Docum-entation	Langu-ages and related	Human-ities	Creative Arts and design	Edu-cation	Combined and General	ALL STUDENTS	MALES	FEMALES
PERSONS										
Higher degree Level										
University (4)	7.3	0.7	2.5	2.2	0.5	3.3	1.2	44.2	27.8	16.5
Other HE	-	-	-	-	-	-	-	-	-	-
Open University (5)	..	..	..	..	..	..	..	1.4	0.8	0.5
Professional quals (6)	0.3	0.1	-	-	0.2	-	0.1	1.8	1.0	0.8
Total Higher Degree Level	7.6	0.8	2.5	2.2	0.7	3.3	1.2	47.4	29.7	17.8
Higher diplomas and certificates										
University (4)(7)	1.9	0.4	0.5	0.3	1.2	12.9	0.2	22.9	9.6	13.3
Other HE (7)	-	-	0.3	0.3	0.3	2.3	0.2	3.9	1.1	2.8
Total Higher Diplomas and Certificates	1.9	0.4	0.8	0.6	1.6	15.2	0.4	26.8	10.7	16.1
First degree Level										
University (4)	15.5	1.5	10.9	7.1	7.7	4.6	20.1	152.8	80.7	72.1
Other HE	1.0	0.2	0.8	0.7	3.2	1.8	6.0	16.2	5.1	11.1
Open University (5)	..	..	..	..	..	..	..	7.2	3.6	3.6
Professional quals (6)	6.1	0.2	1.1	-	0.5	-	0.4	13.0	6.9	6.1
Total First Degree Level	22.6	1.9	12.8	7.9	11.3	6.5	26.4	189.2	96.3	92.9
Sub-degree Level										
First university diplomas and certificates (4)(8)	6.9	-	1.4	0.5	1.2	0.5	5.3	28.9	14.0	14.9
Other HE	2.4	-	-	-	1.8	0.3	0.2	7.3	3.7	3.5
Professional quals (6)	25.7	0.5	1.7	0.2	0.6	0.7	1.3	49.3	22.6	26.7
BTEC higher diploma	10.2	-	-	-	3.4	-	0.6	25.0	15.2	9.9
BTEC higher certificate	5.9	-	-	-	0.2	-	0.1	24.7	18.1	6.7
SCOTVEC higher diploma/certificate	3.7	0.4	-	-	0.7	-	0.1	7.5	3.7	3.8
Total Sub-degree Level	54.9	0.9	3.1	0.8	7.9	1.5	7.5	142.7	77.2	65.5
Nursing and Paramedical courses	.	.	.	.	.	.	.	30.3	2.7	27.6
TOTAL HIGHER EDUCATION 1993	87.1	4.1	19.2	11.4	21.5	26.5	35.6	436.5	216.6	219.8
TOTAL HIGHER EDUCATION 1992 (9)	80.2	4.6	16.9	10.5	17.3	34.2	30.3	406.2	206.7	199.5
TOTAL HIGHER EDUCATION 1979 (2)(10)	..	..	..	..	..	..	..	213.0	143.0	69.0
MALES	46.7	1.5	5.8	5.7	9.7	8.1	15.2	.	216.6	.
Higher degree Level (5)	5.3	0.3	1.0	1.3	0.4	1.4	0.7	.	29.7	.
Higher diplomas and certificates (7)	1.1	0.2	0.2	0.3	0.6	4.8	0.2	.	10.7	.
First degree Level (5)	11.3	0.6	3.6	3.8	4.5	1.3	11.1	.	96.3	.
Sub-degree Level	28.9	0.4	0.9	0.3	4.2	0.5	3.2	.	77.2	.
Nursing and Paramedical courses	.	.	.	.	.	.	.	.	2.7	.
FEMALES	40.4	2.5	13.4	5.7	11.8	18.5	20.4	.	.	219.8
Higher degree Level (5)	2.3	0.5	1.5	0.9	0.4	1.9	0.6	.	.	17.8
Higher diplomas and certificates (7)	0.8	0.2	0.6	0.3	1.0	10.4	0.2	.	.	16.1
First degree Level (5)	11.3	1.3	9.1	4.0	6.8	5.2	15.3	.	.	92.9
Sub-degree Level	26.0	0.5	2.2	0.4	3.7	1.0	4.3	.	.	65.5
Nursing and Paramedical courses	.	.	.	.	.	.	.	.	.	27.6

See previous page for footnotes

33b(33)

QUALIFICATIONS AND DESTINATIONS
Students obtaining higher education qualifications by subject of study (1) (2), gender and type of awarding body in year ending 31 December 1994 (3)(4)

Thousands

	Medicine and Dentistry	Allied Medicine	Biological Sciences	Agri-culture and related	Physical Sciences	Mathematical and Computing Sciences	Engineering and Technology	Archi-tecture building, planning	Social Studies
PERSONS									
Higher degree Level									
University	1.8	1.6	2.7	1.1	3.5	2.8	5.7	0.9	7.5
Other HE	-	-	-	-	-	-	-	-	-
Open University (5)(6)	..	..	..	..	..	..	..	..	..
Professional quals (7)	-	0.4	-	-	-	-	0.4	0.3	0.1
Total Higher Degree Level	1.8	2.0	2.7	1.1	3.5	2.8	6.0	1.2	7.6
Higher diplomas and certificates									
University (5)(8)	0.5	0.5	0.2	0.1	0.2	0.7	0.8	0.4	2.2
Other HE (8)	-	-	0.1	-	0.2	0.1	-	0.0	0.1
Total Higher Diplomas and Certificates	0.5	0.5	0.3	0.1	0.4	0.9	0.8	0.4	2.3
First degree Level									
University	4.6	6.0	9.3	1.7	11.5	11.3	19.2	5.3	24.3
Other HE	-	0.6	0.4	0.2	0.5	0.4	0.3	0.1	0.9
Open University (5)(6)	..	..	..	..	..	..	..	..	..
Professional quals (7)	-	-	0.1	-	0.1	0.6	1.4	0.8	1.6
Total First Degree Level	4.6	6.7	9.7	1.9	12.1	12.3	20.9	6.3	26.8
Sub-degree Level									
First university diplomas and certificates (9)	0.1	3.0	0.7	0.4	0.7	2.5	2.7	1.2	3.0
Other HE	-	0.9	-	0.3	0.1	0.3	0.7	0.1	0.5
Professional quals (7)	-	7.0	0.1	0.3	0.2	1.0	2.4	1.7	6.9
BTEC higher diploma	-	0.2	0.4	1.0	0.6	3.7	4.3	1.3	0.6
BTEC higher certificate	-	0.3	0.3	0.1	0.7	1.7	9.7	3.2	0.5
SCOTVEC higher diploma/certificate	-	0.1	0.1	0.4	0.1	0.8	1.1	0.2	0.7
Total Sub-degree Level	0.2	11.4	1.5	2.5	2.4	9.9	20.8	7.8	12.2
Nursing and Paramedical courses	.	32.1	.	.	.	.	.	.	.
TOTAL HIGHER EDUCATION 1994	7.1	52.7	14.3	5.6	18.5	25.9	48.6	15.7	49.0
TOTAL HIGHER EDUCATION 1993	8.3	46.9	12.9	4.9	16.6	24.4	47.5	16.5	44.6
TOTAL HIGHER EDUCATION 1979 (2)(10)	..	..	..	..	..	..	..	..	..
MALES	3.7	7.1	6.2	3.3	12.3	18.2	39.4	12.0	21.9
Higher degree Level (6)	1.0	0.7	1.4	0.7	2.7	2.1	5.2	0.9	4.2
Higher diplomas and certificates (5)(8)	0.3	0.1	0.1	-	0.3	0.6	0.7	0.2	1.1
First degree Level (6)	2.4	1.6	3.9	0.9	7.8	8.8	18.0	5.0	12.4
Sub-degree Level	0.1	1.8	0.7	1.6	1.6	6.7	15.5	5.9	4.2
Nursing and Paramedical courses	.	2.9	.	.	.	.	.	.	.
FEMALES	3.3	45.6	8.1	2.3	6.2	7.7	9.2	3.7	27.1
Higher degree Level (6)	0.9	1.3	1.3	0.4	0.9	0.7	0.8	0.3	3.4
Higher diplomas and certificates (5)(8)	0.2	0.4	0.2	-	0.1	0.3	0.1	0.2	1.2
First degree Level (6)	2.2	5.0	5.9	0.9	4.3	3.4	2.9	1.3	14.4
Sub-degree Level	0.1	9.7	0.8	0.9	0.9	3.2	5.4	1.9	8.0
Nursing and Paramedical courses	.	29.2	.	.	.	.	.	.	.

(1) Teacher training results are shown in Table 8. However, these overlap with results shown here.

(2) Due to changes in subject classification in 1987/88, a comparable subject split of the qualifications for earlier years is not available.

(3) Excludes qualifications from the private sector.

(4) Provisional.

(5) Includes 1992/93 data.

(6) Open University degrees subject detail is not available in this format. Included only in 'All students', 'Males' and 'Females' totals.

(7) Public sector only. DfEE estimates based on final year of course data.

(8) Includes Postgraduate Certificates in Education (PGCEs).

(9) Excludes students who successfully completed courses for which formal qualifications are not awarded.

(10) Excludes degrees validated by universities (but taught in other institutions) and nursing and paramedic qualifiers.

33b(33) QUALIFICATIONS AND DESTINATIONS

Students obtaining higher education qualifications by subject of study (1) (2), gender and type of awarding body in year ending 31 December 1994 (3)(4)

Thousands

	Business and admin studies	Communi- cation and Docum- entation	Langu- ages and related	Human- ities	Creative Arts and design	Edu- cation	Combined and General	ALL STUDENTS	MALES	FEMALES
PERSONS										
Higher degree Level										
University	7.3	0.7	2.5	2.0	0.6	3.2	1.1	45.0	28.0	17.0
Other HE	-	-	-	-	-	-	-	-	-	-
Open University (5)(6)	..	..	..	..	..	..	..	1.4	0.8	0.5
Professional quals (7)	0.3	0.1	-	-	0.2	-	0.1	1.8	1.0	0.8
Total Higher Degree Level	7.6	0.8	2.5	2.0	0.8	3.2	1.2	48.2	29.9	18.4
Higher diplomas and certificates										
University (5)(8)	2.0	0.4	0.5	0.3	1.4	13.3	0.3	23.9	9.9	14.0
Other HE (8)	0.1	-	0.4	0.2	0.3	2.1	0.3	3.8	1.2	2.7
Total Higher Diplomas and Certificates	2.1	0.4	0.9	0.5	1.7	15.4	0.6	27.7	11.1	16.7
First degree Level										
University	19.4	1.7	12.7	8.2	8.9	5.4	22.2	171.7	89.8	81.9
Other HE	1.2	0.3	1.3	0.9	3.5	1.6	6.2	18.3	6.1	12.3
Open University (5)(6)	..	..	..	..	..	..	..	7.2	3.6	3.6
Professional quals (7)	6.3	0.3	1.4	-	0.4	-	0.5	13.6	7.0	6.6
Total First Degree Level	26.9	2.2	15.5	9.1	12.8	7.0	28.8	210.8	106.5	104.3
Sub-degree Level										
First university diplomas and certificates (9)	7.6	-	1.4	0.6	1.2	0.9	6.0	32.0	15.2	16.8
Other HE	2.2	-	-	-	1.7	0.1	0.4	7.6	3.5	4.0
Professional quals (7)	26.7	0.6	2.2	0.3	0.5	0.7	1.8	52.3	23.0	29.4
BTEC higher diploma	11.4	-	-	-	4.1	0.1	0.9	28.5	17.2	11.4
BTEC higher certificate	6.3	-	-	-	0.2	-	0.1	23.0	16.4	6.5
SCOTVEC higher diploma/certificate	4.2	0.5	-	-	0.8	-	0.3	9.2	4.5	4.8
Total Sub-degree Level	58.3	1.1	3.6	0.9	8.6	1.8	9.5	152.7	79.8	72.9
Nursing and Paramedical courses	.	.	.	.	.	.	.	32.1	2.9	29.2
TOTAL HIGHER EDUCATION 1994	94.9	4.5	22.5	12.5	23.9	27.4	40.1	471.6	230.1	241.5
TOTAL HIGHER EDUCATION 1993	87.1	4.1	19.2	11.4	21.5	26.5	35.6	436.5	216.6	219.8
TOTAL HIGHER EDUCATION 1979 (2)(10)	..	..	..	..	..	..	..	213.0	143.0	69.0
MALES	50.2	1.8	6.9	6.0	10.7	8.3	17.7	.	230.1	.
Higher degree Level (6)	5.2	0.3	1.0	1.2	0.4	1.4	0.6	.	29.9	.
Higher diplomas and certificates (5)(8)	1.2	0.2	0.2	0.2	0.6	4.9	0.3	.	11.1	.
First degree Level (6)	13.5	0.8	4.5	4.2	5.2	1.3	12.6	.	106.5	.
Sub-degree Level	30.3	0.5	1.2	0.3	4.5	0.7	4.2	.	79.8	.
Nursing and Paramedical courses	.	.	.	.	.	.	.	.	2.9	.
FEMALES	44.8	2.8	15.6	6.5	13.1	19.1	22.3	.	.	241.5
Higher degree Level (6)	2.3	0.5	1.5	0.8	0.4	1.8	0.5	.	.	18.4
Higher diplomas and certificates (5)(8)	0.9	0.2	0.7	0.3	1.1	10.5	0.3	.	.	16.7
First degree Level (6)	13.5	1.4	11.0	4.9	7.6	5.7	16.3	.	.	104.3
Sub-degree Level	28.0	0.6	2.5	0.5	4.1	1.2	5.2	.	.	72.9
Nursing and Paramedical courses	.	.	.	.	.	.	.	.	.	29.2

See previous page for footnotes.

QUALIFICATIONS AND DESTINATIONS

34

First destinations of first degree graduates at 31 December 1994 by gender and subject group

(i) First degree graduates- All destinations - From academic year 1993/94   Thousands

	UK EMPLOYMENT		Overseas employment	Further education/ training	Believed unemployed	Other (2)	Unknown	Total
	Permanent (1)	Temporary						
PERSONS								
Medicine and Dentistry	4.2	-	-	0.1	-	0.1	0.2	4.6
Studies allied to medicine	4.4	0.2	0.1	0.7	0.2	0.3	0.6	6.6
Biological sciences	3.1	0.7	0.1	3.0	0.9	0.8	1.0	9.7
Vet. science, agriculture etc	0.9	0.1	-	0.3	0.1	0.2	0.3	1.9
Physical sciences	3.8	0.9	0.2	3.8	1.2	0.9	1.3	12.0
Mathematical sciences	5.5	0.5	0.2	1.9	1.0	1.1	1.4	11.6
Engineering and technology	8.0	0.8	0.2	2.8	1.8	3.5	2.3	19.4
Architecture etc	2.6	0.3	0.1	0.7	0.4	0.6	0.8	5.5
Social sciences	7.6	1.4	0.4	7.5	2.0	2.7	3.5	25.2
Business and financial studies	9.4	1.5	0.4	1.7	1.6	3.3	2.8	20.6
Librarianship & into. science	0.9	0.2	-	0.2	0.2	0.1	0.3	1.9
Languages	4.5	0.9	1.0	3.5	1.2	1.1	1.8	14.1
Humanities	3.1	0.6	0.2	2.4	0.9	0.7	1.3	9.1
Creative Arts	4.6	0.8	0.2	0.7	1.3	0.9	2.9	12.4
Education	4.0	0.8	0.1	0.2	0.3	0.3	0.7	6.4
Multi-disciplinary studies	10.1	2.1	0.6	5.4	2.7	2.3	5.1	28.3
All subjects	76.7	11.8	3.9	35.8	15.8	19.0	26.4	189.3
MALES								
Medicine and Dentistry	2.2	-	-	0.1	-	-	0.1	2.4
Studies allied to medicine	0.9	-	-	0.3	0.1	0.1	0.2	1.6
Biological sciences	1.1	0.3	0.1	1.2	0.5	0.3	0.4	3.9
Vet. science, agriculture etc	0.5	0.1	-	0.1	0.1	0.1	0.1	0.9
Physical sciences	2.3	0.5	0.1	2.5	0.9	0.6	0.9	7.7
Mathematical sciences	4.1	0.3	0.1	1.3	0.8	0.7	1.1	8.4
Engineering and technology	6.7	0.7	0.2	2.3	1.6	3.1	2.0	16.7
Architecture etc	2.1	0.2	0.1	0.5	0.4	0.4	0.6	4.3
Social sciences	3.4	0.7	0.2	3.5	1.1	1.3	1.7	11.9
Business and financial studies	4.6	0.7	0.2	0.9	1.0	1.6	1.6	10.4
Librarianship & into. science	0.3	0.1	-	0.1	0.1	-	0.1	0.7
Languages	1.1	0.2	0.3	0.9	0.4	0.3	0.6	3.9
Humanities	1.3	0.3	0.1	1.1	0.5	0.3	0.7	4.2
Creative Arts	1.9	0.3	0.1	0.6	0.6	0.3	1.3	5.0
Creative Arts	0.1	0.1	0.1	-	-	0.3	1.2	1.9
Education	0.8	0.1	-	0.1	0.1	0.1	0.2	1.4
Multi-disciplinary studies	4.3	0.9	0.2	2.1	1.4	1.0	2.4	12.3
All subjects	37.5	5.4	1.7	17.4	9.4	10.4	14.0	95.8
FEMALES								
Medicine and Dentistry	2.0	-	-	0.1	-	-	0.1	2.2
Studies allied to medicine	3.4	0.2	-	0.5	0.1	0.2	0.5	5.0
Biological sciences	2.0	0.4	0.1	1.8	0.4	0.6	0.6	5.8
Vet. science, agriculture etc	0.5	-	-	0.1	0.1	0.1	0.1	0.9
Physical sciences	1.5	0.3	0.1	1.3	0.3	0.3	0.4	4.3
Mathematical sciences	1.4	0.2	0.1	0.6	0.2	0.4	0.3	3.2
Engineering and technology	1.3	0.1	-	0.4	0.2	0.4	0.3	2.8
Architecture etc	0.5	0.1	-	0.2	0.1	0.1	0.2	1.2
Social sciences	4.2	0.7	0.2	4.0	0.9	1.4	1.8	13.3
Business and financial studies	4.8	0.8	0.2	0.8	0.6	1.7	1.3	10.2
Librarianship & into. science	0.6	0.1	-	0.1	0.1	0.1	0.2	1.2
Languages	3.4	0.7	0.7	2.6	0.7	0.8	1.2	10.1
Humanities	1.8	0.3	0.1	1.3	0.4	0.4	0.6	4.9
Creative Arts	2.8	0.5	0.1	1.1	0.6	0.6	1.6	7.4
Education	3.3	0.6	0.1	0.1	0.2	0.2	0.6	5.1
Multi-disciplinary studies	5.8	1.2	0.4	3.3	1.3	1.3	2.8	16.0
All subjects	39.2	6.4	2.2	18.4	6.4	8.6	12.4	93.5
Total all subjects								
1993/94	76.7	11.8	3.9	35.8	15.8	19.0	26.4	189.3
1992/93	63.9	10.1	3.6	34.2	16.9	16.1	20.2	165.0
1991/92	54.8	8.3	3.5	32.1	16.8	14.6	18.4	148.4
1990/91	52.8	6.8	3.5	27.8	13.5	13.8	17.8	135.9
1985/86 (3)	55.7	3.5	2.4	20.9	8.2	6.4	15.2	112.4
1980/81 (4)	..	..	..	..	..	..	..	91.9

(1) Includes those remaining with or returning to a previous employer.
(2) Includes overseas graduates leaving UK and graduates not available for employment.
(3) Great Britain.
(4) Due to revisions in the format of the survey it is not possible to provide detailed breakdown for 1980/81.

QUALIFICATIONS AND DESTINATIONS
First destinations of first degree graduates at 31 December 1994 by gender and subject group

(ii) Employment categories of first degree graduates known to have entered permanent home employment (1) - 1993/94 — Thousands

	Admin. Management services	Scientific, Engineering	Marketing	Financial, Legal	Personnel, Medical Social	Teaching, Lecturing	Other and Unknown (2)	Total entered permanent employment
PERSONS								
Medicine and Dentistry	-	-	-	-	4.2	-	-	4.2
Studies allied to medicine	0.1	0.2	0.1	-	3.7	0.1	0.3	4.4
Biological sciences	0.4	0.7	0.3	0.2	0.5	0.2	0.8	3.1
Vet. science, agriculture etc	0.3	0.2	0.1	-	0.2	-	0.1	0.9
Physical sciences	0.6	1.0	0.3	0.4	0.2	0.3	0.9	3.8
Mathematical sciences	3.2	0.5	0.2	0.7	0.1	0.3	0.5	5.5
Engineering and technology	1.3	4.8	0.4	0.3	0.2	0.1	1.0	8.0
Architecture etc	0.2	1.9	0.1	0.1	-	-	0.2	2.6
Social sciences	1.3	0.1	0.8	1.5	1.5	0.3	2.0	7.6
Business and financial studies	2.3	0.4	2.0	2.5	0.4	0.3	1.5	9.4
Librarianship & into. science	0.1	-	0.2	-	-	-	0.4	0.9
Languages	0.7	-	0.7	0.4	0.3	0.8	1.6	4.5
Humanities	0.4	-	0.4	0.3	0.3	0.5	1.2	3.1
Creative Arts	0.2	0.1	0.3	-	0.1	1.0	2.9	4.6
Education	0.1	-	-	-	0.1	3.1	0.7	4.0
Multi-disciplinary studies	2.0	0.6	1.3	1.2	1.0	0.9	3.0	10.1
All subjects	13.1	10.6	7.2	7.7	12.9	8.0	17.2	76.7
MALES								
Medicine and Dentistry	-	-	-	-	2.2	-	-	2.2
Studies allied to medicine	-	0.1	-	-	0.8	-	0.1	0.9
Biological sciences	0.2	0.3	0.1	0.1	0.1	-	0.3	1.1
Vet. science, agriculture etc	0.2	0.1	-	-	0.1	-	0.1	0.5
Physical sciences	0.4	0.6	0.2	0.2	0.1	0.1	0.6	2.3
Mathematical sciences	2.6	0.4	0.1	0.4	-	0.1	0.4	4.1
Engineering and technology	1.1	4.2	0.3	0.2	0.1	-	0.8	6.7
Architecture etc	0.1	1.6	0.1	0.1	-	-	0.2	2.1
Social sciences	0.6	0.1	0.4	1.0	0.4	0.1	0.9	3.4
Business and financial studies	1.0	0.2	0.9	1.5	0.1	0.1	0.7	4.6
Librarianship & into. science	-	-	0.1	-	-	-	0.2	0.3
Languages	0.2	-	0.2	0.2	0.1	0.1	0.4	1.1
Humanities	0.2	-	0.1	0.2	0.2	0.1	0.5	1.3
Creative Arts	0.1	0.1	0.1	-	-	0.3	1.2	1.9
Education	-	-	-	-	-	0.5	0.2	0.8
Multi-disciplinary studies	1.0	0.4	0.5	0.7	0.3	0.2	1.2	4.3
All subjects	7.7	8.0	3.1	4.6	4.6	1.8	7.7	37.5
FEMALES								
Medicine and Dentistry	-	-	-	-	2.0	-	-	2.0
Studies allied to medicine	0.1	0.1	-	-	3.0	-	0.2	3.4
Biological sciences	0.2	0.5	0.2	0.1	0.4	0.2	0.5	2.0
Vet. science, agriculture etc	0.1	0.1	-	-	0.1	-	0.1	0.5
Physical sciences	0.2	0.4	0.1	0.1	0.1	0.2	0.3	1.5
Mathematical sciences	0.6	0.1	0.1	0.3	-	0.2	0.2	1.4
Engineering and technology	0.2	0.6	0.1	0.1	-	-	0.2	1.3
Architecture etc	0.1	0.3	-	-	-	-	0.1	0.5
Social sciences	0.7	0.1	0.4	0.6	1.1	0.3	1.1	4.2
Business and financial studies	1.3	0.1	1.1	1.0	0.3	0.2	0.8	4.8
Librarianship & into. science	0.1	-	0.2	-	-	-	0.3	0.6
Languages	0.6	-	0.5	0.3	0.2	0.7	1.2	3.4
Humanities	0.2	-	0.2	0.1	0.2	0.4	0.7	1.8
Creative Arts	0.2	-	0.2	-	0.1	0.6	1.6	2.8
Education	-	-	-	-	0.1	2.6	0.5	3.3
Multi-disciplinary studies	1.0	0.2	0.8	0.5	0.8	0.7	1.8	5.8
All subjects	5.4	2.6	4.1	3.1	8.3	6.1	9.6	39.2
Total all subjects								
1993/94	13.1	10.6	7.2	7.7	12.9	8.0	17.2	76.7
1992/93	10.3	8.8	5.3	6.6	11.8	7.1	13.9	63.9
1991/92	8.4	8.4	4.2	6.1	10.6	6.4	10.7	54.8
1990/91 (3)	8.0	9.5	3.7	6.9	9.6	6.4	8.8	52.8
1985/86 (3)(4)	9.1	11.1	4.5	9.4	9.1	5.0	6.9	54.9
1980/81 (5)	..	..	..	..	..	..	..	36.1

(1) Includes those remaining with or returning to a previous employer. University graduates are included in Other and Unknown category.
(2) Includes overseas graduates leaving UK and graduates not available for employment.
(3) Great Britain.
(4) Excludes university graduates remaining with or returning to a previous employer.
(5) Due to revisions in the format it is not possible to provide detailed breakdown for 1980/81.

QUALIFICATIONS AND DESTINATIONS

35a(35)

Highest qualification (1) held by people aged 16-59 by gender and economic activity 1994

United Kingdom

	PERSONS		MALES		FEMALES	
	All	Econ Active (2)	All	Econ Active (2)	All	Econ Active (2)
NUMBERS (thousands)	33,956	26,936	17,103	15,033	16,853	11,904
PERCENTAGE	100	100	100	100	100	100
HIGHEST QUALIFICATION (Percentages)						
NVQ level 5						
Higher degree	2	2	3	3	1	2
NVQ level 4						
First degree	7	8	8	9	6	8
Other degree	2	2	2	3	1	1
Diploma in HE	1	1	1	1	1	1
HNC/HND/BTEC(higher)/SCOTVEC	3	4	5	6	2	2
Teaching	1	1	-	-	2	2
Nursing qualification	2	2	-	-	4	5
Other HE qualification below degree level	-	-	-	1	-	-
RSA higher diploma	-	-	-	-	1	1
Total NVQ level 4	17	20	18	19	17	20
NVQ level 3						
Vocational qualifications (3)	11	12	16	17	5	6
Academic or advanced GNVQ (4)	6	5	6	5	5	5
Total NVQ level 3	16	17	22	21	11	11
NVQ level 2						
Vocational qualifications (5)	11	12	13	14	8	9
Academic or intermediate GNVQ (6)	10	10	9	8	12	13
Total NVQ level 2	21	22	22	22	21	22
NVQ level 1						
Vocational qualifications (7)	6	6	6	6	6	6
Academic or foundation GNVQ (8)	15	15	12	13	18	18
Total NVQ level 1	21	21	18	19	24	25
No qualification at NVQ level 1 or above	22	18	18	16	27	21

(1)   More detailed information on the levels of vocational qualifications has been collected in 1994 allowing a more accurate allocation of such courses to the broad NVQ levels. The information published in previous volumes is not directly comparable at these levels with that published here.

(2)   The economically active are defined as those in employment plus the unemployed (ILO definition).

(3)   Includes RSA Advanced Diploma, BTEC National/ONC/OND, City and Guilds advanced craft and NVQ level 3 Trade apprenticeships and Other professional/vocational qualifications.

(4)   Includes A Levels (more than 1) and NVQ level 3 SCE Highers and Scottish CSYS.

(5)   Includes RSA Diploma, City and Guilds craft, BTEC first diploma and NVQ level 2 Trade apprenticeships and Other professional/vocational qualifications.

(6)   Includes GCSE A-C and equivalent, NVQ level 2 SCE Highers and Scottish CSYS, A level (1 only) and NVQ level 2 AS examinations.

(7)   Includes BTEC general certificate, YT certificate, RSA other qualifications, City and Guilds other qualifications and Other NVQ level 1 professional/vocational qualifications.

(8)   Includes GCSE, CSE, AS examination and GCSE or equivalent not yet mentioned.

QUALIFICATIONS AND DESTINATIONS
Highest qualification (1) held by people aged 16-59 by gender and economic activity 1995

35b(35)

United Kingdom

	PERSONS		MALES		FEMALES	
	All	Econ Active (2)	All	Econ Active (2)	All	Econ Active (2)
NUMBERS (thousands)	34,062	26,940	17,166	15,012	16,896	11,928
PERCENTAGE	100	100	100	100	100	100
HIGHEST QUALIFICATION (Percentages)						
NVQ level 5						
Higher degree	2	2	3	3	1	2
NVQ level 4						
First degree	8	9	9	10	7	8
Other degree	2	2	2	3	1	1
Diploma in HE	1	1	1	1	1	1
HNC/HND/BTEC(higher)/SCOTVEC	4	4	5	6	2	2
Teaching	1	1	-	-	2	2
Nursing qualification	2	2	-	-	4	5
Other HE qualification below degree level	-	-	-	-	-	-
RSA higher diploma	-	-	-	-	-	-
Total NVQ level 4	18	20	18	20	17	20
NVQ level 3						
Vocational qualifications (3)	10	12	16	16	5	6
Academic or advanced GNVQ (4)	6	6	6	5	5	6
Total NVQ level 3	16	17	21	22	11	12
NVQ level 2						
Vocational qualifications (5)	10	11	13	14	7	8
Academic or intermediate GNVQ (6)	11	13	9	10	13	17
Total NVQ level 2	21	24	22	24	20	24
NVQ level 1						
Vocational qualifications (7)	6	6	6	6	7	7
Academic or foundation GNVQ (8)	16	13	13	11	19	16
Total NVQ level 1	22	19	19	17	26	23
No qualification at NVQ level 1 or above	21	17	17	15	25	19

(1) More detailed information on the levels of vocational qualifications has been collected in 1995 allowing a more accurate allocation of such courses to the broad NVQ levels. The information published in previous volumes is not directly comparable at these levels with that published here.

(2) The economically active are defined as those in employment plus the unemployed (ILO definition).

(3) Includes RSA Advanced Diploma, BTEC National/ONC/OND, City and Guilds advanced craft and NVQ level 3 Trade apprenticeships and Other professional/vocational qualifications.

(4) Includes A Levels (more than 1) and NVQ level 3 SCE Highers and Scottish CSYS.

(5) Includes RSA Diploma, City and Guilds craft, BTEC first diploma and NVQ level 2 Trade apprenticeships and Other professional/vocational qualifications.

(6) Includes GCSE A-C and equivalent, NVQ level 2 SCE Highers and Scottish CSYS, A level (1 only) and NVQ level 2 AS examinations.

(7) Includes BTEC general certificate, YT certificate, RSA other qualifications, City and Guilds other qualifications and Other NVQ level 1 professional/vocational qualifications.

(8) Includes GCSE, CSE, AS examination and GCSE or equivalent not yet mentioned.

QUALIFICATIONS AND DESTINATIONS

Highest qualification (1) held by people aged 16-59, by broad age groups and gender, 1994

36a(36)

	United Kingdom					
PERSONS						
AGE GROUPS	16-59	16-24	25-29	30-39	40-49	50-59
NUMBERS (thousands)	33,956	6,785	4,666	8,557	7,797	6,151
PERCENTAGE	100	100	100	100	100	100
HIGHEST QUALIFICATION (Percentage)						
NVQ level 5						
Higher degree	2	-	2	3	3	2
NVQ level 4						
First degree	7	4	11	10	7	4
Other degree	2	-	1	2	2	2
Diploma in HE	1	-	1	1	1	1
HNC/HND/BTEC(higher)/SCOTVEC	3	3	5	4	3	2
Teaching	1	-	-	1	3	2
Nursing qualification	2	1	2	3	3	3
Other HE qualification below degree level	-	-	-	1	-	-
RSA higher diploma	-	-	-	-	-	-
Total NVQ level 4	17	9	21	21	19	15
NVQ level 3						
Vocational qualifications (2)	11	9	10	11	12	11
Academic or advanced GNVQ (3)	6	13	6	4	3	2
Total NVQ level 3	16	21	16	16	15	13
NVQ level 2						
Vocational qualifications (4)	11	7	10	11	13	13
Academic or intermediate GNVQ (5)	10	20	11	10	7	5
Total NVQ level 2	21	28	21	20	20	18
NVQ level 1						
Vocational qualifications (6)	6	3	4	5	8	9
Academic or foundation GNVQ (7)	15	22	24	18	9	5
Total NVQ level 1	21	25	28	23	17	14
No qualification at NVQ level 1 or above	22	16	13	18	26	38

(1)   More detailed information on the levels of vocational qualifications has been collected in 1994 allowing a more accurate allocation of such courses to the broad NVQ levels. The information published in previous volumes is not directly comparable at these levels with that published here.

(2)   Includes RSA Advanced Diploma, BTEC National/ONC/OND, City and Guilds advanced craft and NVQ level 3 Trade apprenticeships and Other professional/vocational qualifications.

(3)   Includes A Levels (more than 1) and NVQ level 3 SCE Highers and Scottish CSYS.

(4)   Includes RSA Diploma, City and Guilds craft, BTEC first diploma and NVQ level 2 Trade apprenticeships and Other professional/vocational qualifications.

(5)   Includes GCSE A-C and equivalent, NVQ level 2 SCE Highers and Scottish CSYS, A level (1 only) and NVQ level 2 AS examinations.

(6)   Includes BTEC general certificate, YT certificate, RSA other qualifications, City and Guilds other qualifications and Other NVQ level 1 professional/vocational qualifications.

(7)   Includes GCSE, CSE, AS examination and GCSE or equivalent not yet mentioned.

36a(36) QUALIFICATIONS AND DESTINATIONS
Highest qualification (1) held by people aged 16-59, by broad age groups and gender, 1994

United Kingdom

MALES

AGE GROUPS	16-59	16-24	25-29	30-39	40-49	50-59
NUMBERS (thousands)	17,103	3,473	2,369	4,315	3,893	3,053
PERCENTAGE	100	100	100	100	100	100

HIGHEST QUALIFICATION (Percentage)

	16-59	16-24	25-29	30-39	40-49	50-59
NVQ level 5						
Higher degree	3	-	2	3	4	3
NVQ level 4						
First degree	8	4	12	11	9	5
Other degree	2	-	1	2	4	4
Diploma in HE	1	-	-	1	1	-
HNC/HND/BTEC(higher)/SCOTVEC	5	4	7	6	5	5
Teaching	-	-	-	-	1	1
Nursing qualification	-	-	-	1	1	-
Other HE qualification below degree level	-	-	-	-	1	1
RSA higher diploma	-	-	-	-	-	-
Total NVQ level 4	18	9	22	22	20	16
NVQ level 3						
Vocational qualifications (2)	16	11	14	18	18	18
Academic or advanced GNVQ (3)	6	12	6	5	3	2
Total NVQ level 3	22	23	20	22	22	20
NVQ level 2						
Vocational qualifications (4)	13	8	11	13	16	17
Academic or intermediate GNVQ (5)	9	18	8	7	5	4
Total NVQ level 2	22	26	20	21	21	21
NVQ level 1						
Vocational qualifications (6)	6	3	4	5	7	8
Academic or foundation GNVQ (7)	12	21	20	13	6	4
Total NVQ level 1	18	24	24	18	13	11
No qualification at NVQ level 1 or above	18	17	12	14	20	28

FEMALES

AGE GROUPS	16-59	16-24	25-29	30-39	40-49	50-59
NUMBERS (thousands)	16,853	3,312	2,297	4,242	3,904	3,098
PERCENTAGE	100	100	100	100	100	100

HIGHEST QUALIFICATION (Percentage)

	16-59	16-24	25-29	30-39	40-49	50-59
NVQ level 5						
Higher degree	1	-	1	2	2	1
NVQ level 4						
First degree	6	5	10	9	6	3
Other degree	1	-	1	1	1	1
Diploma in HE	1	-	1	1	1	1
HNC/HND/BTEC(higher)/SCOTVEC	2	2	3	2	1	-
Teaching	2	-	-	1	4	4
Nursing qualification	4	1	4	5	5	5
Other HE qualification below degree level	-	-	-	1	-	-
RSA higher diploma	1	-	-	1	1	-
Total NVQ level 4	17	9	21	20	19	14
NVQ level 3						
Vocational qualifications (2)	5	6	7	5	5	4
Academic or advanced GNVQ (3)	5	13	5	4	3	2
Total NVQ level 3	11	19	12	9	8	6
NVQ level 2						
Vocational qualifications (4)	8	7	8	8	10	9
Academic or intermediate GNVQ (5)	12	22	14	12	8	6
Total NVQ level 2	21	29	22	20	18	15
NVQ level 1						
Vocational qualifications (6)	6	3	4	5	9	10
Academic or foundation GNVQ (7)	18	24	27	23	11	6
Total NVQ level 1	24	27	31	27	20	16
No qualification at NVQ level 1 or above	27	16	13	21	33	48

See previous page for footnotes.

36b(36)

QUALIFICATIONS AND DESTINATIONS
Highest qualification (1) held by people aged 16-59, by broad age groups and gender, 1995

United Kingdom

PERSONS

AGE GROUPS	16-59	16-24	25-29	30-39	40-49	50-59
NUMBERS (thousands)	34,062	6,625	4,578	8,773	7,823	6,263
PERCENTAGE	100	100	100	100	100	100

HIGHEST QUALIFICATION (Percentage)

	16-59	16-24	25-29	30-39	40-49	50-59
NVQ level 5						
Higher degree	2	-	2	3	3	2
NVQ level 4						
First degree	8	5	11	10	8	4
Other degree	2	-	1	2	2	2
Diploma in HE	1	-	1	1	1	1
HNC/HND/BTEC(higher)/SCOTVEC	4	3	5	4	3	3
Teaching	1	-	-	1	3	2
Nursing qualification	2	-	2	3	3	3
Other HE qualification below degree level	-	-	-	-	-	-
RSA higher diploma	-	-	-	-	-	-
Total NVQ level 4	18	10	20	21	20	16
NVQ level 3						
Vocational qualifications (2)	10	8	10	11	12	11
Academic or advanced GNVQ (3)	6	14	5	4	3	2
Total NVQ level 3	16	22	15	15	15	13
NVQ level 2						
Vocational qualifications (4)	10	6	9	10	12	13
Academic or intermediate GNVQ (5)	11	21	11	10	7	6
Total NVQ level 2	21	27	20	20	19	19
NVQ level 1						
Vocational qualifications (6)	6	3	5	5	9	10
Academic or foundation GNVQ (7)	16	22	25	19	9	5
Total NVQ level 1	22	26	30	24	18	15
No qualification at NVQ level 1 or above	21	16	12	16	24	36

(1)   More detailed information on the levels of vocational qualifications has been collected in 1995 allowing a more accurate allocation of such courses to the broad NVQ levels. The information published in previous volumes is not directly comparable at these levels with that published here.

(2)   Includes RSA Advanced Diploma, BTEC National/ONC/OND, City and Guilds advanced craft and NVQ level 3 Trade apprenticeships and Other professional/vocational qualifications.

(3)   Includes A Levels (more than 1) and NVQ level 3 SCE Highers and Scottish CSYS.

(4)   Includes RSA Diploma, City and Guilds craft, BTEC first diploma and NVQ level 2 Trade apprenticeships and Other professional/vocational qualifications.

(5)   Includes GCSE A-C and equivalent, NVQ level 2 SCE Highers and Scottish CSYS, A level (1 only) and NVQ level 2 AS examinations.

(6)   Includes BTEC general certificate, YT certificate, RSA other qualifications, City and Guilds other qualifications and Other NVQ level 1 professional/vocational qualifications.

(7)   Includes GCSE, CSE, AS examination and GCSE or equivalent not yet mentioned.

36b(36)

QUALIFICATIONS AND DESTINATIONS
Highest qualification (1) held by people aged 16-59, by broad age groups and gender, 1995

	United Kingdom					
MALES						
AGE GROUPS	16-59	16-24	25-29	30-39	40-49	50-59
NUMBERS (thousands)	17,166	3,393	2,327	4,431	3,906	3,108
PERCENTAGE	100	100	100	100	100	100
HIGHEST QUALIFICATION (Percentage)						
NVQ level 5						
Higher degree	3	-	3	4	4	3
NVQ level 4						
First degree	9	5	12	12	10	6
Other degree	2	-	1	2	4	4
Diploma in HE	1	-	1	1	1	1
HNC/HND/BTEC(higher)/SCOTVEC	5	4	6	6	6	5
Teaching	-	-	-	-	1	1
Nursing qualification	-	-	-	1	-	-
Other HE qualification below degree level	-	-	-	-	1	-
RSA higher diploma	-	-	-	-	-	-
Total NVQ level 4	18	10	21	22	22	17
NVQ level 3						
Vocational qualifications (2)	16	10	14	17	18	18
Academic or advanced GNVQ (3)	6	14	5	5	4	2
Total NVQ level 3	21	24	19	21	22	20
NVQ level 2						
Vocational qualifications (4)	13	7	11	13	16	18
Academic or intermediate GNVQ (5)	9	19	9	7	6	4
Total NVQ level 2	22	26	21	20	21	22
NVQ level 1						
Vocational qualifications (6)	6	3	5	6	7	8
Academic or foundation GNVQ (7)	13	21	21	14	6	4
Total NVQ level 1	19	24	26	20	14	12
No qualification at NVQ level 1 or above	17	17	12	13	18	26
FEMALES						
AGE GROUPS	16-59	16-24	25-29	30-39	40-49	50-59
NUMBERS (thousands)	16,896	3,232	2,251	4,342	3,916	3,155
PERCENTAGE	100	100	100	100	100	100
HIGHEST QUALIFICATION (Percentage)						
NVQ level 5						
Higher degree	1	-	2	2	2	1
NVQ level 4						
First degree	7	5	11	9	6	3
Other degree	1	-	1	1	1	1
Diploma in HE	1	-	1	1	1	1
HNC/HND/BTEC(higher)/SCOTVEC	2	2	3	2	1	-
Teaching	2	-	-	1	4	4
Nursing qualification	4	1	4	5	5	5
Other HE qualification below degree level	-	-	1	-	-	-
RSA higher diploma	-	-	-	-	1	-
Total NVQ level 4	17	9	20	21	19	15
NVQ level 3						
Vocational qualifications (2)	5	6	7	5	5	4
Academic or advanced GNVQ (3)	5	14	5	4	3	2
Total NVQ level 3	11	20	12	9	8	6
NVQ level 2						
Vocational qualifications (4)	7	5	7	7	9	8
Academic or intermediate GNVQ (5)	13	23	13	13	9	7
Total NVQ level 2	20	28	20	20	18	15
NVQ level 1						
Vocational qualifications (6)	7	3	4	5	11	11
Academic or foundation GNVQ (7)	19	24	29	24	13	7
Total NVQ level 1	26	27	33	29	23	18
No qualification at NVQ level 1 or above	25	15	13	20	30	45

See previous page for footnotes.

37

QUALIFICATIONS AND DESTINATIONS

Highest qualification (1) held by people aged 16-59 by gender and broad age group 1985, 1994 and 1995

United Kingdom

PERSONS

AGE GROUP	16-59			16-29			30-59		
YEAR	1985	1994	1995	1985	1994	1995	1985	1994	1995
NUMBERS (thousands)	32,730	33,956	34,062	12,268	11,451	11,203	20,391	22,505	22,859
PERCENTAGE	100	100	100	100	100	100	100	100	100
HIGHEST QUALIFICATION (Numbers)									
NVQ level 5									
Higher degree	1	2	2	-	1	1	1	2	3
NVQ level 4									
First degree	5	7	8	4	7	7	5	7	8
Other degree	2	2	2	1	1	1	2	2	2
Diploma in HE	-	1	1	-	-	-	-	1	1
HNC/HND/BTEC(higher)/SCOTVEC	2	3	4	2	4	4	2	3	3
Teaching	2	1	1	-	-	-	3	2	2
Nursing qualification	2	2	2	2	1	1	3	3	3
Other HE qualification below degree level	-	-	-	-	-	-	-	-	-
RSA higher diploma	-	-	-	-	-	-	-	-	-
Total NVQ level 4	12	17	18	9	14	14	14	19	19
NVQ level 3									
Vocational qualifications (2)	7	11	10	6	9	9	7	11	11
Academic or advanced GNVQ (3)	4	6	6	7	10	10	3	3	3
Total NVQ level 3	11	16	16	12	19	19	10	15	15
NVQ level 2									
Vocational qualifications (4)	8	11	10	6	8	7	9	12	12
Academic or intermediate GNVQ (5)	11	10	11	17	16	17	7	7	8
Total NVQ level 2	19	21	21	23	25	24	16	19	19
NVQ level 1									
Vocational qualifications (6)	5	6	6	5	4	4	6	7	8
Academic or foundation GNVQ (7)	13	15	16	25	23	23	6	11	12
Total NVQ level 1	19	21	22	30	26	27	12	18	20
No qualification at NVQ level 1 or above	39	22	21	26	15	15	46	26	24

(1) More detailed information on the levels of vocational qualifications has been collected for 1994 and 1995 allowing a more accurate allocation of such courses to the broad NVQ levels. Data for 1985 have been restructured to fit the NVQ levels. The information published in previous volumes is not directly comparable with 1994 and 1995.

(2) Includes RSA Advanced Diploma, BTEC National/ONC/OND, City and Guilds advanced craft and NVQ level 3 Trade apprenticeships and Other professional/vocational qualifications.

(3) Includes A Levels (more than 1) and NVQ level 3 SCE Highers and Scottish CSYS.

(4) Includes RSA Diploma, City and Guilds craft, BTEC first diploma and NVQ level 2 Trade apprenticeships and Other professional/vocational qualifications.

(5) Includes GCSE A-C and equivalent, NVQ level 2 SCE Highers and Scottish CSYS, A level (1 only) and NVQ level 2 AS examinations.

(6) Includes BTEC general certificate, YT certificate, RSA other qualifications, City and Guilds other qualifications and Other NVQ level 1professional/vocational qualifications.

(7) Includes GCSE, CSE, AS examination and GCSE or equivalent not yet mentioned.

QUALIFICATIONS AND DESTINATIONS
Highest qualification (1) held by people aged 16-59 by gender and broad age group 1985, 1994 and 1995

United Kingdom

MALES

AGE GROUP	16-59			16-29			30-59		
YEAR	1985	1994	1995	1985	1994	1995	1985	1994	1995
NUMBERS (thousands)	16,380	17,103	17,166	6,202	5,842	5,720	10,143	11,262	11,446
PERCENTAGE	100	100	100	100	100	100	100	100	100
HIGHEST QUALIFICATION (Numbers)									
NVQ level 5									
Higher degree	2	3	3	1	1	1	2	3	3
NVQ level 4									
First degree	5	8	9	5	7	8	6	9	9
Other degree	3	2	2	1	1	1	4	3	3
Diploma in HE	-	1	1	-	-	-	-	1	1
HNC/HND/BTEC(higher)/SCOTVEC	3	5	5	3	5	5	4	5	6
Teaching	1	-	-	-	-	-	1	1	1
Nursing qualification	-	-	-	-	-	-	-	-	-
Other HE qualification below degree level	-	-	-	-	-	-	-	1	-
RSA higher diploma	-	-	-	-	-	-	-	-	-
Total NVQ level 4	12	18	18	9	14	14	15	20	20
NVQ level 3									
Vocational qualifications (2)	10	16	16	8	12	12	11	18	18
Academic or advanced GNVQ (3)	4	6	6	7	10	10	3	4	4
Total NVQ level 3	15	22	21	14	22	21	15	22	21
NVQ level 2									
Vocational qualifications (4)	12	13	13	9	9	9	13	15	15
Academic or intermediate GNVQ (5)	9	9	9	14	14	15	5	6	6
Total NVQ level 2	20	22	22	23	24	24	19	21	21
NVQ level 1									
Vocational qualifications (6)	7	6	6	6	4	4	7	7	7
Academic or foundation GNVQ (7)	11	12	13	21	21	21	4	8	9
Total NVQ level 1	18	18	19	28	24	25	11	15	15
No qualification at NVQ level 1 or above	34	18	17	26	15	15	39	20	18

FEMALES

AGE GROUP	16-59			16-29			30-59		
YEAR	1985	1994	1995	1985	1994	1995	1985	1994	1995
NUMBERS (thousands)	16,350	16,853	16,896	6,066	5,609	5,483	10,248	11,243	11,413
PERCENTAGE	100	100	100	100	100	100	100	100	100
HIGHEST QUALIFICATION (Numbers)									
NVQ level 5									
Higher degree	1	1	1	-	1	1	1	2	2
NVQ level 4									
First degree	4	6	7	4	7	7	3	6	7
Other degree	1	1	1	-	-	1	1	1	1
Diploma in HE	-	1	1	-	1	-	-	1	1
HNC/HND/BTEC(higher)/SCOTVEC	1	2	2	1	2	3	-	1	1
Teaching	3	2	2	1	-	-	4	3	3
Nursing qualification	4	4	4	3	2	2	5	5	5
Other HE qualification below degree level	-	-	-	-	-	-	-	-	-
RSA higher diploma	-	1	-	-	-	-	-	1	-
Total NVQ level 4	12	17	17	9	14	14	13	18	18
NVQ level 3									
Vocational qualifications (2)	3	5	5	3	6	6	3	5	5
Academic or advanced GNVQ (3)	4	5	5	7	10	10	3	3	3
Total NVQ level 3	7	11	11	10	16	17	6	8	8
NVQ level 2									
Vocational qualifications (4)	4	8	7	3	7	6	5	9	8
Academic or intermediate GNVQ (5)	13	12	13	20	19	19	9	9	10
Total NVQ level 2	17	21	20	23	26	25	13	18	18
NVQ level 1									
Vocational qualifications (6)	4	6	7	3	4	4	5	8	9
Academic or foundation GNVQ (7)	16	18	19	29	25	26	8	14	15
Total NVQ level 1	20	24	26	32	29	30	13	22	24
No qualification at NVQ level 1 or above	44	27	25	26	15	14	54	33	30

See previous page for footnotes.

Sources of United Kingdom Education Statistics

1 GENERAL SOURCES

1.1 Various summaries of statistics for all four parts of the United Kingdom, and for universities both in Great Britain and Northern Ireland are contained in the Annual Abstract of Statistics, Regional Trends and Social Trends publications prepared by the Central Statistical Office. Some education statistics also appear in the Digest of Welsh Statistics, the Scottish Abstract of Statistics (which has superseded the former Digest of Scottish Statistics) and the Annual Abstract of Statistics, Northern Ireland.

1.2 Details of how to obtain copies of the various volumes of education statistics published by the Department for Education and Employment are shown inside the back cover, together with information on other publications.

1.3 Each of the home education departments publish statistics in a variety of press notices, bulletins and statistical volumes.

2 CSO PUBLICATIONS

The Central Statistical Office publishes a quarterly journal entitled 'Statistical News' (price £12.00) which contains short articles and notes on the latest developments in all fields of government statistics, including education.

'Social Trends' is produced annually, No 25 1995. £27.00. ISBN 0 11 620662 4 being the current edition. This publication brings together some of the more significant statistical series relating to social policies and conditions and presents a series of articles, followed by tables and charts. One chapter concentrates on education.

'Regional Trends' is also published annually, No 30 1995. £34.95. ISBN 0 11 620707 8 being the current edition. This publication brings together detailed information highlighting regional variations in the United Kingdom and covering a wide range of social, demographic and economic topics. One chapter concentrates on education and training.

'A Guide to Official Statistics' No 5 (Revised 1990) (price £24.00) sets out to give the user a broad indication of the range of government statistics available and, if so, the publication in which they appear. Edition number 6 is due for publication in January 1996.

3 EDUCATIONAL REPORTS

A number of important education reports of recent years contain statistical tables and results of special surveys. They are set out below. Previous editions of this publication include a list of pre-1991 reports.

Education and Training for the 21st Century. (CM 1536) HMSO, 1991. £11.00. ISBN 0 10 115362 7

Higher Education: a New Framework. (CM 1541) HMSO, 1991. £6.60.   ISBN 0 10 115412 7

National Pupil Absence Tables 1994. DFE, 1994

School and College Performance Tables 1994 (16-18 age group). DFE, 1994

Secondary School Performance Tables 1994. DFE, 1994

Testing 7 Year Olds in 1994: Results of the National Curriculum assessments in England. DFE, 1994

Testing 14 Year Olds in 1994: Results of the National Curriculum assessments in England. DFE, 1994.

Truancy in English Secondary Schools: a report prepared for the DFE. HMSO, 1994. £9.95. ISBN 0 11 270870 6

Education at a Glance: OECD Indicators 1995. Organisation for Economic Co-operation and Development. HMSO, 1995. £35. ISBN 92 64 144056

Higher Education Statistics for the United Kingdom 1992/93. Higher Education Statistical Agency, 1995 £15.00. ISBN 1 899840 001

School and College Performance Tables 1995 (16-18 age group). DfEE, 1995

Secondary School Performance Tables 1995. DfEE, 1995

National Pupil Absence Tables 1995. DfEE, 1995

Explanatory Notes

GENERAL

Differences in the way that the statistics are returned or recorded by the contributors have been mentioned in the explanatory notes or footnotes where they are considered to be significant. For reasons of space it is impracticable to identify all the differences.

1   GEOGRAPHIC COVERAGE

1.1   For statistical purposes the United Kingdom is England, Wales, Scotland and Northern Ireland. Statistics for Institutions in the Isle of Man and the Channel Islands are not included in this publication. Great Britain excludes Northern Ireland. Tables show summary data for individual countries as far as possible.

1.2   The following is a brief account of the education system as it operates in the United Kingdom. It ignores many detailed aspects in order to give a general picture.

2   STRUCTURE, ADMINISTRATION AND METHOD

2.1   United Kingdom educational establishments are administered and financed in one of three ways:

a   by local education authorities (LEAs)[1], which form part of the structure of local government partly through funds provided by central government;

b   by governing bodies, which have a substantial degree of autonomy from public authorities but which receive grants from centrally financed funding bodies and from central government sources directly;

c   by the private sector, including individuals, companies and charitable institutions.

This volume excludes students, staff and finance of institutions within the private sector of further and higher education.

2.2   In general, the detailed provision and delivery of education in the United Kingdom are not subject to central administration. School quality assessment is undertaken in England by an inspectorate (OFSTED), in Wales by the Office of Her Majesty's Chief Inspector of Schools (OHMCI) and in Scotland by Her Majesty's Inspectors of Schools (HMI). Further education quality control is undertaken by the FEFC Inspectorate. Higher education institutions are subject to quality assurance procedures of the HE Funding Councils and the Higher Education Quality Council (HEQC). In practice, within the quanta of funds distributed by Funding Councils and Education Departments, institutions are managed by their governing bodies which are able to select their own staff and decide how best to allocate funds to suit local needs.

Some central control is, however, exercised over the curriculum taught during compulsory schooling. In particular, the Education Reform Act 1988 introduced the National Curriculum in England and Wales which includes the core subjects of English, mathematics and science (Welsh in Wales) and seven (eight in Wales) other foundation subjects. The 1988 Act also provided for local authorities to delegate the management of school budgets to the schools themselves and for schools to seek withdrawal from LEA control and become self governing. Unlike England and Wales, the curriculum in Scotland is not statutorily prescribed. Pupils aged 5-14 study a broad curriculum based on national guidelines which set out the aim of the study, the ground to be covered and the way that pupil's learning should be assessed and reported. Post-14 pupils take courses which lead to an award at Standard Grade of the Scottish Certificate of Education.

2.3   The four home Government Departments responsible for education are:

a   Department for Education and Employment (following the merger of the employment and training functions of the Employment Department with the Department for Education) on 6 July 1995: all sectors of education in England.

b   Welsh Office, Education Department: schools and higher and further education in Wales, excluding matters connected with the qualifications, probation remuneration, superannuation and misconduct of teachers. From 1 April 1993, WOED has responsibility for the colleges of the University of Wales.

c   The Scottish Office Education and Industry Department: schools and further and higher education in Scotland.

---

1   *Corresponding to counties, metropolitan districts, the Inner and Outer London Boroughs. Most local education authorities in England and Wales had their boundaries redrawn with effect from 1 April 1974 and those in Scotland from 16 May 1975. From 1 October 1973, the local education authorities in Northern Ireland were replaced by 5 Education and Library Boards.*

d Department of Education, Northern Ireland: schools, institutes of further education, teacher training colleges and universities in Northern Ireland.

2.4 From April 1993 separate unitary **Higher Education Funding Councils** for England, Scotland and Wales replaced the Universities Funding Council and the Polytechnic and Colleges Funding Council referred to in paragraphs 2.6 and 2.7. **The Further Education Funding Councils** for England and Wales were set up in April 1993 in the main to allocate grant to further education and sixth form colleges. From April 1994, the Teacher Training Agency (TTA) has responsibility for funding students on courses of Initial Teacher Training(ITT) leading to Qualified Teacher Status (QTS) in England together with certain specified in-service courses for school teachers, including those operative in further and higher education colleges.

2.5 The FE and HE Funding Councils of England and of Wales, and the Scottish Higher Education Funding Council are responsible, respectively, for distributing funds made available by the Secretaries of State to further education colleges in England and Wales, and higher education institutions in England, Wales and Scotland. Allocation of funds to further and higher education establishments in Northern Ireland are the responsibility of the Northern Ireland Education Department, and the Scottish Office Education and Industry Department apportions funds to 43 of the 46 further education colleges in Scotland. The remaining 3 are still funded by the relevant regional authorities. The publicly financed further education colleges became self-governing corporations; the colleges supported by the FEFC include the following types:

  -   general further education and tertiary colleges

  -   sixth form colleges, (which were in the schools sector until 1993)

  -   specialist designated colleges

The FEFC also fund schedule 2 provision in higher education institutions, in external institutions, in external institutions such as LEA Adult education centres, and also certain non-prescribed higher education.

2.6 The Universities Funding Council, UFC (up to March 1993) (Universities Grants Committee, before April 1989) distributed grant to, and advised the Department for Education on the needs of the UK universities (excluding the Open University and University of Buckingham), and provided support to the Department of Education, Northern Ireland on the co-ordinated planning and development of the Northern Ireland universities.

2.7 The Polytechnics and Colleges Funding Council, PCFC (up to March 1993) (National Advisory Body (NAB) prior to April 1989) advised the Secretary of State for Education on the management and funding of higher education institutions in England outside the universities. The Wales Advisory Body (WAB) similarly advised the Secretary of State for Wales until 1992 and the establishment of HEFCW. From 1992 the Welsh Office took over the responsibility for colleges of higher education.

3 STAGES OF EDUCATION

3.1 There are five stages of education: nursery, primary, secondary, further and higher education. Primary and secondary education is compulsory for all children between the ages of 5 and 16 years, and the transition is normally at age 11. However some local education authorities in England operate a system of middle schools which cater for pupils on either side of the transition age, and these are deemed either primary or secondary according to the age range of the pupils. In any case the majority of children in England who are rising 5 are in state education. In Northern Ireland, children who attain the age of 4 on or before 1 July are required to commence primary school the following September, while in Scotland, children generally commence primary school in August when aged between $4\frac{1}{2}$ and $5\frac{1}{2}$ years, transferring to secondary after seven years of primary schooling. Advanced further education courses, leading to qualifications at NVQ level 3 or equivalent such as advanced GNVQ or GCE A level usually take 2 years of full-time study; while courses for level 1 or 2 usually take one year. No fees are payable at any primary or secondary school wholly maintained by the local education authorities but it is open to parents, if they choose, to pay for their children to attend other schools.

3.2 The non-compulsory fourth stage, further education, covers non-advanced education which can be taken at both further (including tertiary) education colleges, higher education institutions and increasingly in secondary schools. It can include courses usually taken in secondary education. Full-time students under 19 in further education colleges are not charged tuition fees. The fifth stage - higher education - is study beyond A levels and their equivalent which, for most full-time students, takes place in Higher Education Institutions.

4 DATES OF PUPIL/STUDENT COUNTS

4.1 Pupils and students are counted at the following dates, mainly at the end of the calendar year:

Schools - January - except for Scotland (session 1974/75 onwards) when the count is at September and Northern Ireland (session 1992/93 onwards) when the count is at October.

Further education and higher education outside universities formerly funded by the UFC

- 1 November - England and Wales and FE for Northern Ireland. October - Scotland (full sessional count is also available from the Scottish Office Education and Industry Department) - 31 December for Teacher Training in Northern Ireland.

Former UFC Universities - 31 December from 1965/66 onwards - previously overall enrolments were counted.

Higher Education Institutions - 31 December from 1994/95 onwards. 31 July (full session count) for Scotland. From 1994/95 the data collection for all HEIs in the UK is being undertaken by the Higher Education Statistics Agency.

With some minor exceptions, students leaving or completing their courses before the appropriate census date, or joining courses thereafter, are excluded from the statistics presented in this Volume.

5   AGE MEASUREMENT

5.1   The 1982 edition introduced age measurement at 31 August, i.e. immediately prior to the start of the school academic year, so yielding complete academic year cohorts and in particular correct post-compulsory school age data. Time series tables use the original basis of 31 December for 1965/66, 1970/71 and 1975/76, with data on both bases for 1979/80, shown in the 1982 and 1983 editions. Scotland and Northern Ireland have provided estimates for schools and school leavers.

5.2   Tables 12a, 12b and 13 which use the August basis, inflates nursery figures with 'rising 5s' in primary education. Rising 5s are pupils who were 4 on 31 August but whose fifth birthday fell between 1 September and 31 December and were thus of compulsory school age in January.

6   YOUNG PERSONS' POPULATION

6.1   Population data in table 1 are derived from estimates provided by the Office of Population Censuses and Surveys and from the Government Actuary's Department 1992 based projections. The latter embodies the following principal assumptions:

a   fertility rates, declining rapidly in the period up to 1977 and increasing erratically since then, will continue to rise gradually and level off by the year 2000. The rates assumed for 2000 and beyond are equivalent to an average family size of 1.9 children per woman;

b   net inward migration to the United Kingdom of 35,000 persons aged under 25 (heavily concentrated at ages 15-24) each year until 2007;

c   morality rates of persons under 20 will decline further from their present low levels.

7   FINANCE

7.1   The statistics in tables 5 to 7 are based on the statements of expenditure and income of the Education Departments of the four countries as included in the Civil Appropriation Accounts presented annually to Parliament; on annual returns submitted by local education authorities and educational institutions; and on the statement of grants paid through the Universities Funding Council, Polytechnics and Colleges Funding Council and to the Open University (all included in the Civil Appropriation Accounts) and of grants paid by the Department of Education, Northern Ireland, in the case of two Northern Ireland universities.

7.2   The tables exclude:

a   expenditure on education by other Government Departments other than through a local education authority;

b   all public expenditure on libraries, art galleries and museums;

c   receipts and payments by the Government Departments in connection with, teachers' superannuation;

d   private expenditure on education.

7.3   To facilitate the use of the statistical material in economic and social analysis, public expenditure on education proper has, as far as possible, been separated from 'related' expenditure - mainly on welfare and other amenities connected with the educational system.

7.4 The tables do not purport to show how the burden of the cost of educational expenditure is divided between the central government and local authorities. Generally, the expenditure is attributed in the tables to the authority initially responsible for making the payments. The tables do not, therefore, reflect the redistribution of the cost of the service arising from:

    a payments by the central government to local authorities in England, Wales and Scotland of general grant and other grants;

    b the arrangements in Northern Ireland for sharing educational expenditure between the Department of Education, Northern Ireland and local education authorities.

7.5 Throughout this publication the terms 'expenditure' and 'income' are used, even though in some cases the amounts, being based on a cash accounting system, are strictly on a 'payments' and 'receipts' basis. The latter is the case for all central government expenditure and for local education authority capital expenditure.

7.6 Amounts related to capital expenditure appear in these tables under three heads:

    a capital expenditure financed from revenue contributions;

    b capital expenditure financed by loans;

    c loan charges.

All capital expenditure by central government and a relatively small part of the expenditure by local education authorities is financed from revenue contributions; most of local education authority capital expenditure is financed by loans. The gross capital formation of public authorities is obtained by combining items a. and b. The total expenditure chargeable against revenue is obtained by combining items a. and c. The latter are the financing costs of capital expenditure and they combine loan repayments and interest thereon. However, from 1991-92, loan charges are not identified separately from other local authority services and capital expenditure is shown under one head.

7.7 In table 5, UK total public expenditure on education is expressed as a proportion of UK Gross Domestic Product (GDP) at market prices (factor cost plus taxes on expenditure and less subsidies). GDP represents the value of total economic activity on UK territory before allowances for depreciation of capital goods. An alternative comparison could be made with Gross National Product (GNP), which is equivalent to GDP plus net property income from abroad. In table 5, Value Added Tax on United Kingdom educational expenditure has been incorporated into the total United Kingdom educational expenditure. This enables the educational expenditure percentage of GNP or GDP at market prices to be calculated on a basis that incorporates taxes both in the numerator and the denominator. An additional adjustment for capital consumption, which is included in the compilation of National Accounts aggregates, is not included in the table, but is footnoted.

7.8 Included under the appropriate heads in the LEA expenditure, is money received by them for expenditure on work-related further education, the Technical and Vocational Education Initiative (TVEI), and Adult and Youth Training. This money now comes from the Department for Education and Employment (and since 1992 the Welsh Office Education Department, for Wales) superseding the former Employment Department who, from November 1990, took over the responsibility for the provision of public employment and training services from the Training Agency (formerly the Manpower Services Commission), which from that date ceased to exist.

8   AWARDS

8.1 The statistics in tables 3 and 4 have been compiled from annual returns from local education authorities, Research Councils and data held by the Education Departments.

Post-graduate Awards
8.2 Postgraduate awards in the physical natural and social science subjects are made by the five Research Councils in Great Britain (in Northern Ireland this is the responsibility of the Department for Education Northern Ireland). In the main, awards for art subjects and other professional and vocational courses are made by the Education Departments, the Department for Education and Employment being responsible for England and Wales. The British Academy is responsible for making awards in the humanities.

Undergraduate Awards
8.3 Students in England, Wales and Northern Ireland who are normally, habitually and lawfully resident in the United Kingdom and follow full-time first degree and equivalent courses or post-graduate initial teacher training courses are usually entitled to mandatory awards covering tuition fees and a contribution to maintenance from their local education authority. Students domiciled in other EC member states are also usually entitled to payment of tuition fees from the LEA in which their institution is resident. Mandatory awards paid by LEAs have 2 components: a means tested contribution towards maintenance and payment,

usually in full, of the costs of tuition. Students in England, Wales and Northern Ireland deemed ineligible for a mandatory award because of personal illegibility or because the course is not designated under the Mandatory Award Regulations may be considered for a discretionary award. Similar support arrangements apply in Scotland under the Students' Allowances Scheme administered by the Students Awards Agency for Scotland. Since 1991/92 the Northern Ireland Education and Library Boards have provided awards for initial teacher training and postgraduate certificate in education courses.

Further Education Awards

8.4   Students following further education courses may be eligible for discretionary awards (education authority bursaries in Scotland). These are usually at a lower rate than mandatory awards as they are not intended to cover the full cost of fees and maintenance.

Student Loans

8.5   In l 990/91 maintenance grants were frozen at their then current levels and student loans introduced to supplement the grants. The eligibility requirement for loans are similar to those for mandatory grants. The student is required to start repayments soon after leaving the course although deferment is allowed in cases of low income.

Access Funds

8.6   Access Funds are administered by further and higher education institutions and are available in cases where access to education might be inhibited by financial considerations, or where students, for whatever reasons, face real financial difficulties. For 1995-96 provision for institutions in England will be £28 million, of which £6 million is for students in the further education sector. In 1993/94 77 per cent (59,400 out of 77,000) of total applications for higher education access funds were successful.

9   TEACHERS

Initial Teacher Training

9.1   In order to teach in a maintained school, teachers are normally required to have qualified teacher status (QTS). This is usually obtained by successfully completing a course of initial teacher training (ITT) at an accredited institution whose provision meets the Secretary of State's criteria for ITT. There are two main routes to achieving qualified teacher status (QTS) in England and Wales; by successful completion of an undergraduate course of initial teacher training or of a course leading to the postgraduate certificate in education (PGCE).

9.2   Both type of courses are run by higher education institutions and from the beginning of the 1993 academic year, some PGCE courses have been offered by groups of schools. Undergraduates normally complete a three- or four-year course leading to the Bachelor of Education (BEd) degree with honours, or a BA or BSc (QTS) course. These courses usually have the same basic entry requirements as other higher education courses, but they also require mathematics and English language (and in primary ITT a science subject or combined science) at the equivalent of Grade C GCSE. In addition to the three- and four-year BEd courses there are some two-year BEd courses (mostly in certain secondary shortage subjects) for non-graduate mature entrants who already have some relevant experience and who have completed at least one year of HE in the appropriate subject.

9.3   The PGCE is for students who hold a first degree or equivalent qualification. The content of the qualification aim must be appropriate to the Primary or Secondary school curriculum. These courses also require mathematics and English Language (and in primary ITT a science subject or combined science) at the equivalent of Grade C GCSE. Courses are normally full-time and last for one year, but there are a few two-year part-time PGCE courses in some subjects, and some two-year 'conversion' PGCE courses in certain shortage subjects. These latter courses are designed to equip students with a specialism by extending the subject study of their initial degree. The Open University has started to run distance learning PGCE courses with effect from the start of the 1993/94 academic year.

9.4   Qualified Teacher Status can also be achieved via the Licensed Teacher or Overseas Trained Teacher routes. Local Education Authorities or most school governing bodies can, as employers, offer a position as a Licensed or Overseas Trained Teacher to a suitably qualified applicant who will receive tailor-made on-the-job, training. On these routes, it is possible to obtain Qualified Teacher Status after 2 years or less, depending on qualifications and previous experience.

9.5   Applicants for the Licensed Teacher route need to be at least 24 years old or to be recognised as trained teachers outside the UK, and to have successfully completed the equivalent of 2 years' full-time higher education. The Overseas Trained Teacher route is open to graduate trained teachers from overseas who have had at least one year's teaching experience. In common with other routes to Qualified Teacher Status, these routes require applicants to obtain a standard in mathematics and English Language (and in primary ITT a science subject or combined science) equivalent to a minimum of Grade C GCSE.

9.6 New criteria for secondary ITT courses were issued in 1992 and for primary ITT courses in 1993. All secondary courses had to be adapted to meet the new criteria from September 1994. New primary courses also had to meet the criteria from September 1994, and all primary courses must be revised by September 1996. The new criteria mean that schools should play a larger and more influential role in course design and delivery, and that ITT should focus on the subject knowledge and practical skills required by newly-qualified teachers.

9.7 In 1993 a new system of school centered ITT was launched. This is postgraduate training that is designed and delivered by groups of schools. In the first 2 years SCITT was directly funded by the then DFE but is now funded by the Teacher Training Agency (TTA). With effect from 1 September 1995, students are eligible for mandatory awards and student loans for SCITT courses which begin on or after that date.

9.8 In 1994 the Teacher Training Agency (TTA) was established to bring together functions previously discharged by a number of bodies. In ITT it is responsible for the funding of teacher training, the accreditation of providers of initial training for school teachers, and the allocation of student numbers to ITT providers in England. Its statutory objectives in this area are to improve the quality and efficiency of all routes into the teaching profession and to secure the involvement of schools in all courses for the initial training of school teachers. On 1 April 1995, the TTA assumed responsibility for the administration and funding of the Licensed Teacher Scheme. It is also responsible for funding the SCITT Scheme with effect from 1 September 1995.

9.9 The pattern of teacher training and the regulations governing the employment of teachers in primary and secondary schools in Northern Ireland are broadly comparable to those in England and Wales. In Scotland, courses lead to the award of a Teaching Qualification (Primary Education) or a Teaching Qualification (Secondary Education). To gain a primary qualification a graduate is required to complete a one-year training course. A non-graduate may undertake a four-year vocational degree course, leading to the award of a BEd and the Primary qualification. In all but some secondary practical and aesthetic subjects, intending secondary teachers will be graduates, or holders of equivalent qualifications, who will complete a one-year training course.

Teachers and Lecturers in Post

9.10 The regulations governing the employment of teachers in primary and secondary schools in England, Wales and Northern Ireland require teachers to hold one of the qualifications mentioned in paragraphs 9.1 to 9.9, with the exception that in

Northern Ireland the licensed teachers route is not accepted for qualified teacher status (QTS). However, in England and Wales pre-1970 graduates were accepted as teachers in primary schools, and pre-1974 graduates in secondary schools, without having to complete a course of professional training. The position is the same in Northern Ireland in relation to secondary schools, but a professional qualification is required to teach in a primary school. In Scotland the primary teaching courses currently available are a one-year postgraduate course (PGCE) for graduates and a four-year vocational degree course (BEd). Most intending secondary teachers will be graduates, or holders of equivalent qualifications, who will complete a one-year training course (PGCE). The exceptions to this are the four-year BEd courses available in music, technology and physical education, and the concurrent degree and diploma in education course which is run by the University of Stirling. All teachers who teach in nursery, primary or secondary schools in Scotland must undergo initial training and gain a Teaching Qualification before they can register as a teacher with the General Teaching Council for Scotland.

9.11 Statistics of full-time school teachers are derived mainly from returns completed by LEAs and, in the case of self-governing (GM) and independent schools, the institutions themselves. In Scotland, statistics on full- and part-time teachers are derived from information provided biennially by individual teachers in the school census. Statistics of part-time school teachers are derived from returns completed by LEAs and self governing schools. Teacher counts can differ depending on the coverage of the particular return used and resulting factors (such as PTRs) will differ accordingly. From 1994/95 (1993/94 for sixth form colleges) data on staff in further education colleges are collected by the FEFC.

9.12 School teachers cover all qualified staff (registered in Scotland) plus in table 14 those unqualified however the employment of such unqualified teachers has been strictly limited since 1970.

9.13 The teachers' tables 9 and 10 use a count at 31 March or a date in January, with the exception of Scotland (September since the mid-seventies). The count for table 14 is at mid-January. Otherwise each category is in general counted during the first quarter of the calendar year.

9.14 The numbers of academic staff in the former UFC-funded institutions and in the former PCFC-funded polytechnics and colleges are collected by USR and PCFC respectively. USR numbers refer to a census date of 31 December and counts in this Volume cover all staff on academic and academically-related pay scales whose primary function is teaching and research. Data for PCFC institutions relates to the numbers of staff paid on the lecturers' common interest group of PCEF salary scales as at 1 December and additionally includes any other staff paid mainly as lecturers and/or researchers.

9.15 Lecturers in universities cover teaching and research staff involved in academic work, while in other colleges all staff on teaching scales are included. As not all graduate staff in further education are recorded as graduates this figure is understated in tables 9 and 10.

10 SCHOOLS

10.1 Schools in England, Wales, Scotland and Northern Ireland are generally classified according to the ages for which they cater, or the type of education they provide. Schools with more than one department have been counted once for each department. To avoid confusion standardised terms are used for the purposes of United Kingdom Statistics:

a Public sector - maintained and self-governing (grant-maintained) (England and Wales)

- education authority (Scotland)

- controlled, maintained, voluntary and grant-maintained integrated (Northern Ireland)

b Part-maintained - grant-aided (Scotland) until 1985/86 direct grant (England and Wales) until 1980

c Non-maintained - independent including City Technology Colleges (England) (see paragraph 10.5 also)

With effect from 30 October 1980, all direct grant schools in England and Wales became independent. In 1985/86, all but twelve Scottish grant-aided schools became independent, the remainder being grant aided. In 1994/95, there were ten grant-aided schools in Scotland. In the tables of this volume, the non-maintained sector generally includes the part-maintained establishments throughout the whole of the time series shown, unless the footnotes states otherwise. The term 'public school' as commonly

used in the United Kingdom is now a misnomer. It refers for historical reasons to certain of the major independent schools.

10.2 Nursery education is provided for children below compulsory school age in nursery schools or nursery or infant classes in primary schools, on either a full-time or part-time basis. Part-time pupils are counted in full in tables 11, 12a and b, 13a and b and 15 (except for England). In table 14 they are counted as 0.5, except for Scotland where part-time pupils are included on a actual full-time equivalent basis. In the independent sector in Scotland all pupils are counted as full-time. In England, the size of a school is determined by the number of full-time pupils on the register except for nursery schools where the size is calculated by reference to both full-time and part-time pupils aged under five, each part-time pupil being counted as 0.5.

10.3 In addition to the educational facilities provided by nursery classes, day care and some preliminary training are given in day nurseries (provided either by local authorities or by voluntary bodies), in 'playgroups' set up by voluntary bodies and in self-help playgroups. Information relating to day nurseries and playgroups is not included in this publication as these establishments are registered with the local health authorities, or social work departments in Scotland.

10.4 Primary education consists mainly of infant schools for children up to age 7, first schools for children aged 5 to 10, junior schools for children aged 7 to 11 and middle schools for children variously aged 8 to 13. Some primary schools may be a combination of these categories. In Scotland primary schools are generally classified as those catering for children aged between 5 and 11. In Northern Ireland, primary schools cater for children aged between 4 and 11.

10.5 The structure of secondary education may vary between one local education authority and another. Most local authority areas have comprehensive schools which cater for all children irrespective of ability, and in England and Wales over 86 per cent of secondary school pupils attend such schools. Other secondary schools (modern, grammar and technical) usually have selective entry. City Technology Colleges (CTCs) take the form of charitable companies limited by guarantee, are registered as independent schools and, from January 1989 have been included with independent schools statistics. The majority of education authority secondary schools in Scotland are comprehensive in character and offer six years of secondary education; however in the remote areas there are several two-year and four-year secondary schools.

10.6 Special schools comprise both day and boarding schools and provide education for pupils with statements of special educational needs (see paragraph 10.9) who cannot be educated satisfactorily in an ordinary school. All children attending special schools are offered a curriculum designed to overcome their learning difficulties and to enable them to become self-reliant. Boarding special schools which constitute around 16 per cent of all such schools cater mainly for pupils with severe learning difficulties. Compulsory attendance at special schools is from the ages of 5 to 16 but in many special schools children remain beyond age 16. It should be noted that the non-maintained special school figures in respect of England, which have been included in this volume, relate to those special schools which are funded by charitable bodies and should not be confused with independent special schools.

10.7 The 1981 Education Act (in Northern Ireland the Education and Libraries (NI) Order 1986) gave the impetus to educate children with special educational needs in ordinary schools where possible. In addition to the number of pupils given in tables 12a, 12b and 13, therefore, there were also pupils with statements of special educational needs in maintained primary and secondary schools (see table 16 part (ii)), independent schools, and receiving education otherwise than at school.

10.8 The large increase in the numbers of pupils at special schools after 1971 was due mainly to local education authorities in England and Wales assuming responsibility in April 1971 for all mentally handicapped children (similar responsibility passed to the NI education service in 1987). Previously, the most severely mentally handicapped children had been the responsibility of the health authorities. Under the Education (Handicapped Children) Act 1970, local education authorities took over all establishments catering for such children: these establishments became public sector schools and they are included in the statistics from 1972, either as hospital schools or as other special schools, according to their organisation. To maintain comparability in the statistics, junior occupational centres in Scotland, attended by mentally handicapped children and administered by education authorities, were included in the figures from 1972 to 1975. Thereafter the Education (Mentally Handicapped Children) (Scotland) Act 1974 made children in day care centres and in mental or mental deficiency hospitals the responsibility of education authorities with the exception of a small number of schools still deemed grant-aided and they are therefore now included in all statistics relating to mentally handicapped pupils in education authority schools.

10.9 The Education Act 1981 which came fully into force on 1 April 1983 (in Northern Ireland the Education and Libraries (NI) Order 1984), abolished the ten statutory handicaps into which pupils have hitherto fallen. Instead, local education authorities are required to assess a child's particular special educational needs, providing a statement of those needs where necessary. Statistics from 1984 onwards therefore refer to those children with statements.

11 SCHOOL LEAVING AGE

11.1 The minimum school leaving age was raised from 15 to 16 on 1 September 1972. The subsequent Education (School Leaving Duties) Act 1976 amended the dates in the year when children could leave school in England and Wales. Depending on when the child's 16th birthday falls, he/she may leave at Easter or towards the end of May.

11.2 Because of the transitional rules concerning dates which applied at the time the school leaving age was raised, the first school population figures to reflect the change were those from January 1974.

11.3 In Scotland, the main difference from the situation in England and Wales is the existence of a Christmas leaving date in addition to the summer one. This difference affects the percentages of pupils staying on beyond compulsory schooling in the respective countries. Thus the percentages shown for 15 year olds before 1974 and 16 year olds after 1974 in England and Wales are not comparable with those for Scotland.

11.4 In Northern Ireland with effect from the 1992/93 school year, pupils who become 16 in the period 1 September in any year to 1 July (inclusive) in the following year can leave school on 30 June in that following year. Pupils who become 16 in the period 2 July to 31 August (inclusive), in any year, cannot leave school until 30 June of the following year.

12 FURTHER AND HIGHER EDUCATION

12.1 On reaching the minimum school leaving age pupils have a variety of options. They may leave or continue at school, or they may continue full-time, part-time or evening study at other institutions - usually a college of further education. Those who stay on at school or continue study at FE establishments may, after further study, seek admission to higher education courses at higher education institutions or colleges of further education. The choice depends, amongst other things, on what examination results have been achieved.

Table Coverage

12.2 As a result of the 1992 Further and Higher Education Act all polytechnics and 3 HE institutions were designated as universities in 1992/93. In 1993/94 the coverage of the students in tables 2-10, 19a-27, 33a, 33b and 34 was as follows:

i   47 former UFC universities (including the London Business School and Manchester Business School) offering courses of higher education of which 35 were in England and Wales (counting the Universities of London and Wales as single entities), 8 in Scotland and 2 in Northern Ireland. In addition, data for the Open University are included as far as possible (12.6 refers also). The independent University of Buckingham is not included.

ii   Further and higher education outside the former UFC universities provided in:

    a   England and Wales: Former polytechnics and HE colleges now funded by the HE Funding Councils, FE colleges funded by the FE Funding Councils, previously maintained by English and Welsh local education authorities, institutions which were grant-aided by the Department for Education, the Open University, Cranfield Institute of technology (now Cranfield University) and the Royal College of Art and adult education centres (formerly known as evening institutes). On 1 April 1993 Sixth Form Colleges were incorporated into the FEFC and have transferred out of the schools sector[1].

    b   Scotland: Higher Education Institutions funded by the Scottish Higher Education Funding Council (SHEFC); the Scottish Agricultural College funded by the Scottish Office Agriculture and Fisheries Department (SOAFD); Further Education Colleges and centres funded by the Scottish Office Education and Industry Department (SOEID).

    c   Northern Ireland: Colleges of Education funded by the Northern Ireland Department of Education, institutes of further education maintained by Education and Library Boards and, up until the academic year 1983/84, when it merged with the new University of Ulster to become the University of Ulster, the Ulster Polytechnic, which was controlled by an independent Board of Governors and assisted by grants from the Northern Ireland Department of Education.

There are in addition many independent specialist establishments, such as secretarial colleges and correspondence colleges which are not included in the statistics in this volume.

12.3 The majority part of the finance of higher education institutions is provided through central government grants and agencies. Funding Councils advise Educational Departments on institutional needs and on the distribution of these grants, and act as channels of communication between the universities and the Government. Students do not have an automatic right of entry even though they may hold the minimum usual standard of entry to higher education and must seek acceptance through individual applications for admission. To assist the admission process and to act as a clearing house for University application the Universities Central Council on Admissions (UCCA)[2] was established by the former UFC universities in 1961. The Polytechnic Central Admissions System (PCAS) was set up in 1986 by the Polytechnics of England and Wales to act as a clearing house for admissions to full-time degree and HND courses in polytechnics and up to and including 1993 entry, the larger colleges in England many of whom were funded by the PCFC and some Welsh colleges, and some institutions in Scotland. UCCA and PCAS merged with effect for entry to HE institutions in Autumn 1994 to form UCAS, the University and Colleges Admission Service.

Other Points

12.4 Industrial Training Boards covering seven major sectors of industry were established under the 1982 Industrial Training Act. These are construction, clothing, engineering, hotel and catering, off-shore petroleum, plastics processing and road transport. Most Boards offer, through a system of levy and grant arrangements, incentives to employers to release their employees for courses in further education at all levels. Release may be for some type of part-time study, sandwich course, or special full-time short course (note 12.12 refers). Most other sectors of industry are covered by non-statutory training organisations (NSTOs). Their chief sources of income are membership subscriptions from employers and fees for providing training courses and consultancy. The level of NSTOs income varies as does the extent to which they can offer financial incentives to employers to release employees for further education courses.

12.5 Training for young people mainly aged 16-17 years has been run since 1983 by the Manpower Services Commission - later the Training Commission, the Training Agency, the Employment Department and, following a 1995 merger of the former Employment Department and Department for Education, the Department for Education and

---

1   *In January 1993, the 115 Sixth Form Colleges were still schools and are included in the secondary school results.*

2   *Entry to universities and colleges of education in Scotland now take places via the Universities and Colleges Admissions Service (UCAS).*

Employment. This training has been known since 1990 as Youth Training (YT) (previous scheme titles have been: Youth Opportunities Programme YOP) 1978-83; Youth Training Scheme (YTS) 1983-86; and two-Year YTS 1986-90). A new option of Modern Apprenticeships has been available in a range of prototype industry sectors from September 1994 and more widely from September 1995. Youth Credits, available from all Training and Enterprise Councils TECs) in England since April 1995, enable young people to gain access to YT or Modern Apprenticeships. Students attending further education courses as part of their training under these initiatives are included where appropriate in tables 18 to 24b.

12.6 The Open University, financed by the Education Departments, started its courses in 1971. The University enables students to obtain degrees by studying at home by means of correspondence courses and radio and television programmes. There is a network of study centres, usually based on further and higher education colleges, to provide assistance to students, and full-time summer schools of a week's duration per course unit are held annually, often at universities. The Open University study year is from February to October with students being counted in enrolment figures beginning in the previous autumn.

12.7 Adult Education Centres are establishments maintained by local education authorities. Education for adults is also provided by other Bodies, such as the extra-mural departments of universities, the Worker's Educational Associations, residential colleges and the Welsh National Council of the Young Men's Christian Associations. These establishments are often housed in premises used by day for similar or other educational purposes. They provide a wide range of courses, some of a recreational nature.

12.8 Normally, students participating in post-school education are counted once only, but if enrolled for two or more courses they are generally counted once for each separate course. However, in Scotland, with effect from October 1975, and in England and Wales from November 1976, a student enrolled in SCE/GCSE/GCE/CSE studies is counted once only irrespective of the levels or grades taken. Similarly in Northern Ireland students taking one or more GCSE/GCE courses are counted once only.

12.9 All students enrolled for courses leading to specified qualifications (see paragraph 13.5) are included whether or not they are following the complete course. Part-time day students attending classes which form part of a full-time course are included as part-time students.

12.10 Students from overseas are defined as those whose usual place of domicile or residence is outside the United Kingdom. Up to and including 1983/84 the definition was those students who were charged a fee at the overseas rate irrespective of domicile, and EC domiciled students charged at the home fee rate.

12.11 First year students (table 27) include a small number who are on a second, or further course of higher education at undergraduate or postgraduate level.

12.12 Mode of study can be either full-time or part-time.

a **Full-time students.** These are on taught or research courses which, up to and including academic year 1993/94, in former UFC-funded institutions, last the equivalent of one full-time academic year of study (or more), and in FE and other HE institutions were on courses recorded as full-time irrespective of length. From and for academic year 1994/95, full-time students are those on courses lasting more than 18 weeks during the academic year and to which they are expected (as previously) to denote the whole of their time.

b **Sandwich course students.** These are also full-time students. The essential feature of a sandwich course is that the period of full-time study averages 19 or more weeks per academic year, and is broken by a period (or periods) of industrial training forming an integral part of the course.

c **Block release courses.** These are courses for which students are released from industrial training or employment by their employer for a period (or periods) of full-time education averaging less than 19 weeks per academic year. They have been included with part-time day courses.

d **Part-time day courses.** Students on these courses study part-time during the day or day and evening, some of these students are released to study by their employers. Part-time students now include all those on full-time courses lasting 18 weeks or less.

e **Open or Distance Learning courses.** The students study privately using specially prepared learning material and are provided with marking and comment services for their written work which may be accompanied by some counselling and tutorial support.

f **Evening courses.** Evening only students are those who attend evening courses only. Where the students also undertake full-time or part-time day study they are included under those headings. Evening students who have been released from work to undertake study are included with part-time day courses.

12.13 A revised subject classification was introduced for university courses in 1985/86 and for other HE institutions in 1988/89 with the result that direct comparisons with data from earlier years cannot be made for tables 21a and 34.

13 QUALIFICATIONS

13.1 Examinations offered by external examination boards and moderating bodies are not normally taken before the minimum school leaving age. At that time school pupils usually take examinations in a range of subjects offered by the examining board, namely the GCSE (General Certificate of Secondary Education) which replaced the CSE (Certificate of Secondary Education) and GCE (General Certificate of Education) 'O' level in the summer examinations of 1988 - and in Scotland, the SCE (Scottish Certificate of Education) from the Scottish Examination Board). At the end of a further two years' study (one year in Scotland), further examinations are available - A levels and AS examinations from the GCE boards and Highers from the SEB. Two or more GCE A level passes (3 or more Higher Grades) or their equivalent are usually considered the minimum entry requirements for higher education.

13.2 a England, Wales and Northern Ireland: GCSE examinations were first taken in 1988, replacing the previous system of GCE O-level and CSE (Certificate of Secondary Education) examinations. The GCSE is awarded at grades A* to G. The A* grade was introduced in 1994 and is aimed at distinguishing exceptional performance. The GCE O-level was awarded at grades A-E and the CSE at grades 1-5. GCSE grades A-C are deemed equivalent to O-level grades A-C (formerly 'pass' grade) and CSE grade 1. (In Wales pupils also sit for the Certificate of Education.)

In 1989 the AS (Advanced Supplementary) examination was introduced alongside the existing GCE A level examination. AS qualifications are awarded at grades A to E and are deemed to be the equivalent to half of one A level in terms of content. AS examinations are also designed to be taken after two years of secondary study. In the tables, students are shown as having a pass at GCE A level if they have at least one GCE A level or two AS examination passes.

b In Scotland pupils study for the Standard (S) grade, a two-year course leading to examinations at the end of the fourth year of

secondary schooling. These cater for a wide range of academic ability including GCSE equivalent, and have replaced the SCE ordinary (O) grade course. The Higher (H) grade course requires one further year of secondary schooling. For the more able H grade candidate the range of subjects covered may be almost as wide as the S grade and it is not unusual for candidates to study 5 or 6 H subjects spanning both Arts and Science. Pupils who remain at school until their sixth year may opt to study for the Certificate of Sixth Year Studies (CSYS).

13.3 Passes in these examinations provide the normal minimum entry requirements for the majority of courses in further and higher education. Two GCE A level passes (or equivalent AS examination passes) or three SCE H grades together with appropriate passes at GCSE level or equivalent are usually regarded as the minimum qualification necessary for entry to a degree course, but the conditions of entry to particular courses vary and depend, in part, on the balance of supply and demand for places. CSYS is not normally considered as a university entrants qualification but, as an examination giving the experience of independent study and, in many cases by completing a piece of research, is often taken into account by universities making offers of places.

13.4 Up to and including 1990/91 data on school leavers' qualifications and destinations was collected annually using a 10 percent sample survey of leavers in England and Wales. The 1991/92 results were based on only a 3 percent sample of school leavers for England - this was the last year that information was collected on a 'school leavers' basis. For each year since 1991/92 databases of GCSE and GCE A level/AS examination results for all candidates has been assembled for the publication of school and college performance tables for England and Wales. The Scottish Office Education and Industry Department collect annual qualified school leaver data and, annually from 1993, destinations data based on a 10 percent sample of leavers. The data for Northern Ireland now come from an annual survey (surveys were biennial until 1985/86).

13.5 Courses leading to specified qualifications, which include those leading to GCSE, GCE, CSE, SCE and degrees, are usually divided for statistical purposes into 'higher' and 'further' education. Those courses reaching standards above GCE A level, SCE H grade and BTEC National Diploma and Certificates, or their equivalents, are regarded as higher education. In earlier editions of this publication 'higher' education was referred to as 'advanced' and 'further' education as 'non-advanced'. Courses, mainly non-advanced, leading to Royal Society of Arts qualifications cover a wide range of subjects, including business and commerce, languages, administration, shorthand and typing and passenger and freight transport. Other non-advanced courses lead to qualifications of the BTEC and the City and Guilds of London Institute. Statistics in respect of these and other non-advanced courses are shown in tables 24a and 24b.

13.6 The National Council for Vocational Qualifications (NCVQ) was set up in 1986 to reform and nationalise the vocational qualifications system in England, Wales and Northern Ireland. It is establishing a new framework of National Vocational Qualifications (NVQs) based on 5 defined levels of achievement. Coverage will be virtually completed by the end of 1994. The Government's target is that 60 per cent of the employed work force should have attained NVQ level 3 or equivalent by the year 2000.

13.7 The council has also introduced General National Vocational Qualifications. GNVQs are broadly based vocational qualifications designed to lead onto either employment or higher education. GNVQs develop the knowledge, skills and understanding needed in vocational areas such as Business, Health and Social Care, Engineering and Art and Design. They are available at three levels, Advanced, Intermediate and foundation. Foundation is broadly equivalent to four GCSEs at grades D to G, Intermediate is broadly equivalent to four or five GCSEs at grades A to C and Advanced is broadly equivalent to two GCE A levels. GNVQs can be combined with other qualifications in a single course of study, for example a GCE A level could be taken alongside an Advanced GNVQ.

13.8 The competence-based system is being extended in Scotland through a new system of Scottish Vocational Qualifications (SVQs) along the lines of NVQs. SVQs are accredited by the Scottish Vocational Education Council. NVQs and SVQs have equal recognition throughout Britain.

13.9 All former UFC-funded universities confer their own degrees. Up to 31 March 1993 degrees in polytechnics and colleges were conferred by the CNAA which ceased to exist as at that date. Since then, and as a consequence of the 1992 FHE Act, all former polytechnics in England and Wales and Central Institutions in Scotland (and a small number of the colleges in England) were granted the power to confer their own teaching (and research) degrees and to have the term 'University' recognised officially in their institutional title. Institutions which are not granted these powers will have to have their degrees validated either by institutions which have such powers, or by the Open University which takes over some of the validation responsibilities of CNAA. Other advanced qualifications may be conferred by various professional institutions, individual

establishments, the Business and Technician Education Council (BTEC) and the Scottish Vocational Education Council (SCOTVEC). Some diplomas and certificates are conferred by the universities.

13.10 Undergraduates are students who are either:

a taking a course leading to a first degree; or

b taking a course leading to a certificate or diploma (or other qualification designated as higher education) at undergraduate level; or

c attending a course of an HE standard although not leading to a qualification. From 1994/95, students on courses leading to institutional credits are included.

Students already possessing a first degree or first diploma who are taking a second first degree or first diploma course are nonetheless regarded as undergraduates, even though they may be allowed to complete the course in a shorter period than normal.

13.11 Postgraduates are students who are following courses which normally require a first degree for entry, and who are:

a doing research work for, or taking a course leading to, a higher degree or higher diploma; or

b doing other research work; or

c on a course of higher degree or higher diploma standard, though not leading to a qualification. From 1994/95, students on courses leading to institutional credits are included.

13.12 Tables 35a to 37 contain information on the stock of qualifications held by people of working age. The source is the Labour Force Survey (LFS), carried out by the Department for Education and Employment throughout the year, providing information on the distribution of formal qualifications among the post-16 population in the United Kingdom. The information is derived from answers given by, or on behalf of, people of working age to standard questions about educational, business or technical qualifications gained. All qualifications held by an individual are initially coded but the data presented in tables 35a to 37 (taken, in the main, from the results of the 1994 and 1995 LFS although data from the 1984 LFS are also included in table 37) relate only to the highest qualification held. Although the LFS includes all people of **working age**, which for men is 16-64 and for women 16-59, the data in tables 35a to 37 are for 16-59 only. This enables a more consistent comparison to be made between the data for men and women.

Printed in the UK for HMSO Dd. 301989 C16 1/96 9385 3695